In Lady Audley's Shadow

20/11/20

For Holly,

with friendship

Louise

Edinburgh Critical Studies in Victorian Culture

Series Editor: Julian Wolfreys

Volumes available in the series:

*In Lady Audley's Shadow: Mary Elizabeth Braddon and Victorian
   Literary Genres*
Saverio Tomaiuolo
978 0 7486 4115 4   Hbk

*Blasted Literature: Victorian Political Fiction and the Shock of
   Modernism*
Deaglán Ó Donghaile
978 0 7486 4067 6   Hbk

*William Morris and the Idea of Community: Romance, History and
   Propaganda, 1880–1914*
Anna Vaninskaya
978 0 7486 4149 9   Hbk

In Lady Audley's Shadow

Mary Elizabeth Braddon and Victorian Literary Genres

Saverio Tomaiuolo

Edinburgh University Press

© Saverio Tomaiuolo, 2010

Edinburgh University Press Ltd
22 George Square, Edinburgh

www.euppublishing.com

Typeset in 10.5/13 Adobe Sabon
by Servis Filmsetting Ltd, Stockport, Cheshire, and
printed and bound in Great Britain by
CPI Antony Rowe, Chippenham and Eastbourne

A CIP record for this book is available from the British Library

ISBN 978 0 7486 4115 4 (hardback)

The right of Saverio Tomaiuolo
to be identified as author of this work
has been asserted in accordance with
the Copyright, Designs and Patents Act 1988.

Contents

Series Editor's Preface

'Victorian' is a term at once indicative of a strongly determined concept and, simultaneously, an often notoriously vague notion, emptied of all meaningful content by the many journalistic misconceptions that persist about the inhabitants and cultures of the British Isles and Victoria's Empire in the nineteenth century. As such, it has become a by-word for the assumption of various, often contradictory habits of thought, belief, behaviour and perceptions. Victorian studies and studies in nineteenth-century literature and culture have, from their institutional inception questioned narrowness of presumption, pushed at the limits of the nominal definition, and have sought to question the very grounds on which the unreflective perception of the so-called Victorian has been built; and so they continue to do. Victorian and nineteenth-century studies of literature and culture maintain a breadth and diversity of interest, of focus and inquiry, in an interrogative and intellectually open-minded and challenging manner, which are equal to the exploration and inquisitiveness of their subjects. Many of the questions asked by scholars and researchers of the innumerable productions of nineteenth-century society actively put into suspension the clichés and stereotypes of 'Victorianism', whether the approach has been sustained by historical, scientific, philosophical, empirical, ideological or theoretical concerns; indeed, it would be incorrect to assume that each of these approaches to the idea of the Victorian has been, or has remained, in the main exclusive, sealed off from the interests and engagements of other approaches. A vital interdisciplinarity has been pursued and embraced, for the most part, even as there has been contest and debate amongst Victorianists, pursued with as much fervour as the affirmative exploration between different disciplines and differing epistemologies put to work in the service of reading the nineteenth century.

Edinburgh Critical Studies in Victorian Culture aims to take up both the debates and the inventive approaches and departures from convention that studies in the nineteenth century have witnessed for the last half century at least. Aiming to maintain a 'Victorian' (in the most positive sense of that motif) spirit of inquiry, the series' purpose is to continue and augment the cross-fertilisation of interdisciplinary approaches, and to offer, in addition, a number of timely and untimely revisions of Victorian literature, culture, history and identity. At the same time, the series will ask questions concerning what has been missed or improperly received, misread, or not read at all, in order to present a multi-faceted and heterogeneous kaleidoscope of representations. Drawing on the most provocative, thoughtful and original research, the series will seek to prod at the notion of the 'Victorian', and in so doing, principally through theoretically and epistemologically sophisticated close readings of the historicity of literature and culture in the nineteenth century, to offer the reader provocative insights into a world that is at once overly familiar, and irreducibly different, other and strange. Working from original sources, primary documents and recent interdisciplinary theoretical models, Edinburgh Critical Studies in Victorian Culture seeks not simply to push at the boundaries of research in the nineteenth century, but also to inaugurate the persistent erasure and provisional, strategic redrawing of those borders.

Julian Wolfreys

Acknowledgements

First of all, I would like to thank Francesco Marroni, for his great support, for his perceptive, sharp and sometimes 'implacable' comments, and for having followed this book from the very beginning with his contagious enthusiasm. To him goes my deepest gratitude. Many sections of the original manuscript have profited from the readings and suggestions of the following scholars, who have generously bestowed their professional gifts and profound knowledge on it: Maurizio Ascari, Mariaconcetta Costantini, Allan Christensen, Roger Ebbatson, George Levine, Andrew Mangham and the anonymous readers at Edinburgh University Press. Of course, I am the only one who is to blame for eventual idiosyncracies, mistakes or errors included in the book. I am also grateful to Ann Heilmann for her kindness in sending me precious materials related to the figure of Victorian female vampires. A great thank-you also to Mary Patricia Kane, for her careful reading of the manuscript and for her constant availability.

I am deeply thankful to Giovanni Capelli, Dean at the Faculty of Health and Sport Sciences in Cassino, for his professional and human understanding, and for his 'friendly dinners'. My gratitude to Prof. Paolo Russo, Head of the Department of Health and Sport Sciences, for his attentive promptness in solving problems. My thanks also to all the people I have the pleasure of working with at Cassino University, for their sincere support and for their invaluable presence in my brightest and darkest hours.

Sections of this book have been published, sometimes in a very different form and structure, in the following books and journals, whose publishers and editors I thank for their kind permission to use them: 'Mary Elizabeth Braddon's Quest for Realism: Photographic Paradigms in *The Doctor's Wife*', *Englishes*, 22, 8, 2004, pp. 79–104; 'Towers and Trains: Topologies of Dispossession in M. E. Braddon's *John Marchmont's Legacy*', in *La letteratura vittoriana e i mezzi di trasporto:*

dalla nave all'astronave, ed. Mariaconcetta Costantini, Francesco Marroni, Renzo D'Agnillo (Rome: Aracne, 2006, pp. 187–98); 'Reading Between the (Blood)lines of Victorian Vampires: M. E. Braddon's "Good Lady Ducayne"', in Marilyn Brock (ed.), *From Wollstonecraft to Stoker: Essays on Gothic and Victorian Sensation Fiction* (Jefferson, NC; London: McFarland and Company Inc. Publishers, 2009, pp. 102–19); 'Sensational Letters: Mary Elizabeth Braddon, *Lady Audley's Secret* and the Doom of Truth', in Mariaconcetta Costantini, Francesco Marroni and Enrichetta Soccio (eds), *Letter(s): Functions and Forms of Letter-Writing in Victorian Art and Literature* (Rome: Aracne, 2009, pp. 71–90).

This book is dedicated to Anna and Alessandro, who have accompanied me in these 'roaming' years with love and patience. They are my greatest source of encouragement and my reason to live. This book is also dedicated to the memory of my father Renzo, for his unforgettable teachings.

Pescara, January 2010

Introduction: the Lady Audley Paradigm

> We women can't go in search of adventures – to find out the North-West passage or the source of the Nile, or to hunt tigers in the East. We must stay where we grow, or where the gardeners like to transplant us. We are brought up like the flowers, to look as pretty as we can, and be dull without complaining. That is my notion about the plants; they are often bored, and that is the reason why some of them have got poisonous.
>
> George Eliot, *Daniel Deronda*, 1876[1]

This is a sensational story, which also happens to be a true one. At 5 a.m. on 8 June 1858 Lady Rosina Wheeler had just arrived with her friend Mrs Clarke at Hertford, after a long and difficult journey. Rosina reported that she had 'shivers in every limb' and that her head was burning. She had been forced to borrow money, but she was determined to do what she had planned. According to the people who knew her, at fifty-six Lady Rosina was still a beautiful, tall lady, with a finely chiselled nose, a broad and high forehead, dark hair, bright grey eyes (sparkling and changing in colour with every emotion), perfect teeth, a small mouth and a rounded, delicate face. The day before, on Tuesday, Lady Rosina and Mrs Clarke had taken the 3.20 p.m. train from Taunton, 'but instead of going the direct way by London – for fear of meeting Sir LIAR or any of his gang – [they] went a round which, with the usual delays of the trains, made it 11 at night before [they] got to Bedford'. Then they travelled the whole night and came to the 'little dirty mean town of Hertford' when it was almost daybreak. All of this had been done to attend an important political speech of Sir Edward Bulwer Lytton, Rosina's husband, who had been offered a cabinet post in the Derby-Disraeli government. One of the most famous novelists of the Victorian age, Edward Bulwer Lytton published literary works that rivalled Dickens's for the number of sales (with titles such as *Pelham*, *Paul Clifford*, *Ernest Maltravers*, *The Last Days of Pompeii*, *Lucretia* and *The Caxtons*). As his biographer Leslie Mitchell noticed, Lytton's novels '[were] almost overtly didactic. He saw them as vehicles for moral or political instruction [. . .] The historical works [were] crammed with archaic words that would have sent an average reader in search of a dictionary.' His family house at Knebworth was a sort of mediaeval shrine, both in its architecture and in the family principles inculcated (in particular) by his mother Elizabeth Barbara Lytton, whose obsessive relationship with him was probably one of the reasons for his notorious vanity. In a way, Edward Bulwer Lytton seemed to be the perfect representative of his times, as well as of their literary, cultural and political orthodoxy.

Soon after they came to Hertford, Rosina asked Mrs Clarke to give the people working in the Dimsdale Arms (the inn where they were residing) a sovereign to paste up posters all over the town. By 7 a.m. all of them were posted, bearing the following legend: 'Lady B– L– requests the Electors of Herts to meet her at the Corn Exchange this day, Wednesday, June 8, 1858.' Six hours after the two women's arrival (at nearly 11 a.m.) Edward, who had been re-elected at Hertford, was delivering a public speech. Rosina advanced through the crowd and asked people to 'make way for [their] member's wife', coming to the very scaffolding of the place where Edward Bulwer Lytton was making his speech. It is easy, at this point, to imagine Edward Bulwer Lytton's embarrassment. This seemed to be Rosina's victory, since she delivered her speech to an astonished audience while Edward Bulwer Lytton, whose jaw 'fell like that of a man suddenly struck with paralysis [. . .] made a rush [and] took to flight', humiliated. Here is part of Rosina's speech:

> [After] turning me and my children out of our house to run an unexampled career of vice, you have spent years in promulgating every lie of me, and hunting me through the world with every species of persecution and outrage, your last gentlemanlike and manly attempt having been to try and starve me out: therefore, in return to your *lies*, I have come here to-day to say the *truths* I have to say, openly and publicly.

The so-called 'Hertford scandal' was only the last of a long series of matrimonial battles between Edward Bulwer Lytton and Rosina Wheeler, whose marriage lasted nearly thirty years (the 'fatal' day, as Rosina called it in a letter dated 1851, was on 29 August 1829). During one of the 'ordinary' quarrels for trivial matters, Rosina wrote that Edward seized 'a carving knife', sprang to her 'like a tiger and made his hideous teeth meet in [her] left cheek'. In an essay entitled *Nemesis* (1833), written in the form of a letter from Lord Byron to the men of England, she claimed that in May 1828 Edward beat her when she was eight months pregnant.

Sometimes these episodes were given a fictional form in her novels *Cheveley* (1839), *The Budget of the Bubble Family* (1840), *Miriam Sedley* (1850), *The School for Husbands* (1852), *The World and his Wife* (1858) and *Behind the Scenes* (1854). Compared to her husband, Rosina Wheeler was not a successful writer, and her literary works were basically another means to discredit him for his immoral behaviour and to express her opinions on the 'Boeotian mistake' of marriage, as she defined it in *Miriam Sedley*. Nevertheless, she was also hypercritical of the press and of many literary circles of the times (in her words, 'The Press Gang' of Charles Dickens and John Forster), as well as of Queen Victoria, for having elevated 'Sir Liar' (as she addressed Edward) to the baronetage in 1866. To quote from her ironically-entitled autobiography *A Blighted Life* (completed in 1866 but published only in 1880), 'A more shameful insult, either to the People or to the House of Lords, was never committed; but insult now seems to be the lot of us all, and so VIVAT REGINA!' Edward Bulwer Lytton and Rosina Wheeler had two children, Emily and Robert. The first died at the age of eighteen of typhus fever in a seedy boarding house in 1847, almost totally neglected. Nobody knew the real cause of Emily's death, and Edward and Rosina had been repeatedly accusing each other; in truth both were probably to blame. Indeed, Rosina was far from being a good mother, and her verbal aggression and lack of restraint were probably the outcome of her undisciplined upbringing and personal experiences. Since her father Francis had wanted a boy, her birth (which took place on a 'dreary, drizzling November morning' in 1802) was considered a disagreeable event. In her autobiography, Rosina wrote that the first mistake she made 'was being born at all'. Her mother Anna, of Irish origin, was an intelligent and cultivated person with a good social position, who campaigned for the cause of women. Many contemporary scholars consider Anna one of the most influential feminist writers living between Mary Wollstonecraft and Emmeline Pankhurst. Due to Anna's rebellious ideas, to her eccentricity and to her unconventional behaviour, Victorians (including Rosina's husband Edward) suspected that the taint of madness ran in her blood. According to nineteenth-century reports, Anna's Socialist and Owenite engagements did not leave her much time to look after her two daughters Rosina and Henrietta, who were left to themselves when they were still children. Concerning Edward Bulwer Lytton's mother, Elizabeth, she caused problems at the time when Rosina's romance with Edward was blooming; her firm opposition to the marriage cost Edward his allowance. Consequently, he was forced to earn part of his living through novel writing. As husband and wife, Edward and Rosina were reciprocally unfaithful for years and lived in separate lodgings from 1836.

Two days after the 'Hertford scandal', on 10 June 1858, Rosina was at her residence in Taunton, at Clarke's Hotel, when she received at 11 o'clock the unexpected visit of a sixty-year-old medical practitioner named Hale Thompson, who started asking her strange questions. He was accompanied by two people: a black-haired 'Patagonian woman of six feet high' aged sixty; and a mysterious gentleman, who were both waiting in the adjacent room. The 'Patagonian' woman was a keeper from the Brentford Madhouse of Inverness Lodge, at Fairwater. Victorian newspapers and Rosina's biographical notes related that they were all residing at the nearby Castle Hotel. After his seven-hour medical interview, Hale Thompson (who had been sent by Edward Bulwer Lytton) tried to arrange an economic agreement between Edward and Rosina, who finally asked for an allowance of £500 a year (instead of the £400 she received), and promised not to discredit her husband in public any more. In a first report of his visit, Dr Thompson admitted that he had 'never found a clearer head, or a more logical mind, or sounder flesh and blood'. After Dr Thompson left Rosina's lodgings, Mrs Clarke told Rosina that the mysterious visitor in the other room was none other than Rosina's husband. Edward Bulwer Lytton in fact wanted Thompson and another doctor to sign a certificate of the lady's insanity: according to the Madhouse Act (1828) two doctors' certificates sufficed to lock up a person (usually a woman) in a madhouse. While Dr Thompson '*could* not sign' that certificate at first, another doctor who was later consulted would similarly admit that Rosina was totally sane and was 'no more mad' than he was. Hale Thompson's inquests were soon followed by those of Mr Loader, Edward's attorney, in order to come to a final agreement. In truth, these were subtle attempts to amass evidence of the lady's insanity.

Shortly after 5 a.m. on 23 June 1858 Rosina, who had been persuaded to visit Dr Thompson's house, had just arrived in London by train to complete her economic agreement with her husband. She was accompanied by Miss Ryves and by a lady of Taunton. According to a journalist, this was 'a dreary time to enter the great lumbering city, even when one's business is of no such dreary character as theirs'. When she came to the doctor's house at midday, Rosina started to be suspicious and seemed to have, 'on entering the house, a presentiment that there was no favourable information for her'. Indeed, Rosina was soon informed that 'arrangements' had been made for her removal to Brentford, Inverness Lodge. Her forced incarceration in the 'asylum' was based on the medical certificates signed by Dr Thompson (whose opinions on her supposed insanity had 'mysteriously' changed) and by Dr Ross. In the words of the *Somerset County Gazette and West of England Adviser* dated 13

July, 'the policemen "did their duty" and her ladyship was constrained to enter her carriage [. . .] One or two gentlemen also seating themselves within it, the party was rapidly driven to an asylum in Brentford.' At Dr Gardiner Hill's asylum, Rosina would be in the charge of two keepers and would sleep in a bedroom whose windows had been nailed shut. After her arrival she asked Dr Hill 'to remove [the] two keepers from [her] room, for [she was] not mad [. . .] and [would not] be driven mad by being treated as a maniac' in that 'madhouse', as Rosina put it. Dr Hill replied that Inverness Lodge '[was] not a madhouse' and that he considered her, as well as the other inmates, as his 'children'. Then he agreed to leave Lady Rosina alone in her room, although her windows continued to be nailed. In the meantime Rosina's son Robert commissioned Dr Forbes Winslow and Dr G. Connolly to visit her and then to sign a counter-certificate that ascertained the lady's sanity. British public opinion was divided at the time, and Rosina's case became a matter of discussion in newspapers and in social circles as well. Queen Victoria herself intervened with Prime Minister Lord Derby. On 17 July Rosina was released after three weeks of unjust incarceration, which was evidently motivated by her offensive and humiliating speech at Hertford. However, Rosina's fate was – in a way – already written. After a long and satisfying political and literary career, Edward Bulwer Lytton died in 1873 and was buried in Westminster Abbey after solemn celebrations. At his funeral on 1 February, Benjamin Jowett lauded him as one of England's greatest writers and one of the most distinguished men of the times. In contrast, Rosina died alone and neglected on 12 March 1882. Her remains were laid to rest in an unmarked grave in the Church of St John the Evangelist in Shirley, near Croydon. For many years she was remembered only as Edward's 'mad wife'.[2]

As it has already been suggested, this is a sensational story that also happens to be a true one. Indeed, Sir Edward Bulwer Lytton and Rosina Wheeler's tormented relationship was considered one of the most sensational 'affairs' of the fifties, and anticipated many of the features of the so-called 'sensation novel', which was one of the most complex and ambiguous literary phenomena of mid-to-late nineteenth century. The very term 'sensation' is ambiguous, and there are varying opinions on its origin. The *OED*, for instance, attributes its first appearance to Rev. Henry Longueville Mansel, in a notorious review that appeared in 1863. Along with accusations of immorality (typically addressed to their appealing to the 'public' taste for crime), Mansel focused on the fact that these novels stimulated uncontrollable, unnatural and dangerous bodily sensations, saying that they may be classified 'according to what sensation they are calculated to produce' and that some of them 'carry the whole nervous system by steam'.[3] In many attacks against sensation novels it is not clear if they are considered the *cause* of physical (and moral) excitability in readers, or as the *effect* of a corrupted society, in particular at the dawn of the turmoil of the French Revolution and of the late 1840s. In the opinion of many critics the increasing need for independence turned women from angels of the house into the vampirising femmes fatales who made their appearance in these novels. To use a term which would become famous in late-Victorian culture thanks to Max Nordau's 1892 book, sensation novels were reputed to be the product of a 'degeneration' in cultural, social and moral customs. These novels were thus bound to the most deleterious aspects of so-called 'mass culture' and of the mass literary market (which was an expression of that culture), as well as to the new market laws of demand and supply of strong emotions for strong palates.

Margaret Oliphant was the other critic who became famous for her (unsigned) attacks in the pages of *Blackwood's Edinburgh Magazine*. Apart from her focusing (in an article dated 1867) on the 'French' origin of such immoral narrations that were 'foreign to our insular habits', deriving from the 'imported' unhealthy lesson of writers such as Flaubert and Balzac,[4] she suggested the term 'sensation' derived from those spectacular melodramas – usually originating in the United States or France – which employed complex mechanical 'special effects' (such as train crashes, fires and floods on stage) to produce excitement in theatre audiences. These melodramas induced intense 'sensational' emotions in the public. Such a definition of sensation literature as directly indebted to 'spectacular' theatrical exhibitions must be interpreted with reference to the intrinsically 'dramatic' quality of sensation fictions, whose characters played their 'roles' according to what Peter Brooks has defined as the melodramatic 'mode of excess'. The characters' bodies were in fact the main means through which their opinions, their points of view and their identities were voiced. However, notwithstanding these premises, sensation novels partially differed from traditional popular melodramas (introduced to Britain by French dramatists such as Guilbert de Pixérécourt and developed by Dion Boucicault), because the roles of the stereotypical male and female characters of the past, which embodied the principles of evil and good, were often revised and altered. Indeed sensation fictions blurred the boundaries separating justice and crime, legal punishment and moral infamy, with the consequence that the very notion of 'respectability' (which represented for Victorian Britain a fundamental issue) became a fluid and ambiguous concept. The exaggerated melodramatic gestures of those who were once constructed as stock-characters (the 'immaculate' heroine, the unscrupulous villain and the noble hero), and who were now turned into decayed noblemen, independent women and ambiguous middle-class professionals, were given plausible motivations which made them more 'dangerously' credible to the critics. Sensation novels partially derived many of their plots from contemporary trials and journalistic cases (featuring murders, poisonings, concealed identities and sexual scandals) in a sort of 'refined' updating of Newgate calendars and of the 'Newgate fictions', whose masters included, among others, Charles Dickens, William Ainsworth and Edward Bulwer Lytton himself. Contrarily to what happened in the past, readers from 'respectable' classes had started to appreciate tales that were once enjoyed only by the lower classes in third-rate penny serials. This mixture of elements coming from the 'high' and 'low' social scales was an uncanny and blameable feature which almost all critics put into the foreground. According to them, the chaos menacing the social, political, cultural and sexual order found in these sensational narrations a perfect mirror, as well as an instrument to spread its word to a wider audience.

Another concern for critics was represented by the depiction of female assertiveness, along with the creation of a new species of 'fair-haired demon' (as Margaret Oliphant called it) whose aim was to interrogate the rightfulness of the institution of marriage and the role of women within the Victorian family. Female economic, social and sexual oppression became the leading topic of sensation fictions, but with an important 'twist' on the past. Contrarily to traditional Gothic fictions (where women were usually the victims of male villains), female characters reacted, even violently, against their own pre-inscribed fate through changes of identity, subtle machinations, seductive practices and the use of illicit means to survive the struggle for life. In this sense, the word 'desire' can be adopted as an all-compassing term which summarises these (sensation) women's legitimate need of economic gratification, their necessity to be recognised as social subjects and their sexual yearning, after centuries of oblivion. In the case of female sensationalist writers in particular, novels were a complex (and sometimes even contradictory) attempt to express a state of dissatisfaction through a voice of their own, as well as a way to offer an alternative perspective on middle-class femininity. But sensation novels did not represent an isolated literary case in the Victorian literary panorama. On the contrary, they were a fundamental piece in its construction and also in its dissolution, since they questioned the very pillars upon which the illustrious literary canons of the British novel were built.

In truth, it would be misleading to say that there was a single model of sensation novel, because the same issues and questions were often given different textual forms. If Wilkie Collins is reputed to be the father of the sensation school and the creator of intricately-plotted novels such as *The Woman in White*, *No Name* and *Armadale* (while *The Moonstone* anticipates late-century detective fictions), Charles Reade is renowned for having taken inspiration from contemporary sources and documents in 'matter of fact romances' (as he called them) such as *Hard Cash* and *It's Never Too Late to Mend*. Mrs Henry (Ellen) Wood's paradoxically moralising sensation *East Lynne* represents another variant to the sensational recipe, while Mary Elizabeth Braddon is unanimously recognised as one of the most prolific, talented and controversial of these writers, in her uneven attempts to reconcile her desire to offer alternative views of the patriarchal order and her conservative attitude to familial politics. Despite these heterogeneous elements and the different writing-styles of its representatives, in all sensation novels (and in Mary Braddon's *oeuvre* most notably) narrations centred on the Victorian family, seen as a social, political, sexual and moral institution, as well as a micro-representation of Victorian Britain in a particular, critical phase, during which the values of the past clashed with the changed cultural patterns of the present. In the words of Andrew Radford, 'The genre employed its paraphernalia of psychic disintegration, duplicates, spectres, and transposed identities to erode the seemingly solid and respectable structures of mid-Victorian domesticity.'[5] The family, conceived in the past as a shelter and an example of moral rectitude, was depicted by sensation novelists as infected and corrupted to its root by 'endemic' maladies such as economic eagerness, violence, (inherited) madness and repressed sexual drives. The more the social level of its representatives was elevated, the more their fall from grace looked tragic and irredeemable.

Edward Bulwer Lytton and Rosina Wheeler's vicissitudes seem to raise the same 'familial' questions as those asked by sensation novelists and, particularly, by Mary Elizabeth Braddon, the so-called 'queen of circulating libraries'. In a way, their story can be compared with that of Braddon's most famous novel *Lady Audley's Secret* (1862), a text centred on a family crisis and on a determined heroine who is punished for her unconventional behaviour and for her criminal actions. Like other sensation fictions, Braddon's novel was the target of multiple attacks from both male and female critics (headed by Margaret Oliphant), who blamed the presence of an apparently 'respectable' lady concealing unspeakable secrets behind her golden ringlets and her angelic physical traits:

> Lady Audley is at once the heroine and the monstrosity of the novel. In drawing her, the authoress may have intended to portray a female Mephistopheles; but if so, she should have known that a woman cannot fill

such a part [. . .] Her manner and her appearances are always in contrast with her conduct. All this is very exciting; but it is also very unnatural. The artistic faults of this novel are as grave as the ethical ones. Combined, they render it one of the most noxious books of modern times.[6]

But there is a stronger connection between Edward and Rosina's history and Braddon's 'noxious' novel. Just as Rosina Wheeler's 'shadow' haunted Edward Bulwer Lytton throughout his life, Braddon's sensational blockbuster would similarly be her ineluctable Nemesis during her long literary career, in the course of which she brought up eleven children (six of whom were hers), published more than eighty novels, wrote a large number of short stories, edited two magazines (*Belgravia* and *Misletoe Bough*), and conducted a busy social life in Richmond. Her first biographer Robert Lee Wolff underlines the fact that, notwithstanding her efforts to experiment with many literary genres and new narrative forms, Braddon 'all of her life [. . .] remained "the author of *Lady Audley's Secret*". Even today, when she is remembered at all, she is still associated with her artless and somewhat trashy first great success.'[7] Thus, for better or worse, this sensational tale of bigamy, female assertiveness, seduction, violence, male detection and incarceration represents Braddon's haunting 'ghost', as well as a paradigmatic text on a biographical, parabiographical and narrative level.

First, there are emblematical similarities between Lady Audley's story and Rosina Wheeler's vicissitudes recounted in *A Blighted Life: a True Story* that cannot be neglected. Most of the events in these two texts take place in 1858, the year in which Rosina Wheeler publicly humiliated her husband (and was forcibly locked up in an asylum) and Lady Audley committed many of her crimes, and was punished. Despite the different social origin of the two women and their different choices in life (in Braddon's novel Helen Talboys, after her husband's sudden departure, decides to abandon her child to start a new life as a governess with the name of Lucy Graham and then succeeds in marrying Lord Audley), both are strongly assertive persons who do not accept the roles of mute and passive madonnas. In the course of her confession to Robert Audley – Lord Audley's nephew who has been collecting evidence against his aunt – Lady Audley reveals that she has inherited her madness from her mother. Like Rosina Wheeler (whose mother had been similarly accused of being mad), Helen Talboys/Lucy Graham/Lady Audley justifies her 'pathological' behaviour as the only means a woman has to survive:

[George Talboy's] father was rich; his sister was living in luxury and respectability; and I, his wife, and the mother of his son, was a slave allied forever to beggary and obscurity. People pitied me; and I hated them for their pity.

I did not love the child; for he had been left a burden upon my hands [. . .]
At last these fits of desperation resolved themselves into a desperate purpose.
I determined to run away from this wretched home which my slavery supported [. . .] I determined to go to London, and lose myself in that great chaos
of humanity.[8]

Like the many doctors who studied Rosina Wheeler's 'case' and
examined her, Dr Alwyn Mosgrave (who had been sent by Robert
Audley to sign a certificate of madness) does not believe at first that Lady
Audley is mad:

[There] is no evidence of madness in anything that she has done. She ran
away from her home, because her home was not a pleasant one, and she left
it in the hope of finding a better. There is no madness in that. She committed
the crime of bigamy, because by that crime she obtained fortune and position.
There is no madness there. When she found herself in a desperate position,
she did not grow desperate. She employed intelligent means, and she carried
out a conspiracy which required coolness and deliberation in its execution.
There is no madness in that. (Book 3, Chap. 5, p. 383)

Like the 'Hertford scandal', Lady Audley's plan 'required coolness
and deliberation in its execution', but no madness. In addition, even
when Robert suggests to the physician that Lady Audley has killed her
first husband George Talboys, Dr Mosgrave can only say that '[the]
lady is not mad' and that she *probably* inherited the taint of madness
from her mother. However, the fact that she can be 'dangerous' (Ibid.,
p. 385) is enough to condemn Lucy Graham (and Rosina Wheeler) to
imprisonment in an asylum.

Although *A Blighted Life* was written in 1866 and published only in
1880, there are too many similarities to be dismissed as merely coinci-
dental between Lady Audley's vicissitudes and Rosina Wheeler's case,
whose story Braddon had probably read in the press. For instance, is
it just a coincidence that the name of the residence of Hale Thompson
and Bulwer Lytton at Taunton during their interview with Rosina is
the 'Castle Hotel' and that Robert Audley risks losing his life during his
stay at the 'Castle Inn'? Moreover, the arrival of Dr Mosgrave at Audley
Court from London, and in particular the reasons behind it, reminds
readers of Dr Hale Thompson's visit at Rosina Wheeler's house on 10
June 1858:

Mr Robert Audley [. . .] sat long over his solitary cup of tea, smoking his
meerschaum pipe, and *meditating darkly upon the task that lay before him.*
    'I will appeal to the experience of this Dr Mosgrave,' he thought, '*physi-
cians and lawyers are the confessors of this prosaic nineteenth century.* Surely
he will be able to help me.'

The first fast train from London arrived at Audley at half-past ten o'clock, and at five minutes before eleven, Richards, the grave servant, announced Dr Alvyn Mosgrave. (Book 3, Chap. 5, p. 381, my italics)

The description of the Villebrumeuse asylum in Belgium echoes the newspaper reports of Inverness Lodge, and Lady Audley's dialogue with a Frenchwoman who works there bears a strange resemblance to Rosina Wheeler's words addressed to Dr Gardiner Hill (she said she would not 'be driven mad by being treated as a maniac'), and to his reply (he said that for him Inverness Lodge 'was not a madhouse' and that its inmates were his 'children'):

'*A maison de santé*,' [Lady Audley] repeated. 'Yes, they manage these things better in France. In England we should call it a mad-house. This is a house for mad people, this, is it not, Madame?' she said, in French, turning upon the woman, and tapping the polished floor with her foot.
    'Ah, but no, Madame,' the woman answered, with a shrill scream of protest. 'It is an establishment of the most agreeable, where one amuses oneself –.' (Book 3, Chap. 6, p. 392)[9]

In Braddon's writings and in her personal biography insanity and asylums play an important role. In 1861 (when she was still writing *Lady Audley's Secret*) she started a stable, sentimental and editorial relationship with John Maxwell, who was already married to Mary Ann Crowley, and with whom he had seven children. However, after the birth of her last son in 1860 Mary Ann had started suffering from what was defined at the time 'puerperal insanity' (the same pathology affecting Lady Audley and her mother) and had entered an asylum near Dublin. When Maxwell publicly announced his marriage to Mary Braddon in newspapers such as *The Court Journal*, *The Sun* and the *Morning Adviser* a scandal was raised by Mary Ann's brother-in-law and journalist Richard Brinsley Knowles in 1864. Indeed, at the time Maxwell was still legally married to Mary Ann. By then, Braddon and Maxwell had two children of their own, while 'the author of *Lady Audley's Secret*' was actually looking after Maxwell and Mary Ann's other children. *De facto*, Maxwell led, like Lucy Graham, a bigamous life. Only ten years later, when their family had ten children, would Maxwell and Braddon be legally married on 2 October 1874, less then a month after Mary Ann's death at the age of forty-eight, on 5 September.
    Braddon's novel contrives an important twist upon Rosina's story, because Lady Audley will slowly die in the asylum. On the contrary, Rosina will be saved and liberated after three weeks of incarceration. Besides the traditional explanation for Braddon's decision to 'kill' Lady Audley, conceived to give a morally edifying ending to her novel and to

avoid (unsuccessfully) critical attacks, another possible explanation may be suggested by the novel's dedication:

DEDICATED
TO THE
RIGHT HON. SIR EDWARD BULWER LYTTON, BART
MP, DC., &C., &C.,
IN GRATEFUL ACKNOWLEDGEMENT
OF
LITERARY ADVICE MOST GENEROUSLY GIVEN
TO THE AUTHOR

As her letters, her biographers and her famous dedication proves, Edward Bulwer Lytton was Braddon's first and most important literary mentor. She probably met him in London in 1854, through the intercession of her cousin John Delane, editor of *The Times* and a friend of the Lyttons. Their meeting took place during her formative years as an actress to support her family after her mother's separation from her husband Henry Braddon. Like Edward Bulwer Lytton, whose literary interests ranged from Newgate fiction to historical novels, Braddon in the course of her literary career explored and experimented with many literary forms in order to exorcise Lady Audley's pervasive presence, and to be considered a respectable novelist. If on the one hand in 1854 Edward Bulwer Lytton represented for Braddon a 'literary master' and an artistic model, on the other hand Rosina Wheeler described him, in a letter to A. E. Chalon written on 15 June of the same year, as an 'iced cucumber cant of Society', concluding that 'what English society requires and bows down to and worships is a loathsome, leprous, incarnate Infamy like Sir Edward Coward Bulwer Lytton'.[10] Although Braddon did not share Rosina's acrimonious opinions of her husband (which are the expression of a mutual intolerance and of a matrimonial mismatch), it would be misleading to say that Braddon reflected in her literary works Lytton's social principles and literary ideas completely. For instance, her relationship with the reading public was less tense than Lytton's. All of his life Lytton despised the reading public and felt misunderstood by readers, displaying an 'aristocratic' attitude in literary matters that differs from Braddon's more complex self-questioning. In a letter to him, she even admitted: 'I want to serve two masters. I want to be artistic & to please you. I want to be sensational, & to please Mudie's subscribers.'[11]

These reflections shed light on Braddon's famous dedication of *Lady Audley's Secret* to Edward Bulwer Lytton, and introduce an alternative analytical perspective on her sensational bestseller, as well as on her future literary activity. As readers know, paratextual features such as titles, prefaces or dedications of books can be considered important textual 'thresholds' which represent, according to Gérard Genette, not only zones of 'transition' but also of 'transaction'. They are 'a privileged place of pragmatics and [. . .] influence on the public'.[12] Braddon's decision to dedicate *Lady Audley's Secret* to Edward Bulwer Lytton enables Lucy Audley's history to become paradigmatic on a biographical and parabiographical level. First, this dedication suggests that Braddon owes him much in terms of 'literary advice'. Moreover, Braddon's words inform Edward Bulwer Lytton that the book is written *for him* and addressed *to him* in multiple ways. It follows that the similarities between Lady Audley's attitudes and vicissitudes (in particular her imprisonment in the Belgian asylum) and Rosina Wheeler's story suggest an approach to *Lady Audley's Secret* as a fictional alternative rewriting of Lady Lytton's incarceration. In what will be her first successful novel Braddon, so to speak, pays her literary debt to Bulwer Lytton and, at the same time, offers him Lady Audley's death in an asylum as a sort of fictional gift and a surrogate solution to his battle with Rosina, giving an alternative epilogue to his wife's 'improper' behaviour. In addition, through Lady Audley's final incarceration Braddon was in part trying to exorcise her own personal ghost, in the figure of John Maxwell's 'mad wife'.

Nevertheless, Edward Bulwer Lytton's influence on Braddon cannot be reduced to her passive assimilation of his experiences, of his writing principles and of his opinions. Braddon was in fact a strongly assertive woman (like Rosina Bulwer Lytton), her political ideas were sometimes on the verge of radicalism (despite her general scepticism about late-century feminism and about socialism)[13] and her novels portrayed male characters who were far from being heroic representatives of Victorian institutions, as the example of Robert Audley in *Lady Audley's Secret* demonstrates. In the course of her literary career Braddon often oscillated between Lytton's views and Lady Audley's defiance of conventions. Braddon's most renowned sensation novel represents a complex attempt to negotiate a spirit of rebellion (rooted in Braddon's personal experiences and in the tragic history of Rosina Wheeler, which she knew well) and a 'domesticating' approach to narrative issues indebted to Bulwer Lytton's lesson. *Lady Audley's Secret* can thus provide an analytical filter to evaluate her ideological, cultural and literary positions, as well as her evolution as a writer. In this context, Harold Bloom's analysis of authorial anxiety about intertextual influence can explain to some extent Braddon's complex negotiation of the heritage of Edward Bulwer

Lytton, concerning which she had contradictory feelings. According to Bloom, 'Poetic influence – when it involves two strong, authentic poets – always proceeds by a misreading of the prior poet, an act of creative correction that is actually and necessarily a misinterpretation.'[14] In her sensational bestseller Braddon borrows from and 'misinterprets' Edward Bulwer Lytton's lesson, indirectly playing up to him by killing the rebellious mad wife and creates, at the same time, a female character who fascinates readers to the point of surviving its own fictional death. The biographical, parabiographical and narrative paradigmatic value of *Lady Audley's Secret* explains its centrality in Braddon's literary macrotext and motivates her continuous attempt to cope with the enormous impact of this novel on the Victorian literary public. Far from being her masterpiece, Braddon's novel remains in fact an indisputable reference point for understanding her nature as a writer. The importance of *Lady Audley's Secret* in Braddon's macrotext not only lies in its articulated implications, but also in the fact that many of her future novels will alternatively replicate or deny its most recurring ideological, epistemological and narrative paradigms.[15]

Braddon's narrative strategies in *Lady Audley's Secret* are an expression of her complex ideological approach to the Victorian episteme, whose uneven nature and contradictory quality (suspended as it were between opposing worldviews) probably finds in the sensation novel one of its most comprehensive textual forms. Together with Wilkie Collins's *The Woman in White*, Braddon's *Lady Audley's Secret* is considered by readers and critics to be one of the founding texts of the sensation school because it features all of the typical ingredients, such as a tendency to melodramatic characterisation, the use of 'theatrical' effects, the inclusion of fascinating villains and the presence of concealed secrets in a typically contemporary setting.[16] All the elements of the 'sensational recipe' are, however, included within generic boundaries that are necessarily elastic and permeable because sensation fiction drew inspiration from heterogeneous (and apparently irreconcilable) literary genres such as the Gothic, the detective and the realist novel. As Winifred Hughes puts it, the sensation novel 'was drawn to borderlands; it compulsively blurred and transgressed boundaries and knocked down established barriers'. Moreover, '[its] generic instability at once reflected and encouraged a prevailing thematic instability and an attitude of ambivalence toward its unconventional materials'.[17] Therefore, the ideological boundaries that sensation novels easily 'blurred and transgressed' reflected their generic hybridism and enhanced their ambiguous and contradictory moral lesson. Sensation novels, including *Lady Audley's Secret*, both interacted with and put to the test the ideological assumptions and the readers' expectations upon which the three main fictional genres of the Victorian age (namely, the Gothic, the detective and the realist novel) were based. Indeed, sensation novels were usually defined in relation to or in contrast with these literary genres, so that an analysis on this textual dialectics can encourage a more articulate discussion on sensationalism, as well as on Braddon's negotiation with the limits and boundaries of literary canons in general. It may therefore be useful to investigate Braddon's interaction with Victorian literary genres in light of what her first artistic achievement contained *in nuce*, and to look simultaneously at Braddon's future attempts to free herself from her sensational Nemesis in the figure of the paradigmatic 'shadow' of Lady Audley. Finally, Braddon's engagement with Gothic, detective and realist textual and narrative features, whose articulation corresponds to specific ideological approaches to reality, becomes an occasion to deal with wider questions such as the legal and political condition of women, the role of science and technology in the ninenteenth century, the problems raised by capitalism and issues connected with fictional representation. Literary genres are in fact, first and foremost, expressions of specific world views that take a recognisable textual form and can be defined, in narratological terms, as 'codifications of discursive properties',[18] as Tzvetan Todorov asserts. Braddon's literary career can be thus interpreted as a continuous struggle for independence from the Lady Audley paradigm and as a confrontation with the novel that made her famous in the Victorian literary market.

At this point of the discussion, it is necessary to underline that the definitions of Gothic, detective and realist novel have to be approached as slippery and unstable. These artificial categories can be described as conventionally accepted and recurring narrative traits that are used (misused or even parodied) by writers, and easily recognised by readers. Speaking of genres, Jacques Derrida asserts that 'a text would not *belong* to any genre. Every text participates in one or several genres, there is no genreless text, there is always a genre or genres, yet such participation never amounts to belonging'. Yet what Derrida defines as 'law of genre' is counterbalanced by a 'law of impurity or a principle of contamination', and that, consequently, there is 'no madness without the law'.[19] In Braddon's case, it is possible to say that there is no transgression without convention or, in other words, no Lady Audley (and Rosina Wheeler) without Edward Bulwer Lytton. By looking at Braddon's relationship with Victorian literary genres, taking *Lady Audley's Secret* as a reference point, the aim of this study is to reflect on Braddon's adherence to the 'law of genre', and to the modalities through which she questions this very law. It follows that if this book is divided into separate sections (each devoted to Braddon's use of textual and narrative strategies derived, respectively, from the Gothic, detective or realist novel), there will be many cross-references among the various chapters in order to prove that this rigid division must be considered purely instrumental. By dissecting and separating the various 'generic' components within Braddon's macrotext (with *Lady Audley's Secret* as a paradigmatic text), it will be possible to follow Braddon's evolution as a writer who struggled against the haunting and 'shadowy' presence of her most renowned novel with variable results, but always with the desire to be regarded as a serious artist.

Part I ('Gothic Mutations') opens with an analysis of Braddon's updating of the Gothic mode in *Lady Audley's Secret*, in which mediaeval castles are replaced by contemporary (domestic and clinical) settings as the new embodiment of patriarchal power. The second chapter focuses on *John Marchmont's Legacy*, in which Braddon contrasts Marchmont Towers (as the architectonic expressions and the narrative 'modes' of the Gothic novel)[20] with railways and trains (as icons of the technological present), connecting both images with the theme of 'dispossession' that pervades the whole novel. The third chapter is devoted to the analysis of a vampire story entitled 'Good Lady Ducayne' and discusses the socio-political implications of the vampire in the late-Victorian age. The fourth chapter in Part II ('Darwinian Detections') relates the birth of the sensation and detective novel to the spread of evolutionary issues before and after Darwin's *On the Origin of Species*, developing these premises with reference to Braddon's *Lady Audley's Secret* and *Henry Dunbar*, approached as two examples of 'retrograde' counter-detections. The fifth chapter deals with the presence of the paradigm of visual perception and the 'geological' investigation of familial secrets featured in *Eleanor's Victory*, followed by Braddon's interaction with Darwinian and post-Darwinian issues such as heredity, species and variations in light of the investigations undertaken by the physically-disabled detective Joseph Peters in *The Trail of the Serpent*. The sixth chapter is dedicated to the 'Holmesian' inspector John Faunce and to his 'normalising' detections in *Rough Justice* and *His Darling Sin*. Part III ('Victorian Realisms') considers the various expressions of realism in the Victorian age, in particular as far as questions of figurative representation are concerned. The seventh chapter focuses on the use of 'realistic strategies' such as the presence of letters and of a pre-Raphaelite portrait in *Lady Audley's Secret* (considered by many contemporary critics an anti-realistic novel), while the following one centres on *The Doctor's Wife*. In her rewriting of Flaubert's *Madame Bovary*, Braddon's use of a 'photographic' approach in characterising her heroine shows her awareness of the

problems related to the epistemological revolution that affected the notion of 'reality' after the birth and spread of photography. At the same time, *The Doctor's Wife* offers an occasion to discuss the roles of reader (in the character of Isabel Sleaford) and writer (in the figure of sensation novelist Sigismund Smith) in the mid-Victorian literary market. The last chapter takes into consideration *Phantom Fortune*, centring on colonial and imperialist issues, as well as on the questions raised by capitalistic economic practices in late-Victorian Britain. Despite the fact that Braddon was not a Socialist and can be defined as an 'enlightened' Tory, Karl Marx's *Manifesto* and *Capital* seem to represent the main sub-texts of this Zolaesque novel. As this brief summary suggests, each of the three parts includes a chapter dedicated to a discussion on Braddon's interaction with the Gothic, the detective and the realist novel in *Lady Audley's Secret*, in order to prove that her constant attempt to use (or refuse) its paradigms can be adopted as a critical filter to read her literary productions, and to understand her wish to be accepted as something other than 'the author of *Lady Audley's Secret*', and as something other than an apprentice in Edward Bulwer Lytton's shadow.[21]

It is afternoon (nearly 5 p.m.) on 22 October 2009, and I am sitting in front of my computer. In its afterlife, Braddon's *Lady Audley's Secret* (her most famous 'bigamy novel', as she called it) continues to be published in book and digital format, to be discussed in lectures and taught in university courses. In 2000 a television adaptation of Lady Audley's story (written by Donald Hounam and directed by Betsan Morris Evans) was aired on ITV and PBS. Conferences on Braddon's works continue to be organised, while new articles, essays and books are being published, opening more critical approaches to her writings. Braddon's contradictorily normalising epilogue to her sensational bestseller (along with her decision to attribute Lady Audley's rebellion to inherited madness and puerperal insanity) has not prevented her survival in the memory of the reading public. She is not, to be sure, as famous now as she was during her lifetime, when (according to an anecdote) she received in 1888 a letter from an English teacher in Bologna, Italy, addressed only to 'Miss Mary Elizabeth Braddon, author of *Lady Audley's Secret*, London, Inghilterra'. Yet her reputation has paradoxically eclipsed that of her literary mentor Edward Bulwer Lytton. Walking around Richmond, where she resided with her husband John Maxwell and her large family in the sumptuously-adorned red brick Georgian mansion of Lichfield House, one notices that many roads and streets continue to bear the titles of her novels and the names of her characters, while the small parish church that houses her bust in bronze by John E. Hyett (unveiled in October 1915, some months after her death) is the site of a constant stream of admirers. On the other hand, despite their literary value, Edward Bulwer Lytton's novels are still much neglected by readers and scholars. Due to an ironic twist of fate, he is often remembered and referred to more for his tormented relationship with Rosina Wheeler and for his role as Braddon's literary confidant, rather than because he was considered 'one of England's greatest writers and one of the most distinguished men of our times', as Benjamin Jowett said on the day of Bulwer Lytton's funeral. Ironically again, his name survives in the annual Bulwer Lytton Fiction Contest, in which contestants have to write incipit of imaginary novels inspired by the famous opening of *Paul Clifford* (1830), (unfairly) considered among the worst in literary history. In 1993, 103 years after Rosina Wheeler's death, her family placed a stone on her long-unmarked grave with the inscription she originally requested in her will, but that her contemporaries denied her. The quotation is from Isaiah: 'The Lord shall give thee rest from thy sorrow, and from thy fear, and from the hard bondage wherein thou wast made to serve' (14: 3).[22] After a long struggle, Rosina Wheeler and Lady Audley have had their victory. And this is another sensational story, which also happens to be a true one.

Notes

1. Eliot, *Daniel Deronda*, p. 110.
2. Quotations have been taken from Rosina Bulwer Lytton, *A Blighted Life*; Devey, *Life of Rosina, Lady Lytton*; Mitchell, *Bulwer Lytton* and Christensen (ed.), *The Subverting Vision of Edward Bulwer Lytton*. According to Marie Mulvey Roberts, Rosina's vehement attacks against Victorian society, and in particular against the 'criminal' and 'despotic' Lunacy Laws, refer 'not only to her *own* situation, but also to political irregularities which she regarded as examples of corruption' ('Introduction,' in Rosina Bulwer Lytton, *A Blighted Life*, p. xxx).
3. Mansel, 'Sensation Novels', p. 485.
4. See Oliphant, 'Novels'.
5. Radford, *Victorian Sensation Fiction*, p. 3. Here Radford refers to Charles Dickens's famous opinion of *The Moonstone* as a 'wild yet domestic' novel (see Page (ed.), *Wilkie Collins*, p. 169).
6. Rae, 'Sensation Novelists: Miss Braddon', pp. 186–7.
7. Wolff, *Sensational Victorian*, p. 4. Dealing with Rosina Bulwer Lytton, Allan C. Christensen asserts that '[outside] the covers of his books, Bulwer's wife Rosina became a version of the haunting antagonist or Nemesis to whom he was fearfully bound' ('Introduction', in Christensen (ed.), *The Subverting Vision of Edward Bulwer Lytton*, p. 10).
8. Braddon, *Lady Audley's Secret*, ed. Houston, Book 3, Chap. 3, pp. 361–2. All further quotations will be from this edition.

9. In her book *Unstable Bodies*, Jill L. Matus asserts that '[while] it is remark-able how closely the confinement of Lady Audley parallels accounts of the occasion on which Lady Rosina Lytton was committed, there is no evidence from Braddon's correspondence with Bulwer Lytton that she based her representation of incarceration on circulated accounts of Lady Rosina's confinement' (p. 201). However, it seems highly improbable that Braddon would ever have 'dared' to refer explicitly to Lytton's familiar matters in her letters as 'devoted disciple'.

10. Qtd in Mitchell, *Edward Bulwer Lytton*, p. 58. On the contrary, in a letter to Edward Bulwer Lytton dated December 1862, Braddon expresses her gratitude to him: 'I can scarcely tell you how much it flatters and pleases me to think that *you* will take the trouble to read my very feeble attempts in that rank of literature which you have led so long & gloriously' (qtd in Wolff, '"Devoted Disciple"', p. 10).

11. Letter dated May 1863, '"Devoted Disciple"', p. 14.

12. Genette, *Paratexts*, p. 2.

13. According to her biographer Jennifer Carnell, '[Although] Braddon expressed her belief in 1913 that women should have the vote, she disagreed with the militant wing of the suffragette movement' (*The Literary Lives*, pp. 281–2). In Mary Elizabeth Braddon's words, reported in an interview, 'I think women ought to have a vote when every half-educated man, every clodhopper may have his say in the government of his country. Suffragists, I think, are both self-sacrificing and daring. Militants, however, have gone the wrong way about asserting their rights. Nothing is to be gained by the destruction of private property, and those actions have done nothing more than alienate even those who are in sympathy with the movement' (Hatton, 'Miss Braddon at Home', p. 9).

14. Bloom, *The Anxiety of Influence*, p. 30.

15. Although *Aurora Floyd* (1863) seems on the surface very different from the 'bigamy novel' that preceded it (Aurora is not a plotting femme fatale but only a spoiled girl, and there is no reference to madness in the story), even in this case *Lady Audley's Secret* can be adopted as a filter for Braddon's opinions, for instance, on Victorian marriage. In Natalie Schroeder and Ronald A. Schroeder's view, 'Aurora's extraordinary measure of deserting her husband reverses the conventional pattern of spousal abandonment that Braddon established in *Lady Audley's Secret*. In taking this step, Aurora, like Lucy Audley, tries in some measure to lay claim to an autonomous existence' (*From Sensation to Society*, p. 77).

16. On many occasions, Braddon admitted her debt to Collins's *The Woman in White*: 'I always say that I owe "Lady Audley's Secret" to "The Woman in White." Wilkie Collins is assuredly my literary father. My admiration for "The Woman in White" inspired me with the idea of "Lady Audley's Secret" as a novel of construction and character' (Hatton, 'Miss Braddon at Home', p. 28).

17. Hughes, 'The Sensation Novel', p. 264. Richard Fantina and Kimberly Harrison assert that 'sensation novels are generic hybrids, exhibiting char-acteristics of genres including melodrama, romance, the gothic, realism, and Newgate Fiction' ('Introduction', in Fantina and Harrison (eds), *Victorian Sensations*, p. xii), while for Patrick Brantlinger sensation is '[a]

genre of fiction that stands midway between romanticism and realism, Gothic "mysteries" and modern mysteries, and popular and high cultural forms' ('What is "Sensational" about the "Sensation Novel"?', p. 3). On this aspect, see also Loesberg, 'The Ideology of Narrative Form in Sensation Fiction'.

18. Todorov, *Genres in Discourse*, p. 18.
19. See Derrida, 'The Law of Genre'. Thomas O. Beebe opens his analysis on the instability of literary genres saying that '[as] a form of ideology, genre is never fully identical with itself, nor are texts fully identical with their genres. Furthermore, if genre is a form of ideology, then the struggle against or the deviations from genre are ideological struggles' (*The Ideology of Genre*, p. 19). For John Flow, 'Far from being merely "stylistic" devices, genres create effects of reality and truth, authority and plausibility [. . .] These effects are not, however, fixed and stable, since texts [. . .] do not "belong" to genres but are, rather, uses of them' (*Genre*, p. 2).
20. Alastair Fowler defines with the term 'kinds' the historical literary genres, and with the term 'mode' their 'generic signals' (*Kinds of Literature*, p. 52). According to him, each genre 'has multiple distinguishing traits', while '[every] literary work changes the genre it relates to' (Ibid., p. 18; p. 23).
21. Apart from *Lady Audley's Secret*, whose plot is widely known, the analysis of Braddon's texts will be preceded by a brief summary.
22. See Cobbold, 'Rosina Bulwer Lytton', in Christensen (ed.), *The Subverting Vision*, p. 157. Referring to Edward Bulwer Lytton, Andrew Brown notices that '[no] other Victorian writer of note suffered so total an eclipse' ('Bulwer's Reputation', Ibid., p. 29).

Part I

Gothic Mutations

Torn in her own lifetime from the list of the living, the daughter of Philip
Fairlie and the wife of Percival Glyde might still exist for her sister,
might still exist for me; but to all the world besides she was dead. Dead
to her uncle who had renounced her; dead to the servants of the house,
who had failed to recognise her; dead to the persons in authority who
had transmitted her fortune to her husband and her aunt [. . .] socially,
morally, legally – dead.

Wilkie Collins, *The Woman in White*, 1861[1]

Chapter 1

Displacing the Gothic in *Lady Audley's Secret*

In reviewing *Lady Audley's Secret*[2] for *The Times*, an anonymous reader found a precedent to Mary Elizabeth Braddon's most famous novel, which dated back to the seventeenth century. The reviewer hinted at the differences between a quintessential Gothic tale of abuses and violence which took place in the past and the narration of Lady Audley's story, belonging to 'modern times':

> The name of the novel which everybody is just now reading may excite the curiosity of historical students. They may imagine that it refers to that most horrible story which appears in the record of our state trials – the story of Mervyn Touchet, Lord Audley, who was beheaded in the reign of Charles I for inflicting on his wife, Lady Audley, indescribable cruelties. The secret of the imaginary Lady Audley, however, is very different, and the novel in which she figures belongs entirely to modern times.[3]

The story was that of Lord Audley, born in 1552 and executed on 14 May 1631 on Tower Hill because of the daily violence his wife (the Countess of Castlehaven, who died between 1622 and 1624) had to endure, namely rape and sodomy. As far as 'modern times' were concerned, the sad existence of this seventeenth-century Lady Audley would similarly find one of its Victorian counterparts in John Conolly's female patients suffering from puerperal insanity, and in particular in one case regarding a 'sensitive woman, whose mother had been insane, [who] became deranged and melancholic almost as soon as her little child came into the world'. In the opinion of one of the most famous alienists of the times – whose 'merciful' practices of domestic confinement and whose 'homely' approach to the building of asylums were illustrated in *The Construction and Government of Lunatic Asylums* (1847) and in *The Treatment of the Insane without Mechanical Restraints* (1856) – the woman's madness was caused by her husband's sudden leaving. In an uncanny anticipation of George Talboys's decision to abandon his family, this man, according to Conolly, 'left her, and his home, and his country, to seek employment in Australia'.[4] Despite the antithetical nature of these two stories of violence and solitude, set in two different historical periods, they seem to recall (although in an altered and displaced form) the vicissitudes of Lucy Graham and Helen Talboys, who turn out to be the same person in Braddon's novel. The male violence of the past and the clinical procedures of the present are the textual and contextual boundaries that define and characterise Braddon's peculiar treatment of the 'Gothic mode'[5] in a paradigmatic sensation novel which is grafted onto and intertwined with Braddon's biographic, parabiographic and literary experiences (see Introduction). Braddon's borrowing from popular literary genres and her allusion to contemporary themes do not correspond to the creation of manicheistic antitheses between good and evil, or to a traditionally 'melodramatic' construction of the narration. The first and most striking novelty for Victorian readers and critics concerned in particular Lady Audley's physical aspect. An ironic imitation of the insipid but morally edifying heroines of Charlotte Yonge's domestic novels, Lady Audley reverses the association between black-haired women and moral corruption. This disquieting innovation was first noticed by an anonymous reviewer, who was none other than Margaret Oliphant, in an article entitled 'Novels' (*Blackwood's Edinburgh Magazine*, No. 102, September 1867):

> [Braddon] is the inventor of the fair-haired demon of modern fiction. Wicked women used to be brunettes long ago, now they are the daintiest, softest, prettiest of blonde creatures; and this change has been wrought by Lady Audley, and her influence on contemporary novels.[6]

The fact that *Lady Audley's Secret* is a Gothic tale set in Victorian times justifies Braddon's treatment and violation of all the structural, narrative and thematic devices of a literary genre historically born as a reaction and a counter-discourse to Enlightenment. Indeed, the Gothic was given a philosophical and architectural justification first by Edmund Burke in his description of the alluring and fearful (a)symmetry of 'sublime' settings in *Enquiry into the Origins of Our Ideas Concerning the Sublime and Beautiful* (1757) and then by Immanuel Kant in his discussion on 'The Aesthetic of the Sublime' in *Critique of Judgement* (1790). These premises would be translated into a narrative form by Horace Walpole, Matthew Lewis and Ann Radcliffe in their tales of male evil and female persecution taking place in old castles and in Catholic countries such as Italy and Spain. Along with the inclusion of super-natural events in oppressive physical surroundings, the appearance of doubles and the occurrence of dreams or dreamlike states, Eve Kosofsky Sedgwick asserts that the conventions that are typical of Gothic fictions can be reduced to a single 'dynamic structure' characterised by the correspondence between 'within' and 'without', and by a prolonged quest for identity.[7] Although *Lady Audley's Secret* follows this 'law of genre' (as Jacques Derrida defines it), Braddon implodes it from within, in a way that is not too different from Jane Austen's parodic rewriting of Gothic conventions in *Northanger Abbey*. If both Victorian and contemporary critics have noticed the similarities between the Gothic novel and the sensation novel with particular reference to their hybrid quality (as a mixture of romance and realistic narration), the most obvious element that differentiates them is the chronological, geographical and even social proximity of the audience of sensation fictions. Furthermore, the inclusion of assertive female characters, with Charlotte Brontë's *Jane Eyre* as their genotextual model, is another significant feature of the Victorian Gothic.[8] The most remarkable difference between Charlotte Brontë (whom she greatly admired) and Braddon lies in the fact that *Lady Audley's Secret* conflates Jane Eyre, Bertha Mason and Blanche Glover in one single character, with the beautiful and assertive blonde-haired 'madwoman' living on a country estate rather than 'in the attic'. The dangerous modern 'proximity' of Braddon's treatment of the Gothic mode – which she both domesticates and complicates – was noticed by eminent critics soon after the publication of *Lady Audley's Secret*, and was denounced as its most troublesome quality. In his review of over twenty-four sensation fictions, including Braddon's *Aurora Floyd* and Collins's *No Name*, Reverend Henry Longueville Mansel writes that 'Proximity is, indeed, one great element of sensation.'[9]

The first and most apparent revision of the codes of Gothic fictions (once sold as 'penny dreadfuls' and now published as 'respectable' three-volume novels available in Mudie's circulating library) is represented by the beautiful, fair-haired and delicate Helen Talboys/Lucy Graham in the role of the villain, who replaces the morally corrupted males of eighteenth-century Gothic fictions. In Braddon's case the traditional patriarch is none other than the weak and frail aristocrat Sir Michael Audley, who becomes a toy in Lady Audley's skilful hands. In turn, the bohemian barrister, lazy reader of French novels and decadent Robert Audley replaces the heroes of the past and turns into the amateur investigator who finally detects (and counter-detects) Lady Audley's crimes (see Part II, Chapter 4). Despite the fact that Braddon was forced to exploit the stratagem of the hereditary 'fits of madness' to justify Lady Audley's immoral behaviour and include a fundamentally unconvincing happy ending, *Lady Audley's Secret* is a deliberate

attempt at questioning the Gothic mode by means of a constant displacement of its features. Braddon's novel becomes an example of
those fictions Ellen Moers labels as 'Female Gothic', which feature the
emergence of a female narrative subject in search of her autonomous
identity against patriarchal institutions. Braddon's reversal of conventions is more emblematic if we bear in mind Michelle A. Massé's assertion that the *ur-plot* of Gothic novels 'is a terror-inflicted variant of
the Richardsonian courtship narrative in which an unprotected young
woman in an isolated setting uncovers a sinister secret'.[10] On the contrary, in *Lady Audley's Secret* it is the isolated setting that allows Lady
Audley better to conceal her secrets.

The novel opens with the image of Audley Court, described as a
sheltered and 'peaceful' place. Its immutability seems to be shattered
by recognisable Gothic signifiers such as the allusion to the existence of
a convent in the past, the architectural irregularity of the building and
the presence of secret chambers, which in this case function as Victorian
signifieds:

> To the left there was a gravelled walk, down which, years ago, when the
> place had been a convent, the quiet nuns had walked hand in hand [. . .]
> The house faced the arch, and occupied three sides of a quadrangle. It was
> very old, and very irregular and rambling [. . .] A glorious old place [. . .] a
> spot to which Peace seemed to have taken up her abode, setting her sooth-
> ing hand on every tree and flower [. . .] Of course, in such a house there
> were secret chambers: the little daughter of the present owner, Sir Michael
> Audley, had fallen by accident upon the discovery of one. (Book 1, Chap.
> 1, pp. 43–5)

In traditional Gothic fictions convents were either the emblems
of secrecy (as in the Dominican convent of the Spirito Santo where
Schedoni lives in Radcliffe's *The Italian*), corruption, death (in the
convent of St Clare in *The Monk*) or places of repentance (in *The Castle
of Otranto*). On the contrary, in *Lady Audley's Secret* Braddon makes
use of these topological signifiers to introduce us to the criminal nature
of the events which take place on an estate where 'Peace seemed to have
taken up her abode'[11] and where the voice of Lady Audley gradually
replaces the murmurs of the 'quiet nuns', projecting her uneven moral
values in the 'irregular and rambling' architecture of the house. Braddon
gave a new Victorian significance to the Gothic identification between
settings and characters, as well as between the disquieting 'sublimity' of
Audley Court and the inner recesses of the Lady's psyche. The transition
from medieval castles to Victorian country houses as the new sites of
transgression and penetration of the female 'other'[12] becomes a relevant

variation of the Gothic mode. The isotopic reference to the serenity and peacefulness of Audley Court as former convent is an ironically proleptic narrative strategy which anticipates Lady Audley's criminal intents and, later, her incarceration in the Belgian asylum of Villebrumeuse.[13] The image of 'peacefulness' introduced in the opening section of *Lady Audley's Secret* is ironically juxtaposed, some pages after, with Robert Audley's explicit reference to notorious crimes such as the Glasgow poisoning of 1857:

> We hear every day of murders committed in the country. Brutal and treacherous murders; slow, protracted agonies from poisons administered by some kindred hand; sudden and violent deaths by cruel blows, inflicted with a stake cut from some spreading oak, whose very shadow promised – *peace*. (Book 1, Chap. 7, p. 91, my italics)

According to Michel Foucault, the general hospitals of the seventeenth century – the first structures that housed people who were considered mentally ill – imitated the working rhythms and the attitudes of religious institutions such as convents.[14] In Braddon's novel, the 'peaceful' retreat of the British country house where Lady Audley lives looks strikingly similar to the Belgian asylum of Villebrumeuse in which she will be secluded. This provocative association emerges between the lines of the final dialogue between Lady Audley and Robert, with the latter comparing the madhouse to a convent:

> 'You have brought me to my grave, Mr Audley,' she cried, 'you have used your power basely and cruelly, and have brought me to a living grave.'
> 'I have done that which I thought just to others and merciful to you [. . .] You will lead *a quiet and peaceful life as many a good and holy woman in this Catholic country freely takes upon herself*, and happily endures unto the end.' (Book 3, Chap. 6, p. 396, my italics)[15]

As the double meaning of the word 'asylum' suggests, the house (as a material place and a social institution) becomes a retreat and a potential prison, a shelter and a site of confinement.[16] Braddon complicates these antitheses with the creation of a female villain who is both pursuer and pursued, persecutor and victim. Audley Court thus represents in *Lady Audley's Secret* the enclosed space in which control and surveillance predominate and in which Lady Audley is subjected to the 'Panoptical' gaze of those who, spurred by different motivations, search into her past life: Phoebe Marks (out of curiosity), Luke Marks (to blackmail her) and Robert Audley (to disclose her real identity). Slowly but irreversibly Lady Audley's domestic 'retreat' turns into her clinical 'asylum'. This is in line with the then current reform in the treatment of mentally-deranged people, in particular women, which aimed at their 'domestication' through the performance of simple ordinary duties rather than on the use of physical restraint. In this context, John Conolly's medical, cultural and architectonic innovations introduced in *The Construction and Government of Lunatic Asylums* (1847) can be read through a Foucaultian lens, because the alienist's approach foregrounds the transition from an authoritarian form of management to a paternalistic one based upon a 'Panoptical' control over (female) transgressing behaviours. As Elaine Showalter argues, these new 'asylums' (a word which gradually replaced 'madhouses' and which hinted at the domestic nature of confinement) 'were organised on the family model' and 'imitated the architecture of the English country house, with its carefully demarcated space for men and women, master and servants'.[17]

Another example of Braddon's use of proleptic narrative strategies emerges in the course of her description of Phoebe and Luke's walk into the corridors of the house, which precedes the disclosure of the first of Lady Audley's 'secrets': a lock of hair and the worsted shoe of a baby, concealed in a secret drawer. The Gothic background of Audley Court is given a Victorian significance which does not point to secrets set in 'old times' but towards contemporary issues related to the condition of Victorian women:

> The long, black oak corridors were dim in the ghostly twilight – the light carried by Phoebe looking only a poor speck of flame in the broad passages through which the girl led her cousin [. . .]
> 'It's a mortal dull place, Phoebe,' [Luke] said, as they emerged from a passage into the principal hall, which was not yet lighted; 'I've heard tell of a murder which was done here in old times.'
> 'There are murders enough in these times, as to that, Luke,' answered the girl, ascending the staircase, followed by the young man. (Book 1, Chap. 3, p. 68)

The traditional settings of Gothic fictions such as graveyards and ruined tombs have a totally different value in *Lady Audley's Secret*, because Braddon alters their functional and ideological nature.[18] One of the most sensational scenes of Braddon's text describes George Talboys standing in front of his wife's as yet unwritten tombstone at Ventnor, Isle of Wight, whose text he jots down. Here George Talboys literally and symbolically imposes his patriarchal authority and authorship on Helen Talboys's past life. Moreover, the description of Helen Talboys's grave acquires a further importance because of its allusion to the legalised social death of Victorian women:

They very easily found the stonemason, and sitting down amidst the fragmentary litter of the man's yard, George Talboys wrote in pencil this brief inscription for the headstone of his wife's grave: –

Sacred to the memory of
HELEN,
THE BELOVED WIFE OF GEORGE TALBOYS
Who departed this life
August 24th, 1857, aged 22,
Deeply regretted by her sorrowing Husband (Book 1, Chap. 6, p. 81)

While tombs in Gothic novels were often the emblems of crime or of concealed secrets, in *Lady Audley's Secret* they represent the means through which Helen Talboys, as abandoned wife and mother destined to a life of poverty, dies to give life to the governess Lucy Graham and to the future Lady Audley. Braddon in her novel repeatedly aims at emphasising the connection between the social spaces of the house, the tomb and (finally) the asylum. She depicts them as the three settings in which women's bodies and aspirations are contradictorily managed (and in which women try to manage their lives), during a historical period in which the separation of the spheres – connected to the professionalisation of male jobs and to the domestication of women's activities – became a social, political and economic rule. The mid-century manipulation and updating of Gothic conventions in many Victorian novels (for instance in Charlotte Brontë's *Jane Eyre*, in Emily Brontë's *Wuthering Heights*, in Dickens's *Bleak House* and, generally speaking, in sensation fictions by Braddon, Mrs Henry/Ellen Wood, Charles Reade or Wilkie Collins) 'sought in various ways to register the psychic disturbance of the Victorian middle-class wife, who was confined to the domestic realm at the very time in which that locale ceased to be productive or economically active'.[19] In another 'theatrical' and 'sensational' scene of the novel Lucy Graham/Lady Audley reveals her mental disturbance (rooted in a social, cultural and economic imbalance, rather than in hereditary taints) through a hyperbolic association between rebellion and madness:

'You have used your cool, calculating, frigid, luminous intellect to a noble purpose. You have conquered – a MADWOMAN!.'
 'A madwoman!' cried Mr Audley.
 'Yes, a madwoman. When you say that I killed George Talboys, you say the truth. When you say I murdered him treacherously and foully, you lie. I killed him because I AM MAD! Because my intellect is a little way upon the wrong side of that narrow boundary-line between sanity and insanity; because when George Talboys goaded me, as you have goaded me; and reproached me, and

threatened me; my mind, never properly balanced, utterly lost its balance and *I was mad*!' (Book 3, Chap. 3, pp. 354–5)[20]

Lady Audley's confinement in the Belgian asylum represents a victory for the representatives of middle-class patriarchal power, namely professionals such as Dr Mosgrave, alienist Dr Val and lawyer Robert Audley. But, despite their actions, Lady Audley's rebellion will survive the memory of her defeat. Therefore, apart from the adoption of theatrical effects (in this as well as in other novels), Braddon's Gothic imagery and dramatic sensationalism[21] is functional to her attempt at denouncing Victorian women's social, sexual and cultural discrimination, in particular at the dawn of the passage of the Divorce and Matrimonial Causes Act (1857).

In many sections of *Lady Audley's Secret* Braddon tries to justify the reasons that motivate the criminal actions of Lady Audley, who willingly 'departs this life' (to misquote from her headstone inscription) to choose a better one at all costs. Before being informed of the Lady's attempt at killing her first husband and before delegating (in a Pilate-like manner) the destiny of Lucy Graham to the Belgian physician Dr Val, Dr Alwyn Mosgrave analyses her 'excessive' behaviour and even her hereditary madness through the language of science:

> '[There] is no evidence of madness in anything that she has done. She ran away from her home, because her home was not a pleasant one, and she left it in the hope of finding a better. There is no madness in that. She committed the crime of bigamy, because by that crime she obtained fortune and position. There is no madness there. When she found herself in a desperate position, she did not grow desperate. She employed intelligent means, and she carried out a conspiracy which required coolness and deliberation in its execution. There is no madness in that.' (Book 3, Chap. 5, p. 383)

Dr Mosgrave's changed diagnosis of 'latent' and 'dangerous' insanity, originating in a maternal 'hereditary taint in her blood' (p. 385), is the sign of the precarious condition of Victorian women, left at the mercy of middle-class professional man who acted as their confessors, judges and executioners. Indeed, Braddon's novel was written when the Madhouse Act (1828), according to which a single certificate signed by two medical men sufficed to lock up a private patient in an asylum, still exerted a form of violent coercion, as the case of Rosina Wheeler's forced confinement in 1858 demonstrates. Lady Audley's assertion that madhouses 'are large and only too numerous' (p. 267) seems to be another ironic reference to the politics related to the treatment and management of the insane, and in particular to the Lunatics Act of 1845 (a law despised and reviled by Rosina Wheeler). This Act

increased the number of asylums which were required to be built by
all counties of England and Wales to provide for the care of lunatics in
proper places. In this context, Mosgrave's attitudes coincide with the
newly-established hospital politics and the reformed nineteenth-century
medical gaze.[22] In describing the Belgian madhouse to Robert Audley,
Dr Mosgrave also creates a connection between the spaces of the house,
the tomb and the asylum:

> 'From the moment in which Lady Audley enters that *house*,' he said, 'her
> life, so far as life is made up of action and variety, will be finished. Whatever
> secrets she may have will be secrets for ever. Whatever crimes she may have
> committed she will be able to commit no more. If you were to dig *a grave* for
> her in the nearest churchyard and *bury her alive* in it, you could not more
> safely shut her from the world and all worldly associations.' (Book 3, Chap.
> 5, p. 386, my italics)

Lady Audley's final trip will lead her to Belgian alienist Dr Val, who
will incarcerate her until her death. The loss of her name and identity the
moment she becomes the anonymous 'Madame Taylor' – an invented
name chosen by Robert to save the decorum of the Audley family – will
be the Lady's definitive shutting off from 'all worldly associations' in
the madhouse of Villebrumeuse. The Belgian clinic is introduced by
Braddon through the image of a lamp made of 'iron and glass' that
illuminates its gates. This description creates a disquieting association
between the asylum (as an emblem of the modern and institutionalised
hospital system) and the Crystal Palace of the Great Exhibition at Hyde
Park, whose main structure made of 'iron and glass' was completed and
opened to the public in 1851 (seven years before the main events in *Lady
Audley's Secret* take place):

> My lady gave a little scream as she looked out of the coach window. The
> gaunt gateway was lighted by an enormous lamp; a great structure of iron
> and glass, in which one poor little shivering flame struggled with the March
> wind [. . .]
> 'I know where you have brought me,' she said. 'This is a MAD-HOUSE.'
> [. . .]
> 'It is a *maison de santé*, my lady,' the young man answered gravely. 'I have
> no wish to juggle with or to deceive you.'
> My lady paused for a few moments, looking reflectively at Robert.
> '*A maison de santé*,' she repeated. 'Yes, they manage these things better
> in France. In England we should call it a mad-house. This is a house for
> mad people, this, is it not, Madame?' she said, in French, turning upon the
> woman, and tapping the polished floor with her foot.
> 'Ah, but no, Madame,' the woman answered, with a shrill scream of
> protest. 'It is an establishment of the most agreeable, where one amuses
> oneself [. . .]' (Book 3, Chap. 6, pp. 391–2)

The description of an 'establishment' illuminated by an 'iron and glass' lamp where one 'amuses oneself' seems to be an allusion to the Crystal Palace, the most famous symbol of Victorian progress, prosperity and powerful commercial economy. This weird connection demonstrates the ambivalent nature of Braddon's message. In Villebrumeuse and in the Crystal Palace inmates and goods are both 'on display', in its double meaning of being transparently shown to the public and surveyed by institutional powers. In *Lady Audley's Secret* Braddon depicts madness not simply as a mental malady that affects rebellious women but, more significantly, as one of the conditions of modernity. This association between contemporary 'Victorian things' and madness had been previously suggested by Lady Audley, for whom the 'outward apparatus of existence' clashed with the 'riot and the confusion within':

> Who has not felt, in the first madness of sorrow, an unreasoning rage against the mute propriety of chairs and tables, the stiff squareness of Turkey carpets, the unbending obstinacy of the outward apparatus of existence? [. . .]
> Madhouses are large and only too numerous; yet surely it is strange that they are not larger, when we think of how many helpless wretches must beat their brains against this hopeless persistency of the orderly outward world, as compared with the storm and tempest, the riot and the confusion within [. . .] (Book 2, Chap. 6, pp. 226–7)

Lady Audley's physical, ideological and 'textual' escape from the Gothic prisons of the past leads her to face the medicalised domestication of the present in the shape of a Belgian asylum, whose 'spatialization of disease' (as Foucault defines it)[23] is typical of a panoptically-structured social and architectural institution. In the description of the 'agreeable' *maison de santé* of Villebrumeuse Braddon seems to have taken inspiration from Henry Maudsley and John Conolly's asylums, where no physical restraints were used and whose prevalently female inmates were taught to perform ordinary domestic duties. In these surrogate Victorian houses women's innate fragility and weakness were thought to be better managed.[24] Lady Audley's various 'secrets' are far from being inexplicable Gothic mysteries. On the contrary, they are rooted in the Victorian age. As Elaine Showalter puts it, 'As every woman reader must have sensed, Lady Audley's real secret is that she is *sane* and, moreover, representative.'[25]

Lady Audley is the last in a long series of fictional characters who try to escape male violence and imprisonment, ranging from Samuel Richardson's Pamela and the fragile female characters of Gothic novels to Laura Fairlie in *The Woman in White*. However, Mary Wollstonecraft's eponymous heroine in her unfinished *Maria or the Wrongs of Women* (1788–98) anticipates better than others Braddon's

Nice comparison to Wollstonecraft.

peculiar treatment of the asylum. This novel, written during the season in which the success of the Gothic genre reached its peak, and intended as a sort of fictional translation of the ideas Mary Wollstonecraft illustrated in *A Vindication of the Rights of Women,* tells the story of Maria, who escapes her home and her violent father only to marry an even more brutal man named George Venables. After discovering that Maria has tried to run away with their daughter, George drugs and imprisons her in a madhouse from which she will later escape with the servant Jemina and the fellow-prisoner Henry Darnford, with whom she had fallen in love. The description of Maria's imprisonment in Wollstonecraft's novel can be compared with Braddon's displacement of Gothic conventions and settings in *Lady Audley's Secret,* although in the latter case Lucy Graham's madness has more complex implications:

> Abodes of horror have frequently been described, and castles, filled with spectres and chimeras, conjured up by the magic spell of genius to harrow the soul, and absorb the wondering mind. But, formed of such stuff as dreams are made of, what are they to the mansion of despair, in one corner of which Maria sat, endeavouring to recall her scattered thoughts.[26]

According to the Victorian notion of the separation of the spheres, and to its rigidly-defined gender categories, Lady Audley's social and bodily 'liminality' represents her most disquieting characteristic, since her manners and her beauty allow her to ascend the social scale and to turn from governess into lady. As a matter of fact, Victorians considered governesses as strange creatures moving halfway between irreconcilable realities: outer world and family life, paternal rules and maternal tenderness, the economic independence usually attributed to men and the educational (rather than domestic) duties they performed in families which were not theirs. This fact explains the fascination Victorian writers such as Charlotte Brontë, W. M. Thackeray, as well as sensation novelists such as Wilkie Collins and Mrs Henry Wood, felt for these liminal figures, who easily managed to penetrate domestic settings which were traditionally forbidden to strangers.[27] And, dealing with Lady Audley's duplicitous, indeed, 'amphibious' nature, it is significant that Robert Audley in his nightmares imagines Lucy Graham in the form of a siren:

> In those troublesome dreams he saw Audley Court, rooted up from amidst the green pastures and the shady hedgerows of Essex, standing bare and unprotected upon that desolate northern shore, threatened by the rapid rising of a boisterous sea, whose waves seemed gathering upward to descend and crush the house he loved. As the hurrying waves rolled nearer and nearer to the stately mansion, the sleeper saw a pale, starry face looking out of the silvery foam, and knew that it was my lady, transformed into a mermaid, beckoning his uncle to destruction. (Book 2, Chap. 9, pp. 263–4)

This allusion to supernatural events and dreamlike states recalls Matthew G. Lewis's in *The Monk* and Ann Radcliffe's in *The Italian* (respectively Matilda and the Marchesa di Vivaldi), foregrounding Braddon's problematic emancipation from, and updating of, the Gothic mode. But the most striking difference between Braddon's mermaid and these Gothic female villains lies in the fact that Lady Audley is a 'siren with a story' because she is given (like, for instance, W. M. Thackeray's Becky Sharp in *Vanity Fair*) 'what no siren has ever had: a history, out of which a complex character with complex motivations may be constructed by the reader'.[28] When comparing, for instance, Lady Audley's reasons for her 'improper' actions with Matilda's characterisation in *The Monk* this difference becomes more explicit. If on the one hand Matilda is similarly gifted with 'a profusion of golden hair' and 'rosy lips, heavenly eyes, and majesty of countenance', on the other hand her seduction of Ambrosio and her crimes are given a supernatural explanation.[29] Matilda is in fact sent by Satan. On the contrary, Lucy Graham is a product and a victim of the sexual, legal and social discriminations of her times.

Phoebe Marks, the Lady's maid who is prey to her husband/cousin's physical and psychological oppression, is the only character in the novel who seems to embody the traditional female victim of eighteenth-century Gothic tales. After having alluded to the physical resemblance between herself and Phoebe, Lady Audley tells her maid that the only gap that separates them – at least as far as their bodily appearances are concerned – can be easily bridged:

> 'Do you know, Phobe, I have heard people say you and I are alike?'
> 'I have heard them say too, my lady,' said the girl, quietly, 'but they must be very stupid to say it, for your ladyship is a beauty and I am a poor plain creature.'
> 'Not at all, Phoebe,' said the little lady superbly: 'you *are* like me, and your features are very nice; it is only colour that you want [. . .] With a bottle of hair dye, such as we see advertised in the papers, and pot of rouge, you'd be as good-looking as I any day, Phoebe.' (Book 1, Chap. 7, p. 95)

Braddon implies that the differences between a lady and a maid are due only to the dress they wear, the enamels they use and the presence of fashionable hair dyes, in a world increasingly dominated by advertisements and consumerism. As will become more evident in the case of such novels as *The Lady's Mile* and *Phantom Fortune*, Braddon is aware that the social differences of the past – based upon rigid divisions between classes – tend to disappear in a context that was becoming more and more socially fluid. But it is important to read between the lines of

Lady Audley's discourse on 'similarities', because she also alludes to the fact that the two women represent each other's specular image: Phoebe reflects what Helen Talboys *could have been* if she had accepted her destiny of resignation. On the contrary, Lady Audley is a projection of what Phoebe *could have become* if she had rebelled against her destiny.[30]

A more subtle allusion to Phoebe and Lady Audley's (unexpected) sisterhood emerges when Robert Audley, who starts to be suspicious of his aunt, notices some strange bruises upon the Lady's wrist which are the proofs of her struggle for survival with George Talboys:

> It was not one bruise, but four slender, purple *marks*, such as might have been made by the four fingers of a powerful hand that had grasped the delicate wrist a shade too roughly. A narrow ribbon, bound tightly, might have left some such *marks*, it is true, and my lady protested once more that, to the best of her recollection, that must have been how they were made.
>
> Across one of the faint purple *marks* there was a darker tinge, as if a ring worn on one of these strong and cruel fingers had been ground into the tender flesh. (Book 1, Chap. 11, p. 123, my italics)

The lexical reiteration of the term 'marks' is a semantically significant element and a reminder of the many 'Marks/marks' women like Phoebe had to bear and to suffer. The Lady's attempts to kill her enemies thus function as a 'retribution for cruel behaviour on the part of their husbands or fiancés'.[31] In light of the debate on marital violence on women that followed the passage of the Marriage Act in 1858, the connection between Lady Audley's visible 'marks', Luke Marks's prolonged violence on Phoebe and the shape of George's wedding ring impressed on the Lady's wrist suggest that the prevalent context in which such brutal actions took place was represented by the family.

However, as the novel approaches its conclusion the differences between the two women become greater: Lady Audley decides to commit any sort of skilful machination and crime in order to preserve her status while Phoebe Marks (now married to Luke) accepts being the victim of her husband/cousin's brutality. Luke Marks, who has become the 'landlord' of an inn located on Mount Stanning (not far from Audley Court) named 'The Castle', embodies the figure of the traditional Gothic pursuer. Braddon's final rejection of Gothic conventions will be given a narrative form in the Lady's burning of the 'Castle Inn':[32]

> 'It's Mount Stanning, my lady,' cried Phoebe Marks. 'It's the Castle that's on fire – I know it is, I know it is. I thought of fire tonight, and I was fidgety and uneasy, for I knew this would happen some day' [. . .]
>
> [Lady Audley] walked away in the darkness, leaving Phoebe Marks still kneeling upon the hard road, where she had cast herself in that agony of supplication. Sir Michael's wife walked through the house in which her husband

slept, with the red blaze lighting up the skies behind her, and with nothing but the blackness of the night before. (Book 3, Chap. 1, p. 337)

The image of Lady Audley who contemplates the flames destroying the 'Castle' can be interpreted as Braddon's textual farewell to the Gothic genre in its traditional form and an exemplary introduction to its updated evolution in her future productions, where traumatising trains (in *John Marchmont's Legacy*) or foreign vampires haunting young English ladies (in 'Good Lady Ducayne') will represent the new mutating forms of the Victorian Gothic.

Notes

1. Collins, *The Woman in White*, p. 372.
2. *Lady Audley's Secret* was serialised in *The Robin Goodfellow* from 6 July 28 to September 1861, when the magazine closed. Pressed by readers' requests, Braddon was forced to 'resuscitate' it in *The Sixpenny Magazine* from January to December 1862. The work was then published in three volumes by Tinsley Brothers in October 1862 and dedicated to Edward Bulwer Lytton (see Introduction). Our edition is Braddon, *Lady Audley's Secret*, ed. Houston.
3. [Anonym.], '*Lady Audley's Secret*', p. 4.
4. Conolly, 'The Physiognomy of Insanity' (1858), qtd in Gilman ed., *The Face of Madness*, p. 55. Elaine Showalter, who compares Conolly's case to Lucy Graham/Lady Audley's, asserts that 'Mary Elizabeth Braddon's sensational best-seller *Lady Audley's Secret* (1861) presents a subversive feminist view of puerperal mania and its murderous results' (*The Female Malady*, p. 34). Jenny Bourne Taylor and Russell Croft treat the novel in the context of nineteenth-century mental science and in particular with reference to James Cowles Prichard's definition of 'moral insanity' in his *Treatise on Insanity* (1835). See Bourne Taylor with Crofts, 'Introduction', in Braddon, *Lady Audley's Secret*, ed. Bourne Taylor, pp. xxvi–xxvii.
5. In dealing with the influence of the Gothic genre, Robert Mighall prefers to describe it as a 'mode' rather than a 'genre' (*A Geography of Victorian Gothic Fiction*, p. xix). As for sensation fiction, '[it] adopts the key elements from the Gothic and relocates them in a distinctly "modern", secular and, on the surface, mundane context' (Ibid., p. 128).
6. Oliphant, 'Novels', p. 263. *Pace* Oliphant, Lady Audley is not the first fair-haired demon in literary history. Galia Ofek retraces, among Lady Audley's literary antecedents, two anonymous novels published at the beginning of the 1860s (both entitled *The Woman with the Yellow Hair*), the first by Harry Harleton and the second by Percy Fitzgerald. They describe blonde and evil female characters – named Nelly Raymond and Janet Faithfull – who are seducers, calculators and who attempt to murder all those people who oppose their plans ('Sensational Hair').
7. Sedgwick, *The Coherence of Gothic Conventions*, p. 49.

8. 'Like the Gothic, sensation novels were generic hybrids, in this case combining the journalistic and the fantastic, the domestic and the exotic, realism and melodrama' (Pykett, 'Sensation and the Fantastic in the Victorian Novel', p. 203). For Maggie Kilgour the Gothic is a hybrid genre, a Frankenstein-like creature assembled from fragments of other forms (*The Rise of the Gothic Novel*, p. 4). For the notion of 'genotext', see Genette, *Palimpsestes*.

9. Mansel, 'Sensation Novels', p. 491. An anonymous reviewer in *The Spectator* admits that '[people] think themselves very enlightened now-a-days, and will not read about haughty barons and virtuous bandits, and haunted castles, and innocent victims flying from an unintelligible pursuit to an incomprehensible rescue. But the old dish only wants new seasoning, and the class who would once have read Mrs Radcliffe now pore over stories as absurd as hers, but based upon criminal trials' ('Review of *Lady Audley's Secret*', p. 1196).

10. Massé, *In the Name of Love*, p. 10. For the definition of 'Female Gothic' see Moers, *Literary Women*.

11. 'Audley Court used to be a convent, and in fact the first human presence in this desolate place overgrown with moss, reminiscent of the ruined mansions dear to the authors of Gothic tales, is that of the quiet nuns who have walked there hand in hand. These women, surrounded by ancient walls, are the first female icon in the text, the first of a series of versions of femininity that is offered, and their presence suggests the possibility that in spite of apparent differences, *Lady Audley's Secret* may still be struggling with the legacy of the Gothic tradition' (Briganti, 'Gothic Maidens and Sensation Women', pp. 190–1).

12. 'Architecture, particularly medieval in form, signalled the spatial and temporal separation of the past and its values from those of the present [. . .] In later fiction, the castle gradually gave way to the old house: as both building and family line, it became the site where fears and anxieties returned to the present' (Botting, *Gothic*, p. 3).

13. A precedent for Braddon's treatment and description of Audley Court can be found in Charlotte Brontë's novel *Villette* (1853). The Belgian boarding house in which Lucy Snowe works as a teacher is a former convent, described through the use of recognisable eighteenth-century Gothic signifiers (in particular the ghost story of the black and white nun). However, also in this case its significance is totally Victorian and it is related to the condition of emotional, professional and legal seclusion of nineteenth-century women. Charlotte Brontë was one of the British female novelists Braddon included (together with George Eliot) among her masters, as she admits in many of her letters to Edward Bulwer Lytton (see letter dated 21 June 1872, qtd in Wolff, '"Devoted Disciple"', p. 150). In an article entitled 'At the Shrine of Jane Eyre' Braddon goes back to her years as a schoolgirl, when, 'laid with a sick-headache', she was given *Jane Eyre* 'for a solace': 'I forgot my headache. The story gripped me from the first page' (p. 174).

14. See Foucault, *Histoire de la folie*. In an essay entitled 'Enclosure Acts: Framing Women's Bodies in Braddon's *Lady Audley's Secret*', Elizabeth Langland focuses on the linguistic and cultural connection between the Belgian asylum and the convent, concluding that 'Braddon's description

of the "*maison de santé*" ironically echoes the early description of Audley Court, with its darkening shelter, its intensely painful repose, and its death-like tranquillity' ('Enclosure Acts', p. 13).

15. The isotopy of 'peacefulness' reappears in Braddon's final remarks on Lady Audley's death: 'It is more than a year since a black-edged letter, written upon foreign paper, came to Robert Audley, to announce the death of a certain Madame Taylor, who had expired peacefully at Villebrumeuse, dying after a long illness, which Monsieur Val describes as a *maladie de langueur*' (p. 444, my italics).

16. According to Kate Ferguson Ellis, '[T]he middle-class idealization of the home, though it theoretically protected a woman in it from arbitrary male control, gave her little protection against male anger [. . .] The Gothic novel of the eighteenth century foregrounded the home as fortress, while at the same time exposed its contradictions' (*The Contested Castle*, p. xi).

17. Showalter, *The Female Malady*, p. 28; p. 34. This aspect is also treated by Jenny Bourne Taylor, who underlines the peculiar gender implications in the politics related to asylum-building and managing: 'The close links between the cultural construction of femininity and of insanity had been forged long before the nineteenth century, but now both draw on and contribute to the ideology of domesticity in new pervasive ways [. . .] The madwoman of every class is cured through learning to be a middle-class gentlewoman' (*In The Secret Theatre of Home*, pp. 37–8).

18. For Julian Wolfreys, '[escaping] from the tomb and the castle, the Gothic in the Victorian period becomes arguably even more potentially terrify-ing because of its ability to manifest itself anywhere. Reciprocally, the Victorians may be read as embracing the Gothic, taking it to themselves in intimate and disconcerting ways' ('Preface: "I Could a Tale Unfold"', p. xii).

19. Milbank, 'The Victorian Gothic in the English Novels and Stories, 1830–1880', p. 155. For Lyn Pykett '[in] the Victorian period female Gothic became an increasingly complex and contradictory genre which not only represented women's fears of domestic imprisonment, but also enacted, and simultaneously, or by turns, managed [. . .] their fantasies of escape from the physical and psychological confinements of the domestic and conven-tionally defined femininity' ('Sensation and the Fantastic in the Victorian Novel', p. 198).

20. Although asylums will continue to reappear in other novels by Braddon as an evolution of the Lady Audley paradigm, *Taken at the Flood* (1874) is probably the text in which their ominous presence is treated in one of the most interesting ways. Here Sylvia Perriam dies a miserable death for having committed her husband to an insane asylum (and later pretending that he was dead) in order to marry her lover, in a sort of reversed and significant rewriting of Lucy Graham, George Talboys and Robert Audley's tale.

21. Many critics have reflected upon the connections between the presence of theatrical strategies and the Gothic mode, since 'Gothic novels are essentially visual in their emphasis on dramatic gesture and action and their pictorial effects, giving the reader an experience comparable to that of a spectator at the theatre' (Howells, *Love, Mystery and Misery*, p. 16).

Richard Davenport-Hines reads Gothic fictions in relation with their theatrical and architectural background: 'Two of the most important Gothic
revival architects, William Kent in the eighteenth century and Augustus
Welby Pugin in the nineteenth, both worked on stage scenery, and used
its techniques to powerful theatrical effect in their buildings' (*Gothic*,
p. 6).
22. According to Michel Foucault, '[it] was no longer the gaze of any observer,
but that of a doctor supported and justified by an institution [. . .] Moreover,
it was a gaze that [. . .] was not content to observe what was self-evident; it
must make it possible to outline chances and risks; it was calculating' (*The
Birth of the Clinic*, p. 109).
23. Ibid., p. 22. Foucault illustrates in *Discipline and Punish* the function
of Jeremy Bentham's Panopticon in nineteenth-century incarcerating
practices.
24. 'The accounts of female insanity by Nightingale [in *Cassandra*], Brontë
[in *Villette*] and Braddon [. . .] suggest that the rise of the Victorian madwoman was one of history's self-fulfilling prophecies. In a society that not
only perceived women as childlike, irrational and sexually unstable but
also rendered them legally powerless and economically marginal, it is not
surprising that they should have formed [the] greater part of the residual
categories of deviance' (Showalter, *The Female Malady*, pp. 72–3).
25. Showalter, *A Literature of Their Own*, pp. 166–7. D. A. Miller states that
'[the] "secret" let out at the end of the novel is not, therefore, that Lady
Audley is a madwoman but rather that, *whether she is or not*, she must be
treated as such' (*The Novel and the Police*, p. 169).
26. Wollstonecraft, *Maria*, p. 75.
27. 'The governess is [. . .] significant for [an] analysis of the ideological work
of gender because of the proximity she bears to two of the most important
Victorian representations of woman: the figure who epitomised the domestic ideal, and the figure who threatened to destroy it' (Poovey, *Uneven
Developments*, p. 127). For a detailed historical analysis of the figure of the
governess, see Hughes, *The Victorian Governess*.
28. Gilbert, *Disease, Desire and the Body*, p. 104. For Nina Auerbach,
'Victorian iconography abounds in less canonical alliances between women
and fairies, goblins, mermaids, vampires, and all varieties of creation's
mutants; the Victorian universe crawls with anomalies from whose weird
energy only man is excluded' (*Woman and the Demon*, p. 65). As far as
Becky Sharp is concerned, she is characterised as follows: 'They look pretty
enough when they sit upon a rock, twanging their harps and combing their
hair, and sing, and beckon you to come and hold the looking-glass; but
when they sink into their native element, depend on it those mermaids are
no good, and we had best not examine the fiendish marine cannibals, rev-
elling and feasting on their wretched pickled victims' (Thackeray, *Vanity
Fair*, p. 617).
29. Lewis, *The Monk*, p. 81.
30. Chiara Briganti writes that 'Phoebe resembles her mistress not just in physical appearance but also in her quickness to glimpse and seize opportunities.
But she lacks her courage and eventually she must marry Luke because
words fail her' ('Gothic Maidens and Sensation Women', p. 197).

31. Tromp, *The Private Rod*, p. 193. For a more recent study on male violence in Victorian literature and culture, see Surrige, *Bleak Houses*.
32. 'In final desperation, [Lady Audley] attempts to destroy the architectural manifestation of the Gothic novel – the Inn, named The Castle, where the detective sleeps – through fire [. . .] only to be reincarcerated in the far more secure Gothic setting of the madhouse' (Elizabeth Tilley, 'Gender and Role-Playing in *Lady Audley's Secret*', p. 199).

Chapter 2

John Marchmont's Legacy and the Topologies of Dispossession

The title of Mary Elizabeth Braddon's *John Marchmont's Legacy* (1864),[1] though extremely indicative of its main theme, seems to confute its own semantic premises. In relating the history of the 'legacy' left by John Marchmont, Braddon deals in fact with a legal, sentimental and existential 'dispossession' which involves all the characters. The novel opens in a London theatre, where Edward Arundel is watching his former college teacher John Marchmont playing in a drama, and realises that John and his daughter Mary are living in poverty. Marchmont, who hopes to inherit a large estate in Lincolnshire, asks Edward to take care of Mary if he should die, since he believes it will be dangerous to leave her in the hands of his brother Paul Marchmont. Mary is secretly attracted by Edward, who is loved by his cousin Olivia Arundel, the daughter of the local vicar at Swampington Rectory. John Marchmont decides to marry Olivia not because he loves her but to protect Mary after his death. Edward and Mary get married secretly, but while travelling back home to his father's deathbed Edward is badly injured in a train crash and is unable to tell anyone of his marriage because he has momentarily lost his memory. Olivia is consumed by hate and on the verge of madness, while Paul Marchmont is determined to use her as his tool to obtain the Marchmont property. After Edward comes back to Marchmont Towers (following a long recovery) Olivia tells him that Mary has disappeared and has probably committed suicide. Convinced of Mary's death, Edward begins courting Belinda, a beautiful and innocent girl. Determined to prevent him from marrying another 'baby-faced girl', Olivia rescues Mary and her child from a deserted farmhouse and takes them to the church to stop the wedding. Olivia reveals that the 'secret' of her madness lies in her unrequited love for Edward. Paul has no intention of returning to poverty and sets fire to Marchmont Towers, dying in the conflagration. Some months later Mary, who is dying, convinces Edward to marry Belinda, while Olivia becomes a local teacher to expiate her guilt.

As this brief summary demonstrates, 'dispossession' represents a pervasive narrative and textual presence in Braddon's novel, to the point that it could be considered as the prevailing 'hypogram'[2] around which all the themes of the text cluster and converge. The first novelty in *John Marchmont's Legacy* is related to Braddon's new approach to characterisation and, as a consequence, to the weaving of the plot. Overcome by the unexpected success of her 'pair of Bigamy novels' *Lady Audley's Secret* and *Aurora Floyd*, and receptive to the negative critical responses to her scandalous stories and immature narrative style, Braddon confesses in her letters to Edward Bulwer Lytton all of her doubts. Braddon tries in fact to gain her literary mentor's approval of the experiment she is doing in her newly-serialised fiction:

> Believe me I feel very little elated by the superficial success of my pair of Bigamy novels, & the hardest things the critics say never strike me as unjust. I know that I have everything to do yet; but it has been my good or bad fortune to be flung into a very rapid market [. . .] I doubt if you will like 'Aurora Floyd' any better than her predecessor. When I began her I didn't mean to finish 'Lady A[udley]' but I venture to hope you will think 'John Marchmont's Legacy', the novel now running in *Temple Bar*, better written than the other two.[3]

The priority Braddon's novel gives to legacy and dispossession, seen as economic and existential paradigms, is related to the fact that, from the Renaissance onwards, the name of a person in literary (and non-literary) texts had been associated with the property of an individual. Indeed, property represented the distinctive mark of a person's existential and legal integrity, as the identity of a person was literally built up upon the possession of a name associated to a place (as in John Marchmont's case). As a consequence, what mattered most – during the seventeenth century and the Victorian age as well – were 'communally secured proprietary rights to a name and place in an increasingly mobile social world', whose aim Stephen Greenblatt defines as the 'fabrication of social identity'.[4] In Braddon's *John Marchmont's Legacy*, Marchmont Towers represents not only the material expression of economic power but also the site of mystery, seclusion and despair, associated with literary and architectural Gothic codes. By making characters interact with Gothic settings Braddon emphasises their uneasiness with the present in terms of 'story' and 'history', of micro- and macro-narrations, as the case of *Lady Audley's Secret* has exemplified (see Part I, Chapter 1). The anachronistic setting of Marchmont Towers becomes the materialisation of a topology of dispossession which features Mary Marchmont and Olivia Arundel as the selected victims of a parasitic and paralysing *locus* in which medieval obscurantism is engrafted into a Victorian cultural context:

> [A] noble mansion in the flat Lincolnshire country: a stately pile of building, standing proudly forth against a background of black woodland; a noble building, supported upon either side by an octagon tower, whose solid masonry is half-hidden by the ivy which clings about the stonework, trailing here and there, and flapping restlessly with every breath of wind against the narrow casements [. . .]
>
> Ancient tales of enchantment, dark German legends, wild Scottish fancies, grim fragments of half-forgotten demonology, strange stories of murder, violence, mystery, and wrong, vaguely intermingle in the stranger's mind as he looks, for the first time, at Marchmont Towers. (pp. 43–4)[5]

Contrarily to other novels located in seemingly peaceful country houses, *John Marchmont's Legacy* dramatises a partial rejection of the sensational stereotypes Braddon contributed to create. Here Braddon adds no mysteries, no terrible crimes and even no bigamous marriages to the plot, using Gothic settings as metaphorical sites of desolation, in which everybody is dispossessed of what he or she desires: John Marchmont of his life, Olivia Arundel of her love for Edward, Mary of her legitimate heritage and finally Paul Marchmont of his money. Braddon uses the Gothic mode as an ideal medium to describe an external as well as an internal condition of seclusion, the epitome of an epistemological paralysis that was affecting Victorian society.[6] Similarly to *Lady Audley's Secret*, Marchmont Towers is a Gothic *signifier* whose *signified* is Victorian. In *John Marchmont's Legacy*, Braddon alludes to the architectural and narrative stereotypes of eighteenth-century Gothic fictions to prove that the psyche of her nineteenth-century characters can be more mysterious and disquieting than any Castle of Otranto.

Marchmont Towers represents the most significant 'chronotope' in Braddon's novel, through which 'time' and 'space' are fused and compressed in one single topological unity. In this 'intrinsic connectedness of temporal and spatial relationships', *the time* in which events take place becomes artistically visible, while *the space* is responsive to the chronological sequence of fictional and historical events. As Mikhail Bakhtin writes with reference to Gothic castles:

> [They are] saturated through and through with a time that is historical in the true sense of the word, that is the time of historical past. The castle is the place where the lords of the feudal era lived (and consequently also the place of historical figures of the past), the traces of centuries and generations are arranged in it [. . .] as various parts of its architecture, in furnishings [. . .] and in the particular human relationships involving *dynastic primacy* and the *transfer of hereditary rights*.[7]

In Bakhtin's view, the chronotope of the castle (along with the 'road' and the 'threshold') determines the semantic structure of a work of art and delimits the boundaries of its specific literary genre. The choice of Marchmont Towers as the setting for this novel helps Braddon to enhance the analogies, as well as the differences, between past and present cultural systems, and to rewrite a traditional and codified literary genre with an interest in the legal status of Victorian women.

Mary Marchmont exemplifies the paradigmatic Gothic female victim; she is 'motherless', fundamentally 'childish' and attached to reading to the point of mixing reality and fictional dreams.[8] An epitome of the female subject of many Gothic fictions, Mary roams around the old and dusty rooms of the Marchmont estate soon after her father's death, at the beginning of a chapter significantly entitled 'The Day of Desolation':

> Yes, the terrible day had come. Mary Marchmont roamed hither and thither in the big gaunt rooms, up and down the long dreary corridors, white and ghostlike in her mute anguish [. . .] [Mary] suffered, and was still. She shrank away from all human companionship; she seemed especially to avoid the society of her stepmother. She locked the door of her room upon all who would have intruded on her, and flung herself upon the bed, to lie therein in a dull stupor hour after hour. (p. 108)

Along with the intertextual allusion to Tennyson's 'Mariana' and a direct quotation ('She suffered, and was still') from Felicia Hemans's poem 'Madeline: A Domestic Tale' (1828),[9] the most relevant feature is represented here by Mary's condition as 'dispossessed' agent of the Marchmont property. Indeed, in the novel she becomes the actual legacy John Marchmont gives into the hands of Edward Arundel as a sort of exchangeable object of power, through which the two men consolidate their friendship. Mary's precarious legal status turns her from a typically Gothic victim to an unjustly-treated Victorian woman, compared to (or, worse, conceived as) a sexual and economic possession. In a letter written to Edward in which mercantile and commercial rhetoric is mixed with a sexually-marked language, John Marchmont refers to his 'legacy' of Marchmont Towers and to Mary's 'helplessness' as two sides of his property:

> Subjoined with this letter I send you an extract from the copy of my *grand-father's will*, which will explain to you how he left his *property*. Do not lose either the letter or the extract. If you are willing to undertake the *trust* which I confide to you to-day, you may have need to refer to them after my death. The *legacy of a child's helplessness* is the only bequest which I leave to the only friend I have. (p. 30, my italics)

The fact that the property of Mary Marchmont reinforces the friendship between John Marchmont and Edward Arundel proves that 'the use of women as exchangeable objects, as counter of value, [was necessary] for the primary use of cementing relations with other men'.[10] In the novel there will be other references to this letter and to Mary's position as economic and sentimental 'legacy'. Mary's condition as dispossessed subject becomes relevant the moment the novel deals with her legal discrimination as a Victorian woman:

> They talked a great deal of John Marchmont. It was such a happiness to Mary to be able to talk unreservedly of her father to some one who had loved and comprehended him [. . .] 'Did papa say that, Edward?', she whispered; 'did he really say that?' 'Did he really say what, darling?' 'That *he left me to you as a legacy*?' 'He did indeed, Polly [. . .] I'll bring you the letter tomorrow.' (p. 151, my italics)

This condition of legal dispossession was denounced by many proto-feminists such as Barbara Leigh Smith Bodichon, one of the first great campaigners for the reform of the property laws. In 'Brief Summary, in Plain Language, of the Most Important Laws Concerning Women: Together with a Few Observations Thereon' (1854) Bodichon lamented Victorian women's physical and legal erasure after their marriage. Until 1882 – the year in which the Married Women's Property Act was finally passed – wives under common law were in fact still legally absorbed upon marriage into the identity of their husbands, according to a principle which was commonly known in law as 'coverture':

> A man and wife are one person in law; the wife loses all her rights as a single woman, and her existence is entirely absorbed in that of her husband. He is civilly responsible for her acts; she lives under his protection or cover, and her condition is called coverture.
> A woman's body belongs to her husband; she is in his custody, and he can enforce his right by a writ of habeas corpus.
> What was her personal property before marriage, such as money in hand, money at the bank, jewels, household goods, clothes, etc. becomes absolutely her husband's, and he may assign or dispose of them at his pleasure whether he and his wife live together or not.[11]

Like many of Braddon's novels, Rosina Wheeler's *The School for Husbands: or Molière's Life and Times* (1852) attacks the Victorian view of marriage and women's legal, economic and existential elision. Indeed, Rosina Wheeler's personal case is a proof of Victorian women's precarious condition in all social settings and demonstrates that literature often represented for them the only means to denounce discriminatory attitudes and policies. Notwithstanding her advantageous economic position before her marriage, Rosina had to depend upon Edward Bulwer Lytton's annual allowance of £400 and had to live in provincial

Welsh and English towns (Llangollen, Taunton etc.) to survive. Along with Edward Bulwer Lytton's real (or presumed) violence, this was one of the main reasons for the private and public attacks which will lead to the 'Hertford scandal' (see Introduction):

> By convention, marriage annihilates a woman's power and renders her a nullity; this disenfranchisement from all individual privilege and independence has not, and cannot have, a moral tendency, for it is unjust; since then, her sphere is placed within the orbit of her husband.[12]

In *John Marchmont's Legacy* Mary Marchmont's daughter is similarly secured into Edward's hands because of a legal 'erasure' founded on her exclusion from the socio-economical mechanisms of Victorian society. This condition finds an architectural embodiment in the 'Panoptical' space of the Marchmond Towers, because in the novel Mary becomes the object surveyed and contended (for contrasting reasons) by John Marchmont, Edward Arundel and Paul Marchmont. The cultural and material topology of the Gothic Towers in *John Marchmont's Legacy* thus represents a further expression of Victorian women's legal and cultural ontology as 'shifting properties'.[13] Since the sensation novel is concerned in particular with the anomalies in the English marriage laws and with the relationship between women, crime and economic power, it is emblematic that the 'quest for property' reaches its climax after Chapter XV, and in what can be considered as the 'sensational' section of the text, which features the love-mad Olivia.

Olivia Arundel[14] is the other female character associated with Marchmont Towers, even though her relationship with the Gothic setting of the novel differs from Mary's. Olivia's condition is introduced through a topological reference to the surroundings of Swampington (a metaphorically significant name), where she lives an uneventful existence with the rector, her father.

> There are two handsome churches, both bearing an early date in the history of Norman supremacy; one crowded into an inconvenient corner of a back street, and choked by the houses built up round about it; the other lying a little out of the town, upon a swampy waste looking towards the sea, which flows within a mile of Swampington. Indeed, there is no lack of water in that Lincolnshire borough. The river winds about the outskirts of the town: unexpected creeks and inlets meet you at every angle; shallow pools lie here and there about the marshy suburbs; and in the dim distance the low line of the grey sea meets the horizon. (p. 61)

The description of the Lincolnshire rectory, surrounded by decayed ruins, tombs and churches, testifies once more to the dynamic use of the Gothic 'mode' in *John Marchmont's Legacy* as a semantic medium introduced to scan the inner recesses of the characters' personality. The oxymoronic semantic structure of the above-mentioned excerpt foregrounds the presence of images connected to useless/excessive abundance ('no lack of water', 'unexpected creeks and inlets') and sterility ('choked by the houses', 'swampy waste', 'shallow pools', 'marshy suburbs'). Olivia has to play the role of John Marchmont's second wife and Mary's stepmother, wasting her unrequited love for Edward in the suffocating atmosphere of Marchmont Towers. The final impression is that in *John Marchmont's Legacy* Braddon attempts to offer her readers a phenomenology of crime that looks more convincing than Lady Audley's, although some of its premises are the same. Like Lady Audley, Olivia will overcome her induced physical and moral paralysis, moving from the 'passive' condition of a Mariana-like woman (epitomised by Mary Marchmont) to that of a Victorian Lady of Shalott who becomes 'half-sick of shadows'.[15]   *— worth specifying B's reading of Tennyson?*

John Marchmont in his will (dated 4 February 1844, two months after his second marriage) states that Olivia's duty is to become a 'guardian, adviser and mother' for Mary, who has to 'place herself under the charge and guardianship' (as the heiress 'of a very considerable property') and guided 'in the choice of a husband' (p. 125). Like Mary, Olivia becomes an exchangeable object to assure men of their power. Deprived of her role as an individual, she is degraded to a means through which John Marchmont's property passes into the hands of Mary and, according to the 'coverture' law, to Mary's husband. The more Olivia rebels and reacts against her existential (and legal) erasure and her dispossessed love – conspiring with Paul Marchmont and his wife Lavinia against Mary – the more her behaviour becomes 'excessive' and turns her unrequited feelings into a monomaniacal 'love's madness', whose persistent and obsessive object of desire is Edward:[16]

> She writhed; this self-sustained and resolute woman writhed in her anguish as she uttered those five words, 'He will never love me!' [. . .] They stood aloof, divided by the width of an intellectual universe. The woman knew this, and hated herself for her folly, scorning alike her love and its object; but her love was not the less because of her scorn. It was a madness, an isolated madness, which stood alone in her soul, and fought for mastery over her better aspirations, her wiser thoughts. (p. 116)

Winifred Hughes defines *John Marchmont's Legacy* as 'a study in sexual repression'[17] because in her secret theatre of home Olivia plays the love-mad woman whose impossible desires and frustrated intellectual aspirations alienate her from codified respectable behaviours. Despite some theatrical scenes featuring Olivia, Braddon chooses not

to make use of traditional melodramatic strategies to create stark anti-
nomies, but dramatises the effects of a madness whose only 'secret' is
love and misfortune. Moreover, Braddon seems also to be interested in
the contextual causes of Olivia's monomania. In medical terms, Olivia's
pathology is based on a masochistic attitude which, by fighting against
the object of impossible love (in her case, Edward) extracts pleasure
from pain, masking the real intentions of its agent.[18] The only way
Olivia has to conceal her dispossessed love for Edward is by concealing
it behind violent gestures. Therefore, it is not surprising to find sections
dedicated to the description of morbid fantasies of amputation which
verge on Gothic nightmares:

> She could cut away this fatal passion with a desperate stroke, it may be,
> just as she could cut off her arm; but to believe that a new love would grow
> in its place was quite as absurd as to believe in the growing of a new arm.
> Some cork monstrosity might replace the amputated limb; some sham and
> simulated affection might succeed the old love. (p. 86)

It follows that the true (un)sensational 'secret' in *John Marchmont's
Legacy* is Olivia's unreturned love, even though many characters attach
the label of madness to her violently assertive behaviour, without realising (or perhaps refusing to realise) that her monomania derives from her
emotional dispossession.

While on the one hand Mary and Olivia's legal and emotional dispossession is topologically associated with Marchmont Towers, on the
other hand Edward Arundel's traumatic experience of dispossession
relates to the undisputed symbol of Victorian technological advance: the
railway. From a chronological point of view, *John Marchmont's Legacy*
is set during the years of the so-called 'Victorian railway adventure' that
began on 15 September 1830 with the official inauguration by the Duke
of Wellington of the Manchester-Liverpool line. From then on, trains
conditioned everyday life and the idea of movement through space in
time, with an enormous impact on the imagination of intellectuals, journalists, painters, poets and novelists. The decade 1840–50 was the most
intense period of activity, during which nearly 6,000 miles of railway
line was built, accompanied by an increase in the trains' own speed (with
the construction of the 'Rocket' by engineer George Stephenson). But the
forties also witnessed the frantic buying of railway stocks (announced
in enthusiastic terms by the *Railway Times* and shared by many, including writers such as W. M. Thackeray). The consequence of this frenzy
would be an enormous economic scandal, which led to the end of those
delirious great expectations during the last part of the 1840s, and which
Thackeray so acutely described in his *Book of Snobs* (1846–7).

Queen Victoria herself decided to experience the 'sensation of the year', travelling from London to Windsor in a special royal carriage richly upholstered in blue and white silk. In that same period William Turner approached the technological innovation as an artistic subject in *Rain, Steam and Speed. The Great Western Railway* (1844). This picture conveys the feeling of exaltation of those years and reproduces in highly impressionistic terms the energetic velocity of locomotives, as well as their potentially destructive power. Some years later, Turner's fellow painter John Martin depicted in *Last Judgement* (1853) the collapsing bridge Satan built over Chaos using a recognisable Gothic iconography. As far as pictorial art is concerned, trains represented during the mid-Victorian times an updated form of the Burkean 'sublime', with Turner and Martin's paintings as the most poignant artistic expressions of what can be defined as 'technological sublime'.[19] In the two painters' case trains were thus figured as the metaphors of a society that seemed to be moving towards a nebulous future. The feelings raised by the railway revolution justify, in a way, the Victorian fears and perplexities related to the destruction of the rural countryside (devastated and levelled to leave space for railway lines), to the alteration of the slow rhythms of the old travel by horse and carriage and to an ecological violence against the English countryside which was associated with a sense of increasing alienation by intellectuals such as John Ruskin (who compared people travelling on trains to living parcels) and writers such as Dickens. England appeared a fluctuating moving spectacle through the carriage windows, whose 'panoramization of the world' (in Wolfgang Schivelbusch's words) altered the way reality – now seen as a chaotic flux of images and fragmented figures – was experienced in terms of visual perception. Accordingly, the railway experience may be considered as an exemplary symbol of technological innovation in the Victorian age, because '[nothing] else in the nineteenth century seemed as vivid and dramatic a sign of modernity as the railroad'. In a little over a generation trains 'had introduced a new system of behaviour: not of travel and communication but of thought, of feeling, of expectation'.[20] This was also due to the fact that trains both *reduced* – because of their unprecedented velocity – and *expanded* the traditional relationship between time and space. Altering, or in some cases destroying, the pre-railway landscapes, trains created a totally new notion of 'spatiality' and represented not just a symbol but also an agent of modernity and progress.[21] Finally, from a socio-political and economic point of view, trains and railways created the premises of Victorian capitalism, since the speed with which 'goods' travelled turned them into 'commodities'.

The first reference to the problematic relationship between Edward

Arundel and the railways occurs when he fails to catch the last train in time and is forced to delay his search for Mary. Edward's inability to interact with the new spatial and temporal paradigms introduced by the railway system is one of the symptoms of his uneasiness with the faster rhythms and pace of the Victorian age:

> The express-train came tearing up to the quiet platform two minutes after Edward had taken his ticket; and in another minute the clanging bell pealed out its discordant signal, and the young man was borne, with a shriek and a whistle, away upon the first stage of his search for Mary Marchmont.
>
> It was nearly seven o'clock when he reached Euston Square; and he only got to the Paddington station in time to hear that the last train for Marlingford had just started. There was no possibility of his reaching the little Berkshire village that night. No mail-train stopped within a reasonable distance of the obscure station. There was no help for it, therefore, Capitan Arundel had nothing to do but to wait for the next morning. (pp. 176–7)

This excerpt includes a series of terms associated with violence ('tearing up', 'discordant signal', and 'shriek'), and culminates with Edward, who is literally swept away by the speed and energy of the train ('the young man was borne [. . .] away'). The second part of the passage is characterised by a prevalence of disphorically-marked sentences which, along with the previous images, are a prelude to Edward's future destiny as dispossessed agent: 'there was no possibility', '[no] mail-train stopped', 'obscure station', 'no help for it' and 'Capitain Arundel had nothing to do but to wait'. Edward Arundel's lost occasion and first defeat possesses a further metaphorical value, because it proleptically alludes to his precarious condition as weak hero of the novel and to his lack of all those attributes which had to be a prerogative of the manly and masculine citizens of the rising Victorian bourgeois class. Like those of many other novels by Braddon, the male characters of *John Marchmont's Legacy* (John, Edward and Paul) are morally, culturally and physically weak, and unable to face the challenges of modernity.[22] Trains also become a sort of surrogate Victorian house in many sections of the text, where they are explicitly associated with domesticity. In light of the etymological origin of the term 'locomotive' (which fuses the domestic-homely 'locus' and the idea of 'motion'),[23] trains and railway carriages seem to offer characters a sheltered place which assures them that their future will be prosperous:

> It was only when [Mary] seated in the carriage with her husband, and the rain cleared away as they advanced farther into the heart of the pretty pastoral country, that the bride's sense of happiness and safety in her husband's protection returned to her. (p. 188)

But the romantic image of the two lovers' travel carriage will be swept away by future events. As the title of the following chapter suggests ('A Stolen Honeymoon'), Mary and Edward's honeymoon will be 'stolen' and ruined forever, since the news of Squire Arundel's 'paralysis' forces Edward to rush home and to be involved, in the course of his trip, in a terrible train accident. Edward's physical movement by train corresponds to a specific cultural process from an enclosed (feminine) space to an open (male) one. Mary's stay in her room replicates her moral, cultural and psychological condition of imprisonment and dispossession, which is topologically associated to Marchmont Towers:

> Mary had locked the door of her bedchamber, and sat with her head upon the sill of the open window, looking out into the dim orchard [. . .] She prayed for him, hoping and believing everything; though at the hour in which she knelt, with the faint starlight shimmering upon the upturned face and clasped hands, Edward Arundel was lying, maimed and senseless, in the wretched waiting room of a little railway-station in Dorsetshire, watched over by an obscure country surgeon. (p. 216)

If in *John Marchmont's Legacy* Marchmont Towers represents a Gothic setting for Mary and Olivia, in Edward's case trains and railways are not simply the exemplary tropes of an uncanny modernity but also contemporary chronotopes, in the sense of 'a whole complex of concepts, an integral way of understanding experience, and a ground for visualizing and representing human life'.[24] The inclusion of a train accident in *John Marchmont's Legacy* demonstrates Braddon's awareness of the emotional impact these tragic events had on public opinion: spectacular crashes, fires and rescues were being discussed and described in newspapers, periodicals and novels, and also staged in theatres, with sensationally dramatic effects on the audience.[25] Edward's train accident is employed by Braddon as a narrative strategy whose aim is to complicate and delay the course of events and as a paradigmatic illustration of a trauma that was affecting individuals and society. In this respect Braddon's reference to train accidents is not isolated in the literary context of her times. Among the writers who explored the negative side of the railway adventure it is possible to include Wilkie Collins's *No Name*, Mrs Henry (Ellen) Wood's successful sensation novel *East Lynne* (1862) and Charles Dickens's novels. In *East Lynne*, for instance, Isabel Vane is convinced by a villainous character named Captain Francis Levison to commit adultery and to flee from home, leaving her husband Carlyle and her three children. In Chapter 33 (entitled 'An Accident') Isabel is travelling on a train near Grenoble. Despite the fact that she has repented of her choice to abandon her family, she is the victim of a train accident which partially disfigures her and kills the child she has borne Levison. Beside the 'sensational effect' of the episode, the accident has an explicit moral function, punishing the lady sinner, changing her identity and giving her the possibility to repent. The physical mutation Isabel experiences and the trauma she suffers are the signs of a spiritual renewal and of a moral absolution.

Although Charles Dickens includes images of trains in many of his novels and articles, *Dombey and Son* (1848) remains his most significant fictional treatment of the railway as the symbol of a cultural and economical change and, more tragically, of destruction and death.[26] The description of Mr Dombey's thoughts during his trip to Leamington after the recent death of his son Paul is indicative of this transformation of railways from means of transport to metaphor. Trains represent for Mr Dombey – and for Edward Arundel, who will be similarly carried 'with a shriek and a whistle, away' (p. 176) – the locus in which the changes affecting Victorian society clash against the aspirations and desires of individuals:

> He found no pleasure or relief in the journey. Tortured by these thoughts he carried monotony with him, through the rushing landscape, and hurried headlong, not through a rich and varied country, but a wilderness of blighted plans and *gnawing jealousies* [. . .]
> Away, with a shriek, and a roar, and a rattle, from the town, burrowing among the dwellings of men and making the streets hum, flashing out into the meadows for a moment, mining in through the damp earth, booming on in darkness and heavy air, bursting out again into the sunny day so bright and wide; away, away, with a shriek, and a roar, and a rattle, through the fields, through the woods [. . .] among objects close at hand and almost in the grasp, ever flying from the traveller, and a deceitful distance ever moving slowly with him: like as in the track of the remorseless monster, Death![27]

As far as Braddon is concerned, her novel follows Dickens's metaphorical approach to trains rather than Wood's 'sensationalistic' use. Edward's railway accident in *John Marchmont's Legacy* (which Braddon does not describe in detail) causes him a temporary loss of memory:

> It was evident that he was ill, very ill, but that he was, if anything, more ill at ease in mind than in body; and that some terrible *gnawing anxiety*, some restless care, some *horrible uncertainty* of perpetual foreboding of trouble, would not allow him to be at peace. It was as much as the three fellow-passengers who sat opposite to him could do to bear with his impatience, his restlessness, his short half-stifled moans, his very long sighs. (p. 226, my italics)

The description of Edward Arundel's illness focuses not only on his physical problems but also on his '*gnawing* anxiety' (an adjective used by Dickens in *Dombey and Son*) and 'horrible uncertainty'. In this case Edward's narrative and 'memorial' ellipsis is the metaphor of the destruction of any possible hope in the past and its legacy. The decision to describe Edward's loss of memory testifies to Braddon's interest in dealing with the problematic interaction with the 'commodified' present represented by trains. For Karl Marx trains were in fact the means and the most evident emblems of the transition from an old economy to a new one, as he underlines in *Grundrisse, Foundations of the Critique of Political Economy*.[28] Trains reproduced the 'march of the intellect' and created the premises for a 'circulation of capital' that was associated with the capitalisation of the English natural environment. In *John Marchmont's Legacy* Edward is turned into a disrupted, broken and useless 'commodity' with no history, no origin and no identity. Compared to a travelling 'parcel', Edward will have neither a real sentimental nor an economic 'compensation' for his trauma and sufferings.[29]

In the course of the following chapters Edward is compared to a 'living ghost'. His physical condition as newly 'risen from the grave' (p. 232) anticipates his role of weak representative of a rising bourgeois class which was the product of a paralysed and decayed aristocracy (represented by Squire Arundel of Dangerfield Park). After the narrator has given partial details of the train accident and of Edward's trauma, his injured body is compared to his father's corpse:

> For eleven weeks after that terrible concussion upon the South-Western Railway, Edward Arundel lay in a state of coma, – helpless, mindless; all the story of his life blotted away, and his brain transformed into as blank a page as if he had been an infant lying on his mother's knees. A fractured skull had been the young Captain's chief share in those injuries which were dealt out pretty freely to the travellers in the Exeter mail on the 15th of August; and the young man had been conveyed to Dangerfield Park, whilst *his father's corpse* lay in stately solemnity in one of the chief rooms, *almost as much a corpse as that dead father.* (p. 229, my italics)

Through the image of this tragic railway journey Braddon was not invoking an anachronistic return to an idyllic past, but she was reflecting on the Victorian present as an age of uncertainties, in which the gradual retrocession of the cultural, social and economic power of the *ancien régime* (metaphorically represented by the corpse of Edward's father and, topologically, by Marchmont Towers) did not correspond with the rise of a new social order.

The remaining sections describe Edward Arundel's medical case and the pathological causes of his loss of memory: a 'splinter pressed upon the brain' which, according to a 'famous London surgeon', had to be removed surgically to restore the patient's memory: 'The critical operation was performed, with such eminent success as to merit a very long description, which afterwards appeared in the *Lancet*' (p. 230). In this section of the novel Braddon alludes to contemporary medical debates on the effects of railway accidents, and in particular to an eight-part pamphlet entitled 'The Influence of Railroad Travelling on Public Health', published in January-March 1862 in *The Lancet*. Its anonymous writer asserted that, because of the 'rigidity' of the machine parts (rails and wheels), the injuries suffered by passengers consisted of a series of small and rapid 'concussions' which caused them a sense of extreme physical fatigue. Two years after *John Marchmont's Legacy* was in the press, *The Lancet* published another famous three-part article written by Thomas Buzzard (entitled 'On Cases of Injury from Railway Accidents'), which followed the traditional pathological approach to railway shocks. However, despite Victorian doctors' tendency to associate these shocks with a 'concussion' of the spinal cord (a phenomenon known as 'railway spine'), Braddon locates the injured area in Edward's brain and suggests the presence of a 'mental trauma' which possesses an individual, as well as an epistemological, relevance. Braddon's direct association between a psycho-physical shock and the 'loss of memory' anticipates Sigmund Freud's conclusions on the effects of traumatic experiences in *Beyond the Pleasure Principle* (1920), where he focuses on the traumas affecting soldiers after the First World War. These traumas usually consisted in momentary (or permanent) amnesia. As Freud remarks, there is a 'condition [which] has been long known and described [and] which occurs after severe mechanical concussions, railway disasters and other accidents involving a risk to life; it has been given the name of traumatic neurosis'.[30]

Paul Marchmont – a character inspired by traditional Gothic villains – is the undisputed protagonist of the novel's 'sensational' epilogue. Dispossessed of his much desired property and exiled from Marchmont Towers to 'a comfortable room' (p. 472), Paul decides to destroy the emblem of John Marchmont's legacy, replicating Lady Audley's burning of the 'Castle Inn'. Braddon's description of the scene can also be seen as a tribute to *Jane Eyre*, where another emblem of a corrupting and corrupted Gothic past (namely Thornfield Hall) was destroyed. At the end of the novel everything is restored: Edward goes to India and returns as Major to marry Belinda, Olivia lives her uneventful life in the 'swampy' Swampington Rectory and the Arundel family is finally reunited in the Sycamore villa in Lincolnshire. Nothing remains of the old Marchmont legacy, because Mary has died, the Marchmont Towers has been reduced to ashes and even the memory of that story made of seclusions and railway accidents seems to be erased forever: 'And so I leave my soldier-hero, to repose upon laurels that have been hardly won, and secure in that modified happiness which is chastened by the memory of sorrow' (p. 487). However, this seemingly happy epilogue suggests that nothing will ever be the way it was before, and that Edward's serenity is built on a 'memory of sorrow'. Far from representing a financially and emotionally satisfying 'legacy', what John Marchmont has left Mary, Olivia, Edward and Paul is an inheritance of pain, in a world where neither old values (Marchmont Towers) nor progress (trains) result in happiness. On a larger scale, an emblematic illustration of this condition is represented by the monumental Crystal Palace, which can be adopted here as a paradigmatic architectural expression of Victorian values and paradoxes. A decade before *John Marchmont's Legacy* was published, the Crystal Palace stood as the model of a perfect communion between the tradition of the past and the technological present. In this view, it is significant that in 1852 (less than a year after its inauguration)[31] this symbol of Victorian progress and of its railway adventure would be dislocated in another area to be successively rebuilt, abandoned and reduced to ashes by a fire, in a sort of emblematic conjunction of the two antithetical topologies of *John Marchmont's Legacy*: Gothic towers and Victorian trains.

Notes

1. Braddon, *John Marchmont's Legacy*, ed. Sasaki and Page. All further quotations will refer to this edition. The novel was serialised in *Temple Bar* from December 1862 to January 1864.
2. For a definition of 'hypogram', see Riffaterre, *The Semiotics of Poetry*.
3. Letter dated 13 April 1863, qtd in Wolff, '"Devoted Disciple"', p. 12.
4. Greenblatt, 'Psychoanalysis and Renaissance Culture', in Parker and Quints eds, *Literary Theory/Renaissance Texts*, p. 221. According to Lawrence Stone, 'it was the relation of the individual to his lineage which provided a man of the upper class in a traditional society with his identity', because lineage was conceived in terms of 'relations of blood or marriage, dead, living, and yet to be born, which collectively form a "house"' (*The Family, Sex and Marriage in England*, pp. 28–9).
5. As far as nineteenth-century epistemology is concerned, Gothic writings are not 'mere fantasies, isolated from "reality", as perceived and represented in contemporary discourse; rather, they depend upon, engage with, and explore history and its representations' (Mighall, *A Geography of Victorian Gothic Fiction*, p. xxiii). Mighall states that Gothic is 'a process, not an essence; a rhetoric rather than a store of universal symbols' (Ibid., p. xxv), because what he defines as the 'Gothic mode' is characterised by 'mobility' (Ibid., p. 78). In the transition from the Romantic age to the Victorian, '[the] Gothic became part of an internalised world of guilt, anxiety, despair, a world of individual transgression interrogating the uncertain bounds

of imaginative freedom and human knowledge [. . .] The Gothic fiction seemed to go underground: its depths were less romantic chasms or labyrinthine dungeons, than the murky recesses of human subjectivity' (Botting, *Gothic*, pp. 10–11).

6. Charles Dickens makes use of Gothic locations to deal with questions connected with the legal and existential incongruities of the Victorian age, in particular in *Great Expectations* (Satis House), in his last unfinished novel *The Mystery of Edwin Drood* (Cloisterham Cathedral) and in *Bleak House* (Chesney Wold), with which Braddon's novel has many elements in common. The character of Olivia has been repeatedly associated to Lady Dedlock and Marchmont Towers to Chesney Wold. For Toru Sasaki and Norman Page, Dickens's *Bleak House* 'has been a precursor and almost a prototype of the sensation novel, and the most obviously "sensational" portion of that novel is also set in a lonely mansion in Lincolnshire. In Sir Leicester Dedlock's ancestral home of Chesney Wold, as in Marchmont Towers, a proud and gifted woman compelled to suppress her passions lives a life of quiet despair' ('Introduction' to Braddon, *John Marchmont's Legacy*, p. xxi).

7. Bakhtin, *The Dialogic Imagination*, p. 246, my italics.

8. Lyn Pykett observes that '[as] in so many nineteenth-century novels by women, the motherless heroine is both more vulnerable and more assertive than was the norm for a properly socialised woman' (*The 'Improper' Feminine*, p. 87).

9. Some pages after, the evil painter Paul Marchmont will also associate Mary's condition in Marchmont Towers to that of Tennyson's Mariana: 'Paul Marchmont dropped the blind, and turned away from the gloomy landscape with a half-contemptuous gesture: "I don't know that I envy my cousin, after all," he said: "the place is dreary as Tennyson's Moated Grange"' (p. 121). Furthermore, Marchmont Towers, with its 'four gray walls', is also reminiscent of Tennyson's 'The Lady of Shalott'.

10. Sedgwick, *Between Men*, p. 123.

11. Qtd in Dolin, *Mistress of the House*, p. 125.

12. Rosina Bulwer Lytton, *The School for Husbands*, vol. III, p. 114.

13. Wilkie Collins treats this peculiarly Victorian topic in novels such as *The Woman in White*, *Man and Wife* and *No Name*. In the last novel he describes the legal and existential dispossession of the two sisters Norah and Magdalen Vanstone, who have 'no name' because they were born out of any marriage bond between their parents. *No Name* also features a railway accident.

14. As far as the creation of Olivia Marchmont is concerned, the influence of Charlotte Brontë's *Villette* (1853) on Braddon's novel is evident. At the beginning of Brontë's novel, Lucy Snowe finds herself poor, plain and friendless, choosing to work as a companion for an old lady named 'Miss Marchmont' (to whom Chapter IV is totally dedicated), described as a 'a rheumatic cripple, impotent, foot and hand, and had been so for twenty years [. . .] a furrowed, grey-haired woman, grave with solitude, stern with long affliction, irritable also, and perhaps exacting' (Brontë, *Villette*, p. 40).

15. *John Marchmont's Legacy* is not of course the only novel in which 'The Lady of Shalott' has been adopted as a paradigmatic figure. Indeed,

this Tennysonian ballad provided 'a legendary dimension for what are recognizably contemporary concerns', since her 'imprisonment is no more inexplicable or irrevocable than that of many Victorian Ladies' (Gribble, *The Lady of Shalott in the Victorian Novel*, p. 1). Gribble, among others, mentions the 'time-paralysed' Miss Havisham in *Great Expectations* and the female protagonist of Dickens's *Little Dorrit*, along with Charlotte Brontë's 'self-enclosed' Lucy Snowe, Dorothea Brooke in *Middlemarch*, Sue Bridehead in *Jude the Obscure* and Isabel Archer in *Portrait of a Lady*.

16. In *Love's Madness* Helen Small retraces the genesis of the 'love-mad woman' from the legendary Crazy Jane to Mary Wollstonecraft's texts, moving to Wilkie Collins's 'woman in white' and Charles Dickens's Miss Havisham, one of the models for Olivia's self-induced seclusion. According to Andrew Mangham, *John Marchmont's Legacy* orchestrates the idea of female violence as a 'mischannelled force', since Olivia's madness 'stems from her frustrated desires for her cousin Edward'. In Mangham's view, '[the] female monomaniac's insane energies [. . .] are mischannelled ambitions and misspelt intellectual activity' (*Violent Women and Sensation Fiction*, pp. 100 and 102).

17. Hughes, *The Maniac in the Cellar*, p. 131.

18. For Ellen Bayuk Rosenman, masochism is 'a negotiating tool in which pain is the source of a chosen desire that violates a moral or ideological norm. The masochist pursues a forbidden pleasure or agency but arranges to suffer from it, and therefore maintains moral credibility' ('"Mimic Sorrows"', pp. 23–4). On masochism, suffering and Victorian women's literature, see Mitchell, 'Sentiment and Suffering'; Oppenheim, *Shattered Nerves*; and Shuttleworth, 'Preaching to the Nerves'.

19. 'No one can have been more alive than Turner to the fact that railways represented a fresh departure from the old tradition of landscape, offering a new vocabulary with which to describe that heightening of emotional tension associated with impressive natural phenomena which is the essence of the "Sublime" experience' (Wilton, *The Life and Works of J. H. W. Turner*, p. 220). For Ian Carter, '[transformed] into the rampant Other threatening this rural idyll, sublimity no longer buttresses the pastoral order. Viewed thus, Turner's painting shocks us today, as his idealised Thames-side garden landscape, with its rounded shape and pastel palate, is ruptured by the ochrous railway's single diagonal knife thrust' (*Railways and Culture in Britain*, p. 54).

20. Schivelbusch, *The Railway Journey*, p. xiii. Wolfgang Schivelbusch uses the term 'panoramization of the world' to define this new perception of space and time which passengers experienced, and continue to experience, during their journeys by train (Ibid., p. 62). For Michael Freeman '[the] speed of even the earliest railway engines outstripped anything that could be observed in nature. To travel at rates of thirty miles an hour was sensational. Travelling in a carriage that was open to the air intensified the shock and exhilaration, as did arising through deep cuttings and tunnels' (*Railways and the Victorian Imagination*, p. 13).

21. In discussing the impact of the railway experience, Francesco Marroni asserts that '[the] upheaval of the natural order becomes the metaphor of a dynamic society which has lost the sense of order from the past in the chaos

of the present and is hoping to find an order in the future. Natural disorder and social disorder make their appearance on the scene linked together with psychological disorder' (*Miti e mondi vittoriani*, p. 124; translated by the author).

22. Edward's inability to conform to the Victorian models of manliness and masculinity is first testified by the 'wound' he received during his mission in the Afghan wars as a lieutenant. He returned to Marchmont Towers from India because he was wounded by a 'bullet in [his] shoulder from an Afghan musket, and [he is] home on sick-leave' (pp. 56–7).

23. The success of the 'railway libraries' and of famous railway bookstalls such as W. H. Smith is another sign of the Victorian approach to trains as 'moving houses' in which one could find shelter, refuge, time to meditate (trains are Sherlock Holmes's most frequented places) and relaxation. For Alessandra Calanchi, the train is a 'room running through nature' (*Quattro studi in rosso*, p. 110, my translation).

24. Morson and Emerson, *Mikhail Bakhtin*, p. 375.

25. In 1869 the programmes of five theatres in London included plays (mostly written by Dion Boucicault) which featured the 'spectacle of terror' of trains (and of railway accidents in particular). Their melodramatic impact was justified by the interest in the 'visibility of feelings' and the 'spectacular-ization of emotions' which characterised sensational drama, journalism and novels. According to Nicholas Daly, '[this] appetite for the "representations of locomotives" [. . .] suggests that spectacular melodrama contributes to the more general "frenzy of the visible" in the second half of the nineteenth century' ('Blood on the Tracks', p. 50).

26. Dickens was the victim of a railway accident on 9 June 1865, which he described in detail in articles and fictional works. Another report of Dickens's accident would be included in the postscript to *Our Mutual Friend*, while in 1866 a short story inspired by that event – entitled 'The Signalman' – would appear in the special Christmas issue of *All the Year Round*. Trains are described for the first time in *Martin Chuzzlewit* (1844), in which Mrs Gamp accuses them of being the cause of premature births. If in Chapter 55 of *Bleak House* Dickens depicts Sir Leicester Dedlock's changing Lincolnshire, which is going to be swept away by the unceasing advance of railways, in *Hard Times* railways are an integral part of the nightmarish and polluted view of Coketown.

27. Dickens, *Dombey and Son*, pp. 311–12. The train is also the nemesis through which Mr Carker's moral villainy is punished. For a detailed analysis of the relationship between Dickens and railways, see Sanders, *Charles Dickens*, pp. 168–75 and Pontrandolfo, *Railway mania*.

28. The fact that a key concept in Victorian economy such as 'commodity' derives from the archaic Italian *còmodo* and from the Latin *commodus* ('vehicle') suggests the association between physical movement, progress and commodification.

29. In another passage the question of Edward's trauma is discussed from a 'commercial point of view' (p. 227). One of his fellow-passengers asks him if he had any compensation from the railway company. Indeed, during the mid-fifties, due to the increase in railway accidents, the railway companies became legally liable for their passengers' safety and health. The Campbell

Act of 1864 required that railway companies pay compensation to victims. As for compensation, there arose a medical and legal debate around those who suffered damages without a pathologically demonstrable cause or tangible physical wounds.

30. Freud, *The Standard Edition of the Complete Works of Sigmund Freud*, vol. 18, p. 12. For a detailed account of these themes, see Matus, 'Trauma, Memory and Railway Disaster'. For an illustration of the medical debate on the effects of train accidents, see Schivelbusch, *The Railway Journey*, pp. 134–49. According to Ralph Harrington, '[the] mysterious disorders suffered by railway accident victims [. . .] acquired a subtext of metaphorical and implied meanings, becoming emblematic of the condition of modern humanity, subject both to the remorseless efficiency of an increasingly mechanized civilization and the violent unpredictability of seemingly irrational and uncontrollable machines' ('The Railway Accident'). Since the early 1880s, the new psychopathological approach had been replacing the purely pathological view of traumas, so that the expression 'traumatic neurosis' became more widely used than the obsolete 'railway spine'. Therefore, in this chapter the use of the term 'trauma' (referring to Edward's condition) has been deliberately anachronistic.

31. The year after the Great Exhibition at Hyde Park (May 1851), the Crystal Palace was moved to south-east London (Sydenham), where it remained until it was destroyed by a fire in 1936. Michael Freeman argues that '[it] appeared (even to its organisers) to be a kind of *gigantic railway station*; its building techniques largely made possible by the construction industry engendered by the railways. Moreover, steam locomotives were central among its exhibits' (*Railways and the Victorian Imagination*, p. 116; my italics).

Chapter 3

Reading between the (Blood)lines of Victorian Vampires: 'Good Lady Ducayne'

Although they are considered an enduring species, vampires do not scare people any more the way they did in the past, probably because the contemporary world has replaced their outmoded look – made up of sharp teeth, dark robes, pallid faces and foreign-sounding accents – with more terrifying realities. What is indisputable is their capacity to survive and to adapt, in almost Darwinian terms, to a society which always needs menacing and vampirising 'others' to haunt its institutions and its (presumably) advanced civilisation. In this view, Nina Auerbach's definition of the 'children of the night' seems appropriate: 'an alien nocturnal species, sleeping in coffins, living in shadows, drinking our lives in secrecy, vampires are easy to stereotype, but it is their *variety* that makes them survivors'.[1] Rather than being unchanging creatures, vampires have undergone a slow evolution from scary 'myths' to mutating 'tropes', with the latter term intended in the double meaning of rhetorical figure (connected to the way vampires have been textually inscribed and described) and ideological strategy, referring to the modalities according to which these creatures have become an expression of the 'political unconscious' of society. Just to give an example of the sociopolitical relevance (and use) of the image of the vampire, it may be useful to refer to Karl Marx's words included in Chapter 10 of *Capital* (1867), where he compared capitalism to a vampiric attack in a sort of updated Gothic tale:

> Capital is dead labour, that, *vampire-like*, only lives by sucking living labour, and lives the more, the more labour it sucks [. . .] The prolongation of the working-day beyond the limits of the material day, into the night, only acts as a palliative. It quenches only in a slight degree the *vampire thirst* for a living blood of labour.[2]

During her literary career Braddon wrote many Gothic stories, among which it is possible to include 'The Cold Embrace' (published in

Welcome Guest, III, 1860), 'Eveline's Visitant' (published in *Belgravia*, I, January 1867), 'At Chrighton Abbey' (published in *Belgravia*, XIV, May 1871) and 'The Shadow in the Corner' (published in *All the Year Round*, Extra Summer Number 1879). In 'The Cold Embrace', for instance, an art student is haunted by the ghost of a former lover who leads him to death, while the Christmas story 'At Chrighton Abbey' deals with the themes of family decay and fear of female sterility. Behind the attempt to give a scientific explanation to a ghostly apparition in the residence of the aristocrat Michael Boscom, 'The Shadow in the Corner' features the servant Maria as the most uncanny presence in the tale and the true human 'shadow' to whom the title alludes. It follows that Braddon's semantic reconfiguration of the Gothic mode becomes, in this case, a means 'to examine the experience of women in a society dominated by men, in a world defined and structured by ways of thinking strongly associated with men'.[3] 'Good Lady Ducayne' (1896) remains one of Braddon's most intriguing explorations of Gothic themes, which she updates through allusions to contemporary scientific debates and socio-cultural questions. It is the story of eighteen-year-old Bella Rolleston, who leads a poor and difficult life with her mother in London because of her father's flight (a theme which is paradigmatic in Braddon's macrotext, from *Lady Audley's Secret* onwards). Following her application to an employment agency, Bella receives an offer from an eccentric aristocrat named Adelaide Ducayne, who needs a young companion to accompany her during her travels abroad. Bella accepts her offer and follows Lady Ducayne to Cape Ferrino, on the Italian Riviera, where she meets Lotta and her brother Herbert Stafford, a young medical practitioner who has studied in Edinburgh and Paris. After her friends leave Cape Ferrino, Bella begins to feel a strange creeping weakness and lassitude come upon her (experiencing strange dreams and sensations), and finds what seems to be a mosquito bite on her arm. In order to cure this wound she asks for the help of a mysterious Italian doctor named Parravicini, a close friend of Lady Ducayne. In the meantime, she casually overhears two elderly Englishmen who discuss the mysterious death of Bella's predecessors in Ducayne's service. During a trip to Bellagio, Bella and her travelling companions meet Lotta and Herbert again, the latter of whom begins to be suspicious of Bella's strange wounds and of her worsened health. Herbert confronts Ducayne and Parravicini, accusing the doctor of having bled Bella through blood transfusions performed with chloroform. This gives a scientific explanation for the girl's strange dreams and for her mosquito bites. Lady Ducayne, who reveals that these transfusions have been performed in order to prolong her life, confesses to having been born on the day when Louis XVI was decapitated. Dissatisfied with Parravicini's services, the Lady sends him away, searching for new methods to survive ageing. The story ends with 'Good Lady Ducayne' discharging Bella and giving her a cheque for £1,000 to be invested in debenture stocks, thanks to which the girl will have the economic means to marry Herbert in England and to live comfortably for the rest of her life.[4]

While on the one hand Braddon's text narrates a form of vampiric exploitation by a wealthy aristocrat, on the other hand this vampire tale suggests many other parallel readings related to decayed female sexuality (and productivity) and, as we will see, to an anti-Semitic racial unconscious that was widespread during the years in which this short story was written. The fact that Braddon's 'Good Lady Ducayne' was published one year before Bram Stoker's *Dracula* (1897) suggests that the writers may have discussed vampires, since Stoker frequently visited Braddon's residence in Richmond. Among other sources, Braddon derived the reference to the vampire-like desire to prolong one's life unnaturally from the story of the sixteenth-century Hungarian Countess Erzsebet Bathory (1560–1614) – better known as Elizabeth Bathory – who used to have baths in the blood of young and healthy servants. Furthermore, her tale is connected with the tradition of vampire stories that featured corrupt male aristocrats travelling throughout Europe (like William Polidori's Lord Ruthven in *The Vampyre*, 1819) along with its female variation in Sheridan Le Fanu's *Carmilla* (1872). Last but not least, it is also necessary to bear in mind the enormous popular success of James Rymner's 'sensational' eight-thousand double-column page saga *Varney the Vampire*, subtitled *The Feast of Blood* (1847), which for the first time introduced the reference to vampiristic sexual seduction. Braddon mixed these intertextual influences with multiple allusions to the new scientific and technological innovations that would also be fundamental in *Dracula*. Indeed, Braddon's and Stoker's texts are examples of what Kathleen L. Spencer terms the 'Urban Gothic', which acknowledges 'the eighteenth-century ancestry [of traditional Gothic fictions] while identifying the major modifications that have been made to adapt the fantastic to the needs of a new era'.[5] Braddon's peculiar vampire story testifies to her desire to draw inspiration from the latest *fin-de-siècle* issues. In 'Good Lady Ducayne' the relationship between the ancient past and the Victorian present embraces concerns related to social discrimination, political questions and scientific debates centred on the female body, which relationship in Braddon's Gothic stories is described in 'monstrous' (or at least 'abnormal') terms, or reduced to 'phantasmal' forms.[6]

From a biographical point of view, 'Good Lady Ducayne' may be described as a reflection on ageing and death by a writer who had been experiencing many tragic losses in the years preceding its composition, and who was realising that her physical energies were decreasing. In 1885 three close friends died, followed in March by her husband.[7] Nevertheless, Braddon's tale is only partially influenced by these biographical events, because the text centres upon the condition of Lady Ducayne as an old and sexually 'unproductive' woman, juxtaposed with Bella as the expression of physical and sexual 'productivity':

> Never had she seen anyone as old as the old lady sitting by the Person's fire: a little old figure, wrapped from chin to feet in an ermine mantle; a *withered, old face* under a plumed bonnet [. . .]
> 'This is Miss Rolleston, Lady Ducayne.'
> Claw-like fingers, flashing with jewels, lifted a double eye-glass to Lady Ducayne's shining black eyes, and through the glasses Bella saw those unnaturally bright eyes magnified to a gigantic size, and glaring at her awfully.
> 'Miss Torpinter [the owner of the employment agency] has told me all about you,' said the *old voice* that belonged to the eyes. *'Have you good health? Are you strong and active?, able to eat well, sleep well, walk well, able to enjoy all that there is good in life?'* (p. 85, my italics)

Ducayne's reference to 'good health' and strength is related to the opinions of many Victorian doctors on menstruation. Despite their heterogeneity in education and background, these professionals shared the same ideas on women's inferiority and weakness due to their bodily cycles. While in 1873 Dr Edward Clarke asserted in *Sex in Education* that menstruation was debilitating and marked out women's physical and 'functional' difference from men (gaining Henry Maudsley's approval in *The Fortnightly Review*, XXI, 1874), James MacGrigor Allen had already listed in 1869 some clear points in Victorian medicine as far as the menstrual 'question' was concerned:

> Although the duration of the menstrual period differs greatly according to race, temperament and health, it will be within the mark to state that women are unwell, from this cause, on the average two days in the month, or say one month in one year. At such times women are unfit for any great mental or physical labour. They suffer under a languor and depression which disqualify them for thought or action and render it extremely doubtful how far they can be considered responsible beings while the crisis lasts [. . .] In intellectual labour, man has surpassed, does now, and will surpass woman, for the obvious reason that nature does not periodically interrupt his thought and application.[8]

However, it was not menstruation *per se* that interested and puzzled Victorian doctors most. Rather, it was its control that represented a discriminating factor in the way female difference was managed and domesticated in cultural, sexual and economical terms. In the words of Sally Shuttleworth, 'The Victorian concern with regulating the circulation of the female uterine economy only takes on its full historical meaning when read as part of the wider social and economic ideologies of circulation that underpinned the emergent social division of labour within industrial England.'[9] Many professionals in the medical field considered the suppression of menstruation during the so-called 'climacteric' stage of womanhood (the menopause) as the most alarming and disquieting bodily event, comparing it to a form of sexual and economic stagnation. Some of the most original and extravagant cures to allow the free circulation of blood included products such as Dr Locock's female pills and Widow Welch's pills. Therefore, in Braddon's short story Ducayne's vampirism is justified not only by her desire to prolong her life and health but also to continue – through the physical regeneration guaranteed by blood transfusions – to enjoy the pleasures of wealth and money. In other words, Lady Ducayne 'capitalises' the young girl's youth and health in order to fight against the consequences of her 'climacteric' stagnation. Although in Ducayne's case blood spilling is not metaphorically associated with sexual intercourse, as in Le Fanu's *Carmilla*, Stoker's *Dracula* or Arabella Kenealy's 'A Beautiful Vampire' (1896), some theories of the period held that 'woman's blood lust came from her need to replace lost menstrual blood'.[10]

In his essay entitled 'The Social Organism' (1891) Herbert Spencer made a significant connection between the 'circulation' of blood and the 'circulation' of commodities in market economy, suggesting an association between economic crisis and female sterility. For Spencer there was a homologous relationship between 'the blood in a living body and the consumable and circulating commodities in the body politic'.[11] As far as Victorian literature is concerned, one of the most famous examples of unproductive female sexuality associated with an arrested economic flow is represented by Dickens's Miss Havisham, who could be considered a paradigmatic literary figure of paralysed reproductive energy. Dressed in her worn wedding dress, surrounded by dusty reminders of her unconsumed wedding feast in the ironically-sounding Satis House (where her dreams of love will never be 'satiated'), Miss Havisham establishes a complex relationship with Estella, the young heroine of *Great Expectations*. This relationship, made up of a strange mixture of sympathy and vampiric affection, anticipates Lady Ducayne and Bella's. Like Miss Havisham, Lady Ducayne represents another 'aging female body [who] figures a dysfunctional market economy'.[12] These cultural and economic concerns are strongly related to political issues, and in particular to Marx's association between capitalist economy and vampirism. This background is complicated by the fact that in capitalistic economies there is a sort of mutual acceptance of roles, which Braddon's story dramatises. Lady Ducayne knows that she has the economic power to do what she wants, but that she needs the girl's blood/labour to survive. In turn, although she has a physical repulsion for the Lady and for Parravicini, Bella accompanies them wherever they go in order to earn money and to live a decent life. Therefore, each of the two women plays her role on the social stage. Bella and Lady Ducayne establish an 'abject' relationship based on repulsion and attraction, given that this vampiristic bond involves the two women in a specular way: Ducayne despises Bella's social condition and naivety although she is attracted by her youth and health, and Bella is confused (and even disgusted) by the Lady's strange behaviour and by her physical appearance, but needs her money. In Julia Kristeva's view, blood can be properly included in the category of the 'abject' because of its troublesome liminal quality. An internal as well as an externally visible substance, suspended between the necessities of the ego and the requirements of the social non-ego, blood is 'abject' because it 'disturbs identity, system, order' and does not respect – as Bella and Lady Ducayne's cases exemplify – social differences, 'borders, position, rules'.[13] At the end of the story this abject exchange of each other's 'services' (Lady Ducayne's money and Bella's young blood) will be brought to a halt by Dr Herbert Stafford, a representative of the new professional classes who, during the Victorian age, were an alternative both to the decayed aristocrat owning capital (Lady Ducayne) and to the proletariat (Bella).[14] In Braddon's short story the Gothic 'mode of excess' runs parallel to the economic discourses connected to Bella's low social condition. This becomes explicit in another scene featuring Lady Ducayne's carriage, which recalls the arrival of Carmilla's mother at the General's castle in Stiria, and anticipates a similar image included in *Dracula*:

> It was a dull October afternoon, and there was a *greyness* in the air which might turn to fog before night. The Walworth Road shops gleamed brightly through that *grey* atmosphere, and though to a young lady reared in Mayfair or Belgravia such shop-windows would have been unworthy of a glance, they were a snare and a temptation for Bella. *There were so many things she longed for, and would never be able to buy* [. . .]
>
> The Person's office was at the further end, and Bella looked down that long, *grey*, vista almost despairingly, more tired than usual with the trudge from Walworth. As she looked, a carriage passed her, an old-fashioned, yellow chariot [...] drawn by a pair of high *grey* horses, with the stateliest of coachmen driving them, and a tall footman sitting by her side. (p. 84, my italics)

This passage displays the lexical predominance of 'greyness' as an expression of the physical, cultural and sexual liminality that is typical of the creatures inhabiting *fin de siècle* Gothic tales. Behind their supernatural Gothic façade, these images allude to socio-political and economic questions related, in this case, to Bella's low social condition and to the seductions of the new commodity culture that were particularly visible in late-Victorian London ('There were so many things she longed for, and would never be able to buy'). By making Lady Ducayne an aged and aristocratic foreigner, instead of a young and attractive Victorian Englishwoman, Braddon violates the Lady Audley paradigm. In this case, Lady Ducayne's unspeakable 'secret' lies in her desire to face the attacks of old age and of the rising middle classes who were menacing her economic stability.

From a chronological point of view, 'Good Lady Ducayne' was published when debates on degeneration – originating from the imperial fears of invasion which would largely inform *Dracula* – were widespread. This justifies a further approach to the figure of Adelaide Ducayne as a representative of the cultural, sexual and racial 'other' who tries to penetrate, corrupt and infect Bella's Englishness. Significantly, the year Braddon's tale was published coincided with the English translation of Max Nordau's *Degeneration* (1892) and with the first French edition of Cesare Lombroso's *L'uomo delinquente* (1876), two texts that Braddon and Stoker had certainly in mind in the characterisation of their alien vampires. A famous passage from Nordau's text, in which the author condemns the phenomenon of cultural degeneration of late nineteenth-century Europe, refers in explicit terms to the intellectual inferiority of Eastern peoples, accused of being inveterate consumers of opium and hashish:

> We have recognised the effects of diseases in these *fin-de-siècle* literary and artistic tendencies and fashions, as well as in the susceptibility of the public with regard to them, and we have succeeded in maintaining that these diseases are degeneracy and hysteria [. . .] That the poisoning of civilised peoples continues and increases at a very rapid rate is widely attested by statistics [. . .] The increase in the consumption of opium and hashish is still greater, but we need not concern ourselves about that, since the chief sufferers from them are *Eastern peoples, who play no part in the intellectual development of the white races.*[15]

In turn, in *The Criminal Man* Cesare Lombroso deals with those physical traits that supposedly help in identifying 'l'uomo criminale', using Peruvians and negroes as examples of atavism and evolutionary regression. Again in turn, Lombroso's and Nordau's opinions on racial inferiority found a precedent in Robert Knox's *The Races of Men* (1850), which contributed to increasing the fear of invasion by monstrous creatures menacing the stability of the most important Victorian institutions: the state, the Empire and the family. Here is an extract from Knox's much debated essay:

> But who are the dark races of ancient and modern times? It would not be easy to answer this question. Were the Copts a dark race? Are the Jews a dark race? The Gypsies? The Chinese, &c.? Dark they are to a certain extent; so are all the Mongol tribes – the American Indian and Esquimaux – the inhabitants of nearly all Africa – of the East – of Australia.[16]

In Braddon's and Stoker's stories vampires embody a fear of invasion and contagion which was widespread during a period in which Britain was experiencing its triumph as an empire – Queen Victoria was crowned Empress of India in 1876 – and which was at the same time facing the difficult and complex problems of the control of its various colonies. However, while Stoker's Dracula evidently comes from a mysterious Eastern 'dark' country (Transylvania), Adelaide Ducayne's racial origin is not easy to trace. The only information given by the text is that she is not English. Like Robert Audley, Lady Ducayne enjoys reading morally-corrupting French novels, considered another 'alien' cultural product infecting (according to many critics) English literary tradition.[17] On the contrary, Dr Herbert Stafford represents the typical model of cultural and medical well-being and exerts a form of censorial control over the potentially dangerous readings of his sister Lotta. In a letter Bella writes to her mother the girl significantly juxtaposes Lady Ducayne's unrestrained reading of novels with Lotta's:

> When [Lady Ducayne] is tired of my reading she orders Francine, her maid, to read a French novel to her and I hear her chuckle and groan now and then, as if she were more interested in those books than in Dickens or Scott [. . .]
> [Herbert Stafford] won't allow [his sister Lotta] to read a novel, French or English, that he has not read and approved. (pp. 88–9)

Nevertheless, in order to solve the mystery of Ducayne's origin it is useful to reflect on two works that occupied Braddon's late eighteen-nineties, when she was writing 'Good Lady Ducayne'. The first was Henry James's *The Portrait of a Lady* (1882), which illustrates a form of sentimental vampirism in the character of Osmond, whose aim is to 'drain' away Isabel Archer's emotions. But it is in particular Braddon's reading of Arthur P. Stanley's *Jewish Church* (1865, 3 volumes) that proves her interest in the Jewish question and her desire to be informed on it during a period characterised by animated debates concerning fears of a Jewish invasion. Considered a degenerate and criminal population, as well as one of the 'dark races' of mankind by Knox, Jews have experienced a long tradition of discrimination and persecution which can be traced back to the Middle Ages, when they were described as monstrous and devilish creatures and accused of having been the main persecutors of Christ during his trial. In many accounts they were even charged with drinking blood (like vampires), eating children and cooking the Passover *matzah* with Christian blood. Jews were constantly associated with a secretive and lethally parasitic behaviour: the difference in their dietary laws, religious rituals and language led to the belief that these attitudes involved the perversion of Christian sacraments. Moreover, during the late years of the nineteenth century Britain was inflamed by a strong anti-Semitic campaign partially related to a massive wave of immigrants that had been coming from Russia since 1884 in order to escape persecution there. The climax of this xenophobia (which reflected the desire to protect the English 'race' from any form of pollution and from any economic invasion) was represented by the institution of the Royal Commission on Alien Immigration in 1903, followed by the Immigration Act of 1905, which were the culminating expression in a long debate concerning racial questions. In a speech given before the Royal Commission in 1903, Arnold White gave voice to a commonly-shared alarmist position as far as the Jewish immigration from the East was concerned, stating that these races were 'feeding off' and 'poisoning' the blood of Londoners, implicitly using the image of the vampire as a metaphor.[18] The figure of the ambiguous and wicked Jew inspired the themes and the characterisations of many eighteenth- and nineteenth-century novels, from Charles Maturin's *Melmoth the Wanderer* and Lewis's *The Monk* (where the character of the Wandering Jew is featured in one of its secondary plots) to Dickens's Fagin in *Oliver Twist*. In late nineteenth-century novels such as Stoker's *Dracula* and Rider Haggard's *She* (where Ayesha embodies another variation on the theme of the Wandering Jew) are expressions of a specific literary sub-genre that Patrick Brantlinger terms 'Imperial Gothic' in his study *Rule of Darkness*.

As a consequence, in portraying Lady Ducayne's traits as a vampire Braddon drew inspiration from a racial (political) unconscious that emerged during the last decades of the nineteenth century. Indeed, apart from the foreign-sounding name of the Lady, many of her physical traits recall those traditionally and (stereotypically) attributed to Jews:

[Her] face was so wasted by age that it seemed only a pair of eyes and a *pointed chin. The nose was peaked*, too, but between *the sharply pointed chin* and great, shining eyes, the *small aquiline nose* was hardly visible. (p. 85, my italics)[19]

Even Ducayne's condition as 'wandering' vampire in search of new methods to fight against the doom of ageing seems to be a parodic revision of the myth of the Wandering Jew and, generally speaking, of the destiny of the Jewish population. But Braddon's vampire is not the only one who is associated with Jews in late-Victorian literature, since Bram Stoker's *Dracula* as well, as Andrew Smith puts it, 'articulates a contemporary anti-Semitic view in the association between the Count, eastern Europe and disease, which tapped into a popular anxiety of an "alien invasion" of Jews'.[20] Indeed, Dracula's physical traits suggest an explicit link between vampires and Jews, seen as the representatives of a 'dark', 'degenerate' and 'enduring' race:

His face was a strong – very strong – aquiline, with a high bridge of the thin nose and peculiarly arched nostrils; with lofty domed forehead, and hair growing scantly round the temples, almost meeting over the nose, and with bushy hair that seemed to curl in its own profusion. The mouth, so far as I could see it under the heavy moustache, was fixed and rather cruel-looking, with peculiarly sharp white teeth; those protruded over the lips, whose remarkable ruddiness showed astonishing vitality in a man of his years. (*Dracula*, p. 48)

Furthermore, it is thanks to the well-paid services of an unscrupulous Jew named Hildesheim, 'with a nose like a sheep, and a fez' (*Dracula*, p. 390), that Dracula will be able to leave London with his coffin on board the *Czarina Catherine*. The intertextual similarities with *Dracula* (the mysterious carriage, the alien intruder, their physical traits, the aristocratic origin, even the capacity to use modern technologies and to profit from new medical researches) prove that, like Stoker, Braddon more or less unconsciously had modelled Lady Ducayne upon what was at the time considered one of the darkest races of humankind.[21]

From a narrative point of view, Braddon's story dramatises the clash between the conventions and strategies of realistic fiction and the Gothic violations of those same conventions, enhancing the uneasy relationship between the Gothic genre and the contemporary setting. While realism aims at giving an organic narrative form and a coherent meaning to events, on the contrary the use of Gothic codes points to the decomposition of traditional literary genres (and of their reassuring implications) through the presence of multiple voices and perspectives. This is the case, for instance, of *fin-de-siècle* 'multivocal' Gothic fictions such as Robert

Louis Stevenson's *The Strange Case of Dr Jekyll and Mr Hyde* (1886) and *Dracula*, where there is a deliberate inclusion of documents, diaries, letters, reports and narrations which do not offer a linear description of the events but a narratively and epistemologically disruptive one. As far as Braddon is concerned, 'Good Lady Ducayne' displays the coexistence of a third-person omniscient perspective and of a first-person narration (mainly, the letters written by Bella to her mother), as if to offer readers two faces of the same story: an objectively realistic one and a subjectively impressionistic one, in which the intrusion of Gothic codes is more easily retraceable. As a general rule, Gothic narrations and stories *do not* represent a total rejection of realism but rather tend to 'vampirise', particularly in late-Victorian literary productions, its formal conventions in order to give more credit to their deforming perspective.[22] Apart from the ironic reference to the mosquitoes which supposedly cause Bella's wounds ('What a vampire!', exclaims Parravicini while curing the girl), Bella's dreams represent, as in *Lady Audley's Secret*, one of the most explicit Gothic elements of the tale:

> The dream troubled her a little, not because it was a ghastly or frightening dream, but on account of *sensations* which she had never felt before in sleep – a whirring of wheels that went round in her brain, a great noise like a whirlwind, but rhythmical like the ticking of a gigantic clock; and then in the midst of this uproar as of winds and waves she seemed to sink into a *gulf of unconsciousness*, out of sleep into far deeper sleep – *total extinction*. And then, after that blank interval, there had come the sound of voices, and then again the whirr of wheels, louder and louder – and again the blank – and then she knew no more till morning, when she awoke, feeling *languid* and oppressed [. . .]
>
> She was homesick, and she had dreams – or, rather, an occasional recurrence of that one bad dream with all its *strange sensations*. It was more like a hallucination than dreaming – the whirring of wheels; the sinking into an abyss; the struggling back into consciousness. (pp. 94–5; pp. 99–100; my italics)

Although the passage quoted above explicitly recalls Le Fanu's *Carmilla*, Laura's dreams (during which she is 'vampirised' like Bella) allude to images of homosexual intercourse and *post-coitum* exhaustion which are absent from Braddon's short story:

> But they left an awful impression, and a sense of *exhaustion*, as if I had passed through a long period of great mental exertion and danger [. . .] Sometimes there came a *sensation* as if a hand was drawn softly along my check and neck. Sometimes it was as if warm lips kissed me, and longer and more lovingly as they reached my throat, but there the caress fixed itself [. . .] I had grown pale, my eyes were dilated and darkened underneath, and the *languor* which I had long felt began to display itself in my countenance. (*Carmilla*, p. 126, my italics)

Opposite to the sensations described in *Carmilla*, associated with traditional vampirism, the strange events occurring in 'Good Lady Ducayne' will be scientifically explained as a side effect of the administration of chloroform. Indeed, Ducayne's peculiar form of vampirism is performed through a syringe with the help of Parravicini (the typical Italian Gothic villain) and consists of blood transfusions. Braddon attempts to de-Gothicise her story through Herbert Stafford's 'realistic' cultural and narrative perspective, which he introduces in the course of his unmasking of Parravicini's and Lady Ducayne's crimes:

> I could take upon myself to demonstrate – by most convincing evidence, to a jury of medical men – that Dr Parravicini has been bleeding Miss Rolleston, after putting her under chloroform, at intervals, ever since she has been in your service. The deterioration in the girl's health speaks for itself; the lancet marks upon the girl's arms are unmistakable; and her description of a series of sensations, which she calls a dream, points unmistakably to the administration of chloroform while she was sleeping. (p. 106)

The use of chloroform and the practice of transfusion was a contemporary theme Braddon chose to include in her tale to give 'realistic' credit to her Gothic story. As a matter of fact, chloroform was introduced by Sir James Young Simpson, Professor of Midwifery at Edinburgh University (the same university where Herbert studied), who had begun to use chloroform instead of ether since 1847.[23] As for blood transfusions, James Bluddell (a British obstetrician) performed the first successful one in the treatment of postpartum haemorrhage in 1818. Using the patient's husband as a donor, Blundell extracted a small amount of blood from the husband's arm and, using a syringe, successfully transfused his wife. Between 1825 and 1830 he performed ten documented transfusions, five of which proved beneficial for his patients, and devised various instruments for blood transfusions. But the most famous Victorian doctor who studied transfusions was Joseph Lister, who introduced the use of antiseptics to control infections during donations. This choice helped in reducing the number of infections caused by lack of hygiene. Not until 1870, however, did the idea of antiseptic firmly catch on. In 1877 Lister (who was later made baronet by Queen Victoria and become namesake of 'Listerine) proved that surgery and blood transfusions through the use of antiseptics reduced the mortality rate by 50 per cent. Contrarily to Stoker's *Dracula* and George Eliot's 'The Lifted Veil' (1859), Braddon in 'Good Lady Ducayne' makes only implicit references to blood transfusions, using a narrative ellipsis which is probably more disturbing than any accurate description.[24] The four transfusions performed in *Dracula* have a strong sexual connotation (where blood metonymically represents sperm) which is absent from Braddon's vampire story. In Stoker's novel, besides conveying the idea of a strong male homosocial bond, the characters' behaviour resembles a rape whose victim is the vampirised Lucy Westenra:

> 'Young miss is bad. She wants blood, and blood she must have or die. My friend John [Steward] and I [Van Helsing] have consulted; and we are about to perform what we call a blood transfusion – to transfer from full veins of one to the empty veins which pine for him. John was to give his blood, as he is the more young and strong than me' – here Arthur took my hand and wrung it hard in silence [. . .]
>
> Then with swiftness, but with absolute method, Van Helsing performed the operation. As the transfusion went on something like life seemed to come back to poor Lucy's cheeks, and through Arthur's growing pallor the joy of his face seemed absolutely to shine. (*Dracula*, pp. 157 and 159)

However, it is the vampire-like use of modern Victorian technology and medical discoveries by 'degenerate' creature such as Lady Ducayne which represents the most problematic and disquieting element in Braddon's tale. Just like Dracula, who takes advantage of innovations such as telegraphs and phonographs, Lady Ducayne's attitude can be interpreted as 'nineteenth century up-to-date with a vengeance':

> 'You are young, and medicine is a progressive science, the newspapers tell me. Where have you studied?'
>
> 'In Edinburgh – and in Paris.'
>
> 'Two old schools. And do you know all the new-fangled theories, the modern discoveries – that remind me of the medieval witchcraft, of Albert Magnus, and George Ripley; you have studied hypnotism – electricity?'
>
> 'And the transfusion of blood,' said Stafford, very slowly, looking at Parravicini.
>
> 'Have you made any discovery that teaches me to prolong human life – any elixir – any mode of treatment? I want my life prolonged, young man. That man there [Parravicini] has been my physician for thirty years. He does all he can to keep me alive – after his lights. He studies all the new theories of all the scientists – but he is old; he gets older every day – his brain-power is going – he is bigoted – prejudiced – he can't receive new ideas – can't grapple with new systems.' (p. 105)

Notwithstanding the conciliatory epilogue of 'Good Lady Ducayne', where a repentant Lady Ducayne offers a large sum of money to Bella, Braddon's happy ending is characterised by an ironic undertone. Her epilogue can be also approached as a parodic rewriting of Dickens's *Great Expectations* (a novel with which Braddon's tale shares many elements), since Ducayne's economic donation recalls Magwitch's. Both are in fact 'aliens' whose money is the product of criminal actions, and who help two young people to gain economic stability. Like the morally unacceptable banknotes which make a gentleman of Pip, the £1,000 cheque Ducayne gives Miss Rolleston, after suggesting that she '[go] and marry [her] doctor' (p. 109), is still drenched in the blood of the other girls who contributed to the unnatural prolongation of Adelaide Ducayne's wealthy life as aristocratic vampire. In this, as well as in the other previous examples from *Lady Audley's Secret* (Chapter 1) and *John Marchmont's Legacy* (Chapter 2), Braddon's mutations of the Gothic code demonstrate her willingness to survive the challenges of the Victorian literary market, proving that it was her 'variety' as a writer that made her a 'survivor'.

Notes

1. Auerbach, *Our Vampires, Ourselves*, p. 1, my italics.
2. Marx, *Capital*, vol. 1, transl. Moore and Aveling p. 233; p. 256. Marx's metaphor is read with an eye to its literary relevance by Franco Moretti in 'Dialectic of Fear' (in *Signs Taken for Wonders*, pp. 83–108). Ken Gelder asserts that '[the] representation of the capital or the capitalist as a vampire was, then, common both to Marx and to popular fiction in the mid-nineteenth century. It would not be an exaggeration to say that this representation mobilised vampire fiction at this time, to produce a striking figure *defined* by excess and unrestrained appetite – whose strength increased, the more victims he consumed' (*Reading the Vampire*, p. 22). Karl Marx was not the only political thinker to use vampires as metaphors. According to Engels, religious beliefs 'serve only to weaken the proletariat and to keep them obedient and faithful to the capitalist vampires' (*The Condition of the Working Class in England*, Chap. 9, p. 270). Engels defines the middle classes as vampires who 'first suck the wretched workers' day so that afterwards they can [. . .] throw a few miserable crumbs of charity at their feet' (Chap. 13, p. 313).
3. Frye, 'The Ghost Story and the Subjection of Women', p. 171. According to Vanessa Dickerson nineteenth-century women writers and ghosts were both perceived as 'powerful and peripheral', while the act of writing a ghost story 'was for the popular woman writer the creation of a public discourse for voicing feminine concerns' (*Victorian Ghosts in the Noontide*, pp. 5–6). Alysia Kolentsis argues that the female ghost story articulates a paradoxical preservation of the patriarchal order ('Home Invasions').
4. 'Good Lady Ducayne' was published in *The Strand Magazine*, vol. XI, February 1896, pp. 185–99 and in *The Sheffield Weekly Telegraph* in two parts, on 21 and 28 March 1896. All quotations are from Braddon, 'Good Lady Ducayne', in *At Chrighton Abbey and Other Horror Stories*.
5. Spencer, 'Purity and Danger', p. 201.
6. According to Kelly Hurley '[the] *fin-de-siècle* Gothic consistently blurs the boundaries between natural and supernatural phenomena, hesitating between scientific and occultist accountings of inexplicable events. The realm of genre explored is the grey area at the borderline between

known and unknown, or extra-rational phenomena, with the supernatural defined not as the occult per se, but as the product of mysterious natural forces the scientist has not yet been able to explain' (*The Gothic Body*, pp. 16–17).

7. The three friends were Madame Delpierre (an intimate of the Braddon family), Miss Elizabeth Philip, a frequent guest at Richmond and Mrs Browne, another family friend. As regards Maxwell's death, Robert Lee Wolff writes that '[as] the autumn of the year turned into winter, the weather grew unusually severe. By January and February 1895, MEB was frequently noting in her diary how bitter cold was at Annesley Bank [. . .] and [later] she wrote: "M. feverish and ill." Across the empty spaces of the days between the first and fifth of March 1895 she drew two heavy lines. These were the days of John Maxwell's final illness – influenza – and death' (*Sensational Victorian*, p. 357).

8. James MacGrigor Allen's speech is published in the *Anthropological Review*, VII, 1869, pp. cxxviii–cxcix. According to Victorian 'progressive' medicine, the menstrual flow was also seen as a form of physical renewal of the bodily fluids which were monthly expelled. In the opinion of P. J. Barthez (1734–1806), an influential French physician, '[probably] women employ this increase [in the menstrual circle] in their average age because of the softness and flexibility of their fibres, and particularly of their periodic evacuations which rejuvenate them, so to speak, each month, renew their blood, and re-establish their usual freshness' (qtd in Jordanova, *Sexual Visions*, p. 28).

9. Shuttleworth, 'Female Circulation', p. 48.

10. Showalter, *Sexual Anarchy*, p. 180. As for 'A Beautiful Vampire' (another variation of the Countess Bathory theme, published in *Ludgate Magazine* in 1896), Kristine Swenson writes that 'whereas Kenealy's menopausal vampire is principally a figure of sexual and racial anxieties, Braddon's operates on a more social and economic level. Lady Deverish steals beauty and sexual energy from those around her in order to remain beautiful and sexually attractive herself. In contrast, Lady Ducayne merely wishes to prolong her life and retain her wealth and privileges' ('The Menopausal Vampire', p. 30). In their analysis of Kenealy's short story and of its allusions to (contradictory) anti-feminist politics, Ann Heilmann and Valerie Sanders assert that '[what] is particularly interesting about this text is the ambivalent and unstable violence of (menopausal) femininity as an emblem of both vampirism and debility' ('The Rebel, the Lady and the "anti"', p. 295).

11. Spencer, 'The Social Organism', in *Essays*, vol. 1, p. 294.

12. Welsh, 'Bodies of Capital', p. 75. Nina Auerbach explores the double status of 'old maids' in Victorian literature and culture, seen as 'plaintive variant of the angel of the house' (*Woman and the Demon*, p. 111).

13. Kristeva, *Powers of Horror*, p. 71.

14. For Lauren Goodlad, 'Lady Ducayne's late-century capitalism-as-vampirism is brought to a halt, almost anticlimactically, by an exemplary English *professional*: Dr Herbert Stafford'. Braddon's tale 'details an anti-capitalist rhetoric, especially prevalent in mid-Victorian middle-class culture, in which professionalism asserts its merits less by reference to its

technological capabilities than to its putative monopoly over gentlemanliness' ('"Go and Marry Your Doctor"', p. 220).

15. Qtd in *Literature and Science in the Nineteenth Century*, pp. 525–7, my italics.
16. Ibid., p. 478.
17. Reviewing Wilkie Collins's *The Woman in White* (1861) in *The Reader* on 3 January 1863, an anonymous critic describes the Victorian novelists' interest in adultery, crimes and moral corruption as a 'plant of foreign growth' imported from France (qtd in Rance, *Wilkie Collins*, p. 31). On the influence of French literature on Braddon's themes and literary techniques, see Part III.
18. 'Edwardian legislation was characterised both literally and metaphorically by the dream of national insurance; a desire to tighten the supervision and welfare of the national stock, to exclude and eliminate degenerate "foreign bodies". Indeed the Royal Commission on Alien Immigration in 1903 and the ensuing Act of 1905 should not be seen as a mere anomaly, nor, exclusively, as part of some timeless, centuries-old phenomenon of anti-Semitism, but in relation to those wider contemporary attempts to construct a racial-imperial identity, excluding all "bad blood" and "pathological elements", literally expelling anarchists, criminals, prostitutes, the diseased, and the hopelessly poor – all those declared "undesirable aliens"' (Pick, *Faces of Degeneration*, pp. 215–16).
19. Although Sander L. Gilman's book *The Jew's Body* deals with the male Jewish body, the author's reflections on physiognomic distinguishing traits such as the peculiar shape of the nose (to which he devotes a whole chapter) can be applied to Braddon's short story: 'In popular and medical imagery, the nose came to be the sign of the pathological Jewish character for Western Jews, replacing the pathognomonic sign of the skin, though closely linked to it' (pp. 180–1). In *Rough Justice*, published two years after 'Good Lady Ducayne', Braddon compares a Jewish character to a vampire in metaphorical terms: 'The solicitor is one Morris Mortimer, a Jew, whose father was concerned with old Greswold in many of his money-lending schemes – in a word a fellow-bloodsucker' (*Rough Justice*, vol. 2, p. 106).
20. Smith, *Victorian Demons*, p. 35. According to Matthew Biberman, who focuses on the connections between *Dracula* and the Jewish question, both the vampire and the vampire-killer represent a scenario of self-policing that was first realised in the ghettos and later in concentration camps (*Masculinity, Anti-Semitism and Early Modern English Literature*). Carol Margaret Davison in *Anti-Semitism and British Gothic Literature* investigates the changing 'spectropoetics' related to the fears of a Jewish invasion from traditional Gothic fictions to Victorian novels.
21. Kathleen L. Spencer compares the medieval witch hunt with many persecuting attitudes that characterised the last decades of the nineteenth century: '[though] the late Victorians did not explicitly attribute evil to whites, they manifested the same fears of pollution from the outsiders, the same suspicion of deviants as traitors, and the same exaggerated estimation of what was at stake – in short, the same social dynamics as more traditional witchcraft societies [. . .] The battle produced numerous cries of "seize the witch!" directed both at groups (Jews, Germans, Slavs, Orientals,

birth control advocates, promiscuous women, decadent French authors [especially Zola], homosexuals) and at individuals – most spectacularly, though by no means solely, Oscar Wilde' ('Purity and Danger', pp. 207–8).

22. For Rosemary Jackson the Gothic and the fantastic exist 'as the inside, or underside, of realism, opposing the novel's closed, monological forms with open, dialogical structures, as if the novel had given rise to its own opposite, its unrecognizable reflection' (*Fantasy*, p. 25).

23. See Stratmann, *Chloroform*. On the debate on the use of chloroform (headed by Sir James Simpson from 1846 to 1856 in *The Lancet*), see Poovey, 'Scenes of Indelicate Character'. Dr Simpson's success arrived only in 1853, when Queen Victoria decided to be anaesthetised with chloroform during the birth of her ninth child: from then on this procedure started to be widely accepted. Simpson was awarded a baronetcy in 1866.

24. In *The Victorians and the Visual Imagination* Kate Flint, who also alludes to Braddon's vampire tale on page 107, asserts that Eliot's story 'in its very construction, is based on a paradigm of morbid anatomy' (p. 99). In his article on 'undead' characters in literature (Miss Havisham, Bertha Rochester, Lady Audley and Ann Catherick), whose apoplectic attacks seemed to replace the use of paranormal images, Andrew Mangham states that '[although] today we are encouraged to think about literature and medicine as two highly disparate avenues of thinking, the links between these two disciplines were, in the nineteenth century, fluid and inspired' (Mangham, 'Life after Death', p. 289).

Part II

Darwinian Detections

That gravel page upon which I might have read so much has
been long ere this smudged by the rain and defaced by the clogs
of curious peasants.

Arthur Conan Doyle, *The Hound of the Baskervilles*, 1901[1]

Chapter 4

From Geology to Genealogy: Detectives and Counter-detectives in *Lady Audley's Secret* and *Henry Dunbar*

In an autobiographical note she wrote a few years before her death, Mary Elizabeth Braddon remarked that while the English reading public was attracted by stories of crime, it was yet more fascinated by the processes of scientific detection. As she put it, '[There] is nothing that English men and women enjoy more than the crime which they call "a really good murder" [. . .] Every man is at heart a Sherlock Holmes, while every woman thinks herself a criminal investigator by instinct.'[2] These words by Braddon confirm the opinion of many contemporary critics, who agree that sensation novels established some of the conditions for the birth of detective fiction and that their 'preoccupation with secrets, and the revelation of those secrets and of crime, are often so intrinsic to the plot that they must be considered as the antecedents of the emergent detective novel'.[3] Basically, sensation novels focused on familial secrets that involved female characters, who became the object of male scrutiny. In this sense, they dramatised a cluster of mid-century Victorian anxieties: the crisis of the old aristocracy, the increasing independence of women in society and the creation of a new juridical (and political) system marked by an institutionalised form of control. In turn, detective stories tended to subordinate this framework to the slow and scientifically oriented process of revelation. This peculiar characteristic, as well as its cultural implications, can be understood also by considering the impact that evolutionary thought had on the Victorian frame of mind. Like many other contemporary intellectuals and writers, Mary Elizabeth Braddon was aware of the importance that researches in the field of geology, palaeontology, natural history and anthropology had in the nineteenth century. Indeed, many of her novels, in which detection plays a major role, testify in direct or indirect ways to the influence of evolutionary studies on the figure and on the achievement of investigators.

Braddon experimented with all the variants and developments of the detective during her long literary career: from morally ambiguous male and female amateur investigators (such as Robert Audley in *Lady Audley's Secret* or Margaret Wilmoth and Clement Austin in *Henry Dunbar*) to the disabled policeman Joseph Peters in *The Trail of the Serpent* and the 'Holmesian' detective John Faunce in *Rough Justice* and *His Darling Sin*. At the same time, the impact of evolutionism on her novels contributed to complicate both her characterisations and the epistemological implications of her narrations.

Generally speaking in the Victorian age, evolutionary, Darwinian and post-Darwinian theory was sometimes misread and put to use as part of a larger political effort to construct an efficient institutional system to control the new developments of bourgeois society and to manage any 'anomaly', whether in the form of 'unfit' citizens, aggressively assertive women, born criminals or racial outsiders. According to a revised notion of subjectivity, which arose in the mid-nineteenth century, citizens were gradually becoming objects of *legal* and *bodily* management:

> That the mystery at the heart of virtually every sensation novel is based on the disappearance and subsequent identification of some 'character' reflects [a] paradigmatic shift in the realm of subjectivity: the replacement of the entire ideologically laden notion of Victorian moral character (something we associate with high realism) with the more physiologically based but socially-defined conception of Victorian identity (the contested issue in a detective plot).[4]

If on the one hand the past was not conceived as a pre-defined certainty but a mystery that usually concealed disquieting truths, on the other hand the criminal stood at the centre of scientific analyses and surveys. Many representatives of nineteenth-century middle-class society thus found in the police force (created in 1829) and later in detectives (as the expression of a more 'humanised' and 'reassuring' exercise of power) their perfect intermediaries. With the introduction of the notion of 'social order' and 'state power', whose origin dates back to Jean-Jacques Rousseau's *Du contrat social* (1762), the idea of crime changed in nature and quality. According to these new social principles, individuals are united by a 'contract' which must be respected by everybody and whose violation has moral and socio-political implications. Criminal behaviours thus turned from an offence against a single individual or a community to a threatening action against the stability of institutions.[5] The first consequence of this change was that punishments changed in form and meaning. Public torture was replaced by a controlled coercion of the body and of the criminal's mind, with a shift in interest from the *effect* of crime (stigmatised with a sentence that was equal if not superior to the infringement) to its *origin*.[6] Moreover, the juridical system profited from modern technological inventions (such as photography) and from new scientific researches in the field of criminology, which made legitimate or illegitimate use of Darwinian notions of heredity. Since it was fundamentally concerned with history and with the question of origins, evolutionary and Darwinian theory suited the public's interest in the detection of the origin of crimes. In the literary field in particular, the sensation novel and the detective novel represented a textualisation of a speculative-analytical approach that offered an archaeology of criminal actions and of the criminal, with the detective turning into a sort of criminal geologist. Dickens, for instance, devoted many articles published in *Household Words* from 1850 to 1853 to the 'science of detection', concentrating on the activities of the London police department and on the deeds of Inspector Field, the source of inspiration for Inspector Bucket in *Bleak House* (1854).[7] The example of scientific investigators such Poe's Chevalier C. Auguste Dupin, of Inspector Bucket in Dickens, of Wilkie Collins's Sergeant Cuff in *The Moonstone* (1868) and of Braddon's amateur and professional detectives is indicative. The deeper was the 'unearthing' of (hi)stories – whether in the natural world or in the fictional universe – the wider became the gap between the certainties of the past and the murky realities discovered by scientists, detectives and readers as well.[8]

The first real step in the modernisation of evolutionary theories, and of the figure of the 'geological investigator', was represented by the publication of the three volumes of the *Principles of Geology* (1831–3) by Charles Lyell. Traditional geological studies were renovated by the presence of a scientist who, via his 'microscopic' eye and his creative imagination, was capable of reconstructing a pre-human past whose chronology pre-dated the Holy Scripture (which traditionally put the origin of the world at 4004 BC). It followed that the human species was relegated to a secondary role in the history of the earth.[9] Although on a 'political' level Lyell's anti-catastrophist and gradualist theory of evolution reflected his conservative fears of revolution and the prejudices against the new rising classes, he was primarily influential in affirming a new scientific method based on the assumption that all natural phenomena might be explained by causes now in operation. For Lyell, the impossible task of offering a complete stratigraphy of the earth's crust justified an imaginative reconstruction of geological history. In this sense, Lyell's 'deductive' science, uniting a professional knowledge of the subject of analysis to an imaginative power, may be compared to the procedures that became the norm for the literary detective. Indeed, in the initial section of *Principles*

Lyell makes use of a hermeneutic code and of a vocabulary which many Victorian detectives would borrow from him:

> Geology is the science which *investigates* the successive changes that have taken place in the organic and inorganic kingdoms of nature; it enquires into the *causes* of these changes, and the influence which they have exerted in modifying the surface and external structure of our planet [. . .] *We trace* the long series of events which have gradually led to the actual posture of affairs; and by *connecting events with their causes*, we are enabled to classify and retain in the memory a multitude of *complicated relations*.[10]

Unlike Lyell's *Principles*, addressed to an educated public which included poets and intellectuals such as Tennyson, Browning and Arnold, Robert Chambers's *Vestiges of the Natural History of Creation* (1844) became a literary case and a popular bestseller that overstepped the boundaries of mere scientific speculation. Chambers's book even turned into a 'sensation' because, for fear of being involved in the religious and cultural debate that would inevitably follow its publication, its author sustained his anonymity for more than twenty years. After the success of the first editions, Chambers decided to prolong the mystery, seducing his readers into a sort of editorial detection. Although Chambers's *Vestiges* did not add anything new to the previous scientific researches, his book was influential because of its peculiar narrative construction. Like the author of a detective story, Chambers – through a careful strategy based on the dissemination of clues and a deliberate reticence about results – led his readers to share his opinions on what the astronomer William Herschel called 'the mystery of mysteries'. Like Lyell before him, Chambers claimed that the real scientific investigator should counterbalance a detailed observation of geological records with an imaginative ability:

> That God created animated beings, as well as the terraqueous theatre of their being, is a fact so powerfully *evinced*, and so universally *received*, that I at once take it for granted. But in the particulars of this so highly supported idea, we surely here see cause for some *re-consideration*. It may now be *inquired* – in what way was the creation of animated beings effected.[11]

By mixing the results of Lyell's 'gradualist' approach, the narrative strategies used by Chambers and Thomas Malthus's arguments in *Essay on the Principle of Population* (1798), Darwin offered in *On the Origin of Species* (1859) an interpretation of the natural world as a battlefield for the survival of species and for the acquisition of food. Its 'complex web' of relations revealed unexpected (and often disquieting) 'family links' among living creatures.[12] The Darwinian scientist and the detectives of many Victorian novels tried to find a final coherence in the disorder and chance which seemed to rule everyday life, moving backwards to a primeval history to find answers. Like a Darwinian study, the plot of many detective stories concealed – to quote Tzvetan Todorov – 'the story of an absence: its most immediate characteristic is that it cannot be immediately present in the book'.[13] Thanks to the 'second story' (properly related to detection, which Todorov compares to the *sjužet*) the real nature of the 'first story' (in formalistic terms, the *fabula*) is revealed, offering its readers and its audience the illusion of a surrogate order and harmony. However, like many novelists, Charles Darwin realised that the attempt to find a reassuring 'plot' led to the vision of an 'entangled bank'. Although Darwin avoided moral questions and often described the grandeur of the world in its wonderful variety, he could not avoid noticing the primacy of struggle and confusion:

> We look at the plants and bushes clothing an *entangled bank*, we are tempted to attribute their proportional numbers and kinds to what we call chance [. . .] What a struggle between several kinds of trees must have gone on during long centuries, each annually scattering its seeds by the thousand; what war between insect and insect [. . .] all *striving to increase*, and all feeding on each other or on the trees or their seeds and seedlings, or on the other plants which first clothed the ground and thus checked the growth of the trees![14]

This is similar to what takes place in Mary Elizabeth Braddon's novels featuring amateur or professional detectives, where 'retrograde investigations' in the present (as Robert Audley calls them) reveal the presence of chaotic and morally compromising counter-stories in the past.[15] Although it was first rejected as a frustrating implication of Darwin's scientific researches, 'chance' seemed to be for Braddon – and for Darwin as well – a disquieting occurrence. This fact explains why, despite the detectives' acute observing eye and imaginative perspective, many cases are solved thanks to fortuitous and casual discoveries, where religious providence is counterbalanced by secular randomness.

In a Foucaultian critical perspective, the control exerted by detectives over the people involved in an investigation turns detective fictions into what can be defined as 'panoptical narrations'.[16] In Braddon's case, Robert Audley's scrutiny of his aunt's actions, detective Carter's attitude in *Henry Dunbar* and John Faunce's surveying gaze reproduce in a fictional form Jeremy Bentham's architectural model of incarceration and control illustrated in his *Panopticon* (1791), where the criminal is constantly observed from an invisible source of institutional power. Real and fictional detectives were thus part of a bureaucratic system that reproduced a politics of policing which opposed social, political and imperial anomalies (or dysfunctions). However, unlike Conan Doyle's perfect detecting machine Sherlock Holmes, who is the expression of a centralised power and who makes use of Lombrosian anthropology,[17] Braddon's investigators discover unsavoury secrets that lead them to reconsider their status as social subjects. She therefore negotiated the necessity to convey a normalised worldview with the 'shadow' of the transgressing Lady Audley. It is not accidental that many of her detectives (with the notable exception of John Faunce) are figures located in a 'liminal' position: Robert Audley is an indolent lawyer, whose desire to avenge his friend George Talboys leads him to abandon his immoral way of living; the weak and fragile Clement Austin in *Henry Dunbar* leaves his job to help Margaret (who, in turn, protects a murderer) with her investigations; Eleanor Vane in *Eleanor's Victory* marries a man she does not love in order to have the economic independence to pursue her father's murderer; the disabled policeman Joseph Peters is a culturally and biologically anomalous figure who has a close relationship with the most degraded representatives of Victorian society. Braddon's predilection for improvised, occasional and amateur investigators (at least before the official 'entrance' of John Faunce) signals a certain diffidence towards professional detectives that was widespread during the 1850s and 1860s. These new figures, usually coming from the lower classes, had the privilege of a direct access to the world of the upper classes that was traditionally denied them. Since the life of the Victorian family had been traditionally associated with a prevalently female space, its penetration was considered a metaphoric violation of the women's domestic space and body.[18]

Aware of the impact that his theory of the evolution of species would have on Victorian society and culture, in a letter to fellow-scientist Joseph Hooker Charles Darwin compared – in sensationalistic terms – his new discovery to a 'murder' that he was going to confess to the Victorian scientific community. For him the scientist is basically a 'collector' of clues who has discovered crimes concealed in the past:

> I was so struck with the distribution of the Galapagos organisms, &c. &c., and with the character of the American fossil mammifers, &c. &c., that I determined *to collect blindly every sort of fact*, which could bear any way on what are species. I have read heaps of agricultural and horticultural books, and have never ceased *collecting facts*. At last gleams of light have come, and I am almost convinced (quite contrary to the opinion I started with) that species are not (*it is like confessing a murder*) immutable.[19]

↳ Nice attention to language.

Contemporary critical studies on *Lady Audley's Secret* have generally followed either a Foucaultian approach aiming at retracing the disciplining practices of the male characters or a gender-oriented reading. The latter is centred upon Lady Audley's rebellious assertiveness, through which she opposes her female language to the *logos* of the representatives of patriarchal institutions (Robert Audley, Luke Marks, Dr Mosgrave and Dr Val).[20] However, it seems useful to introduce a further complementary analysis of this novel centred on the figure of the post-Darwinian detective Robert Audley, whose investigation moves halfway between a scientific search for truth and a reticence born of the fear of chaos. Robert's final victory as a detective and a successful lawyer corresponds to the gradual deletion of the identity of Lady Audley, as an unacceptable Victorian 'species'. Her survival is considered by Robert a social danger, and a menace to his (displaced) homoerotic attraction to George Talboys.

The themes of mystery and the necessity of discovering secrets in the past are introduced in the opening paragraph of *Lady Audley's Secret*, in which the narrator's visual perspective gradually moves from the Essex pastures to the garden and then to the 'glorious old space' of Audley Court:

> It lay low down in a *hollow*, rich with fine old timber and luxuriant pastures; and you came upon it through an avenue of limes, of which the cattle *looked inquisitively* at you as you passed, wondering, perhaps, what you wanted [. . .]
> At the end of this avenue there was an old arch and a *clock-tower*, with a stupid, bewildering clock, which had only one hand; and which jumped straight from one hour to the next, and *was therefore always in extremes*. Through this arch you walked straight into the gardens of Audley Court. (Book 1, Chap. 1, my italics)[21]

Audley Court is dysphorically associated to a geological depression (a 'hollow') and to the moral precipice into which the various characters will fall. The description of the curious faces of the cattle ('looked inquisitively') is an ironic anticipation of Robert's inquisitive attitude. Finally, the sudden jumps of the tower-clock represent the metaphor of a moral and epistemological crisis whose outcome is the apocalyptic image of a time out of joint.

Robert Audley's ambiguous nature is illustrated in many sections of the novel, which describe his position as a good-for-nothing barrister at Fig-tree Court in London Temple Bar who has never practised his profession and was only 'supposed to be a barrister' (Book I, Chap. IV, p. 71). In addition to Robert's failure in the professional field, he is also characterised as a lazy young man and a reader of immoral French novels. Robert owns all of the books of Michael Lévy, who became famous for having published Flaubert's scandalous *Madame Bovary*. Therefore the barrister's behaviour, way of living and 'unhealthy' literary tastes are all symptoms of his moral lassitude.[22] Robert's role as the representative of the professional middle class, juxtaposed with the old country gentility embodied by Sir Michael Audley, foregrounds the ironic 'actantial' construction (as Algirdas Julien Greimas terms it) of *Lady Audley's Secret*. Moreover, the detection of Lady Audley's 'secrets' also has a direct effect on the investigator, who turns from a corrupted bohemian into an active member of the rising middle classes and of Victorian masculinity.[23]

On a topological level, Audley Court is the place where Lucy Audley's desire for a life without solitude and squalor can come true. This country mansion, which on the surface is safe from any criminal incursion, becomes a place of deviance that testifies to a collision between the paradigms of *being* and *appearing*. This becomes explicit in one of the most famous passages of the novel, where the narrator comments on the crimes committed in 'peaceful' country retreats:

> We hear every day of murders committed in the country. Brutal and treacherous murders; slow, protracted agonies from poisons administered by some kindred hand; sudden and violent deaths by cruel blows, inflicted with a stake cut from some spreading oak, whose very shadow promised – peace. (Book 1, Chap. 7, pp. 91–2)[24]

Using the same lexical and rhetorical devices, a few years before Charles Darwin had asserted that beyond the appearances of a peaceful natural world there was a ferocious struggle for existence. In some of the most debated sections of the *Origins*, Darwin looked at the world as an immense arena where an ineluctable natural selection was carried out without any moral restraint:

> *We behold* the face of nature bright with gladness, *we often see* superabundance of food; we do not see, or we forget, that the birds which are idly singing round us mostly live on insects or seeds, and are thus constantly destroying life. (*On the Origin of Species*, p. 133, my italics)

While for Darwin it was the need of food that led creatures to fight with each other, Helen Talboys's criminal actions in *Lady Audley's Secret* are motivated by her need to 'survive' and to rise on the social ladder. Braddon thus relocates the struggle for existence from the natural world to Victorian society, from singing birds living 'on insects or seeds' to the Mannings' 'eight-roomed house':

> What do we know of the mysteries that may hang about the houses we enter? If I were to go tomorrow into that common-place, plebeian, eight-roomed house in which Maria Manning and her husband murdered their guest, I should have no awful prescience of the bygone horror. Foul deeds have been done under the most hospitable roofs, terrible crimes have been committed amid the fairest scenes, and have left no trace upon the spot where they were done. (Book 1, Chap. 18, p. 170)[25]

In Darwinian terms, Lady Audley represents a new female 'species' who struggles to survive in a patriarchal world whose rules she repeatedly violates, first by transgressing her matrimonial bonds and then by gaining access to a higher social class. In turn, Robert Audley embodies a 'variation' of the species to which he belongs (the breed of a decayed aristocracy) and succeeds in integrating himself with those middle classes who were an alternative to the privileged social world of Audley Court.[26] Like *On the Origin of Species*, which oscillated between the reassuring notion of an invisible providential order determining the course of events and the shadow of anarchy, *Lady Audley's Secret* dramatises the clash between the principle of order (as a sign of providence) and the rule of chaos. Here Braddon gives a new interpretation to evolutionary terms such as heredity, genealogy and species, and 'Lucy Audley herself thinks of the world, as evolutionary biologists do, as both product and locus of fluke and chance.'[27] For instance, Robert's providential reading of events takes place during a deathbed scene that does not feature a repenting fallen woman (as traditional narrative norms prescribed) but the male villain Luke Marks:

> 'The clergyman will talk to him and comfort him when he comes to-morrow morning,' Mr Audley thought; 'and if the poor creature needs a sermon it will come better from his lips than from mine. What should I say to him? His sin has recoiled upon his own head; for had my lady's mind been set at ease, the Castle Inn would not have been burned down. *Who shall try and order his own life after this? Who can fail to recognise God's hand in this strange story?*' (Book 3, Chap. 8, p. 433, my italics)

Lady Audley's Secret echoes debates that were then current on female mental maladies and anticipates the future misuses of Darwinian theories by psychiatrists such as Henry Maudsley, who argued that '[the] individual [. . .] is but a link in the chain of organic beings connecting the past with the future' and that the human being represents 'the inevitable consequence of his antecedents in the past, and in the examination of these alone, we do arrive at the adequate explanation of him'.[28] In her novel, Braddon complicates and interrogates evolutionary ideas, by having Lady Audley as a product of her times and of the contextual, rather than the biological, causes which made her a criminal:

> I brooded horribly upon the thought of my mother's madness. It haunted me by day and night. I was always picturing to myself this madwoman pacing up and down some prison cell, in a hideous garment that bound her tortured limbs [. . .] I had no knowledge of the different degrees of madness; and the image that haunted me was that of a distraught and violent creature, who would fall upon me and kill me if I came within her reach. (Book 3, Chap. 3, p. 357)[29]

Detective Robert Audley is the appointed hero, who wants to contrast this cultural and natural disorder. For this reason, he embodies the male characters' desire to confine the pathogenic influence of Lucy Graham within the limits of the Audley family. The epilogue to Braddon's novel proves that the Lady's secret will be concealed behind the domestic walls of Audley Court, and Lucy Graham will be exiled to a modern and updated version of the eighteenth-century Gothic castle in the form of a Belgian madhouse (see Part I, Chapter 1). Unlike professional detectives coming from the 'outside', Robert Audley has free access to Audley Court and has the opportunity to be Lady Audley's judge and, indirectly, executioner. However, his willingness to leave his previous bohemian life and to engage in an active detection has unexpected, and partially 'unspeakable', reasons. First, his investigations are motivated by the mysterious disappearance of his friend George Talboys, for whom he shows a form of love which, in some ways, looks suspect to Victorian eyes. The friendship between Robert and George makes them accomplices in a mutual fight against Lady Audley through a male comradeship aiming at neutralising an agent which disturbs not only the life of the Audleys but, in particular, the homosocial and homosexual bond between these two men.[30] On many occasions, Braddon (in particular through the voice of Michael Audley's daughter Alicia) alludes to this form of love that dare not speak its name. For instance, commenting upon Robert's anxiety over his friend's prolonged and unexplained absence, Alicia refers to the Greek legend of Damon, who offered to sacrifice his life in case his friend Pythias would not appear on the appointed day of his execution: 'What a dreadful catastrophe!' said Alicia maliciously, 'since Pythias, in the person of Mr Robert Audley, cannot exist for half an hour without Damon, commonly known as George Talboys' (Book 1, Chap. 11, p. 119). Alicia's allusion is far from innocent: these two characters from classical mythology were in fact traditionally associated by Victorians with 'Greek friendship' and homosexual love. Moreover, the fact that George Talboys's sister Clara physically resembles her brother George allows Robert to find in this woman a socially acceptable alternative to his affection for George:

> The whole length of the room divided this lady from Robert, but he could see that she was young, and that *she was like George Talboys.*
> 'His sister!' he thought in that one moment during which he ventured to glance away from the master of the house towards the female figure at the window. 'His sister, no doubt. He was fond of her, I know. Surely, she is not utterly indifferent as to his fate?' (Book 2, Chap. 4, p. 210, my italics)[31]

Driven by his 'improper' passion for George, Robert Audley is responsible for a series of controlling practices performed upon the incriminated
subject Lady Audley. In Audley Court, turned by Robert into a sort of
'Panoptical' building, Lady Audley falls prey to the detective's scrutinising eye. Robert's disciplined use of time, juxtaposed with his previous
attitude of wasting it by indulging in 'immoral habits', is exemplified by
his choosing to use a notebook and a journal to write down his personal
reflections (see Book 1, Chap. 13). Through this method of detection,
Robert will attempt to discover the Darwinian 'missing link' to the series
of events that brought Lucy Graham to Audley Court, and that caused
George Talboys's disappearance.[32] In the Darwinian-sounding chapter
entitled 'Retrograde Investigation' (Book 2, Chap. 7) Robert illustrates
his method, which consists of an archaeological investigation of Lucy
Graham's past to understand her present as Lady Audley ('I must trace
the life of my uncle's wife backwards, minutely and carefully, from this
night to a period of six years ago'). Like a geological study, each infini-
tesimal existential fragment is given a first-rate value in the 'backward'
reconstruction of a hidden history. Consequently, Robert decides to
make use of indirect evidence, which he defines in legal terms as 'circumstantial evidence':

> 'Circumstantial evidence,' continued [Robert Audley], as if he scarcely
> heard Lady Audley's interruption, 'that wonderful fabric which is built out
> of straws collected at every point of the compass, and which is yet strong
> enough to hang a man. Upon what infinitesimal trifles may sometimes hang
> the whole secret of some wicked mystery, inexplicable heretofore to the
> wisest upon the earth! A scrap of paper; a shred of some torn garment; the
> button of a coat [. . .] the fragment of a letter [. . .] a thousand circumstances
> so slight as to be forgotten by the criminal, but links of steel in the wonderful
> chain forged by the science of the detective officer [. . .]' (Book 1, Chap. 15,
> p. 152)[33]

The allusion to circumstantial evidence foregrounds Braddon's interest in contemporary debates on juridical questions. Since the 1840s a
plethora of books dealing with this theme had been published, including
A Practical Treatise of the Law of Evidence (1842) by Thomas Starkie.
In a few years, the rules of evidence would be applied to specifically
scientific areas of research such as natural history and palaeontology,
where the impossibility of having the direct experience of an event and
the necessity to reconstruct a detailed chronology of facts justified the
use of retroactive procedures. William Will's *An Essay on the Principles
of Circumstantial Evidence* (1850) included a significant reference
to George Cuvier's studies, followed by a comparison between the
inferential ability of the palaeontologist and that of detectives:

A profound knowledge of comparative anatomy enabled the immortal Cuvier, from a single fossil bone, to describe the structure and habits of many of the animals of the antediluvian world. In like manner, an enlightened knowledge of human nature often enables us [. . .] to follow the tortuous windings of crime, and ultimately to discover its guilty author, as infallibly as the hunter is conducted by the track to his game.[34]

Thanks to his zeal as a detective, Robert at the end of the novel succeeds in committing his aunt to a mental asylum in order to save the Audleys' reputation. His detection becomes a counter-detection the moment he decides to silence and to lock Helen Talboys/Lucy Graham into Villebrumeuse, where her secrets will be buried with her.[35] Here Lady Audley will be rechristened 'Madame Taylor', a Franco-British name that hints at her ambiguous position as liminal subject suspended between Victorian respectability ('Taylor') and continental immorality ('Madame').

But *Lady Audley's Secret* is not the only novel in which a detection finally turns into a counter-detection. Published during Braddon's great sensationalist season, *Henry Dunbar* (1864) is considered one of her best-plotted and most captivating novels, and represents a further step in the evolution and updating of the Lady Audley paradigm. This text, which deals with professional and amateur detectives and double identities, begins with the return home of Henry Dunbar, the former owner of a bank. Dunbar had to choose a forced exile to India because of a scandal (forgery) which had involved him and his close friend Joseph Wilmot in the past. At Winchester Henry has a chance meeting with Wilmot, whose body then turns up brutally murdered and disfigured. After being accused of the murder by police detective Henry Carter, Dunbar is finally released, although Wilmot's daughter Margaret – abandoned by her father when she was still a child – asks for the help of cashier Clement Austin (who works in Dunbar's bank and who is in love with her). Margaret soon discovers that her father has not died but has assumed Henry Dunbar's identity, and he is being blackmailed by the villainous Vernon. Despite police detective Henry Carter's attempts to catch Wilmot, the latter succeeds in escaping with the help of his daughter, who has now become his accomplice. At the end, Margaret comes back to Clement only after her father's repentance and death.[36] As this brief summary demonstrates, along with the use of textual and narrative paradigms derived from *Lady Audley's Secret* (the change of identity, the familial crimes, the presence of morally ambiguous detectives and the final concealment of a criminal secret), and the anticipation of Braddon's interest in white-collar crimes, the novelty of this text lies in the presence of multiple investigators of a very heterogeneous nature. The Scotland

Yard detective Carter is joined by Clement (whose love for Margaret has turned him into an amateur detective) and by a woman detective who is finally subjected to detection. The plot of *Henry Dunbar* follows a very complex and contradictory trajectory, since Margaret Wilmot's first attempt to collect the clues about her father's death (with the support of her lover Clement) fails the moment she realises that the supposed criminal is none other than her father in disguise. Margaret's decision to become her father's accomplice is a demonstration of the moral permeability of detectives in Braddon's macrotext.[37] At the same time, the professional investigator Henry Carter – motivated by economic rather than moral considerations – shares the typical strategies of evolutionary detectives, based upon a sharp observation of the 'relics' of the past:

> Mr Carter was silent for some moments, during which his eyes wandered about the apartment in that professional survey that took in every detail, from the colour of the curtains and the pattern of the carpets, to the tiniest porcelain toy in an antique cabinet on one side of the fireplace. The only thing upon which the detective's glance lingered was the lamp, which Margaret had extinguished. (p. 306)

Detective Carter is first defeated and baffled by Margaret – disguised as one of John Wilmot's servants – and then by Vernon, who challenges him in an adventurous boat chase aboard *The Crow*. This unsuccessful chase results in Vernon's death, in Joseph Wilmot's escape and in the loss of hundreds of pounds in diamonds that end up on the bottom of the sea. Clement Austin, who once trusted the 'science of detection' of professional investigators, shows his disappointment after he happens to read the news of Carter's defeat and humiliation in a newspaper (in a way that recalls *Lady Audley's Secret*). On this occasion Braddon seems to share the prejudice of many Victorian journalists, intellectuals and writers on the ability and moral rectitude of detectives.

The narration of the final part of the story is left to Clement Austin's first-person account. Taking inspiration from Collins's multivocal sensation novel *The Woman in White*, Braddon anticipates the narrative technique adopted in her future detective fictions *Rough Justice* and *His Darling Sin*. Like many of Braddon's contradictory heroes, Clement is described in 'unmanly' terms, replicating the paradigmatic juxtaposition between weak males (Robert Audley, George Talboys, Sir Michel Audley) and assertive females (Lady Audley, Alicia Audley) of *Lady Audley's Secret*: ' The strong man covered his face with his hands and sobbed aloud. Margaret watched him with tearless eyes; her lips were contracted, but there was no other evidence of emotion in her face' (p. 242).

At the end of the story amateur detective Clement reconciles with Margaret and decides to conceal Joseph Wilmot's criminal secrets (namely, Henry Dunbar's homicide and his illegal acquisition of properties and money) from the community. Like Robert Audley before him and like many other detectives in Braddon's future novels, Clement Austin buries Dunbar's criminal actions committed in the past within domestic walls. Austin's and Robert Audley's attitudes are those of two imperfect Darwinian investigators, whose counter-detections conceal, rather than reveal, unspeakable secrets. In Clement's own words, '[We] are very happy. The secret of my wife's history is hidden in our own breasts – a dark chapter in the criminal romance of life, never to be revealed upon earth' (p. 350).

Notes

1. Doyle, *The Hound of the Baskervilles*, p. 71.
2. Braddon, *Beyond these Voices*, p. 185.
3. Carnell, *The Literary Lives*, p. 235. As far as the literary market is concerned, Maurizio Ascari points out that detective stories were generally addressed to a more educated public than sensation novels, and that '[from] its inception, the discourse on detective fiction discarded the sensational lineage of the new genre, grounding its literary status on its association with scientific method and highbrow literature' (*A Counter-History of Crime Fiction*, p. 1).
4. Thomas, *Detective Fiction and the Rise of Forensic Science*, p. 63.
5. 'The citizen is presumed to have accepted once and for all, with the laws of society, the very laws by which he may be punished. Thus the criminal appears as a juridically paradoxical being. He has broken the pact, he is therefore the enemy of society as a whole, but he participates in the punishment that is practised upon him' (Foucault, *Discipline and Punish*, pp. 89–90).
6. Neil Davie states that '[there] was not just a desire to *describe* criminals, but also to *explain* them. What gripped the minds of a wide range of Victorians and Edwardians was thus not simply a taxonomic desire to pin a label on "The Criminal" and place him or her under a bell jar, but to explore the very springs of crime itself' (*Tracing the Criminal*, p. 15).
7. On the relationship between Dickens and the metropolitan police, see Ousby, *Bloodhounds of Heaven*, p. 83 onwards. The expression 'detective novel' is here deliberately anachronistic since, in R. F. Stewart's opinion, the first occurrence of this term dates back to a review of H. F. Wood's volume *The Passenger from Scotland Yard*, published in *The Morning Post* in 1888 (. . . *And Always a Detective*, p. 27).
8. 'Throughout the detective fictions of Poe, Dickens, and Doyle [. . .] there appear terms, figures of speech, and methodological practices indebted to nineteenth-century philosophy, geology and palaeontology, archaeology,

and evolutionary biology, disciplines that by mid-century were to share common preoccupations about the nature of evidence and narratological reconstructions of a past unavailable to the observer' (Frank, *Victorian Detective Fiction*, p. 4).

9. In *The Voyage of the Beagle* (1839), a text that owed much to Lyell's *Principles*, Darwin juxtaposed 'the eye of the body' (limited and subdued to contingencies) with 'the eye of reason', which reflected the imaginative approach of the new scientist. On this aspect, see Willingham-McLain, 'Darwin's "Eye of Reason"'.

10. Lyell, *Principles of Geology*, p. 5, my italics.

11. Chambers, *Vestiges*, pp. 152–3. James A. Secord asserts that in the *Vestiges* '[implied] narrator and implied reader explore the book of nature together, and the relationship runs as a subplot throughout the novel [. . .] *Vestiges* begins with facts. But the possibility of greater intimacy between author and reader is hinted at from the start' (*Victorian Sensation*, p. 99).

12. George Levine reflects on the fact that '[one] of the great Christian metaphors, and one of the central concerns of Victorian writers, becomes in Darwin a literal fact: we are all one family' (*Darwin Among the Novelists*, p. 145).

13. Todorov, 'The Typology of the Detective Fiction', p. 46. For Stephen Knight plot is 'a way of ordering events; its outcome distributes triumph and defeat, praise and blame to the characters in a way that accords with the audience's belief in dominant cultural values – which themselves interlock with the social structure' (*Form and Ideology in Crime Fiction*, p. 4).

14. Darwin, *On the Origin of Species*, p. 141, my italics; all quotations will be taken from this edition, with pages parenthetically indicated. For George Levine 'Darwin's science, continuing self-consciously to expel caprice from the universe by explaining even biological development in naturalistic terms of law of cause and effect, affirmed laws that looked very much like chance and caprice' ('Dickens and Darwin', p. 268).

15. According to Alexander Welsh, 'sensation novels seem to mimic the far-reaching efforts of geology and evolutionary biology to construct continuous narratives of the past' (*George Eliot and Blackmail*, p. 24).

16. 'In relation to an organization so complex that it often tempts its subjects to misunderstand it as chaos, the detective story realizes the possibility of an easily comprehensible vision of order. And in the face – or facelessness – of a system where it is generally impossible to assign responsibility for its workings to any single person or groups of persons [. . .] the detective story performs a drastic simplification of power as well' (Miller, *The Novel and the Police*, p. 69).

17. 'Commentators have related Holmes's methods of investigating crime to other scientific strains in Victorian culture in addition to criminal anthropology, most notably to the interpretative methods of Darwin in biology and Lyell in geology, both of whom conceived of their disciplines as being radically historical in nature' (Thomas, 'Minding the Body Politic', p. 246).

18. Anthea Trodd suggests that '[at] one level [. . .] problems concern etiquette, uncertainties about the social status of the policemen, and the conversational peculiarities of being interrogated by a kind of higher servant or lower tradesman. More significantly, the encounters betray deep fears

about the threat to the world of domestic innocence posed by the new police world of subterfuge and surveillance' (*Domestic Crime*, pp. 12–13).

19. Letter to Joseph Hooker, 11 January 1844, 'Appendix E: Letters', in Darwin, *On the Origin of Species*, p. 475.

20. For Ann Cvetkovich '[One] can read the novel from the detective or masculine point of view as a fantasy of control, surveillance, and power, in which threats to the family can be identified and contained. One can also read it from Lady Audley's or the women's point of view as a fantasy of rebellion, in which women can take their revenge on patriarchy that restrains them, and in which madness is a sign of resistance' (*Mixed Feelings*, p. 55).

21. Braddon, *Lady Audley's Secret*, ed. Houston, p. 43. All further references will be from this edition, with quotations parenthetically indicated. According to R. F. Stewart, *Lady Audley's Secret* is 'the sensation novel to begin all detective novels' (. . . *And Always a Detective*, p. 202).

22. During his investigation Robert always brings with him French novels and indulges in smoking Turkish tobacco, which was considered a sign of immoral behaviour (see Book 1, Chap. 15, p. 145; Book 1, Chap. 17, p. 162; Book 2, Chap. 7, p. 235).

23. '[Robert] Audley's pursuit of Lady Audley's past is also his own quest for a professional fortune, and his investigation of Lady Audley's secret is the means to the establishment of his own identity as professional man' (Petch, 'Robert Audley's Profession', p. 1). On the question of Robert's moral ambiguity, Greg Howard says that '[although] Braddon celebrates the triumph of the entrepreneur [Robert Audley] over his aristocratic predecessor [Sir Michael Audley], Braddon regards the entrepreneurial victory with considerable ambivalence' (Howard, 'Masculinity and Economics in *Lady Audley's Secret*', p. 34).

24. Mary Elizabeth Braddon's explicit influence on Conan Doyle emerges in a passage included in 'The Adventure of the Copper Beeches' (1892) in which, in the course of a trip to Hampshire to solve a case, Sherlock Holmes addresses Watson almost paraphrasing *Lady Audley's Secret*: 'You look at these scattered houses, and you are impressed by their beauty. I look at them, and the only thought which comes to me is a feeling of their isolation, and of the impunity with which crime may be committed there [. . .] They always fill me with a certain horror. It's my belief, Watson, founded upon my experience, that the lowest and vilest alleys in London do not present a more dreadful record of sin than does the smiling and beautiful countryside' (Doyle, 'The Adventure of the Copper Beeches', in *The Adventures of Sherlock Holmes*, p. 277).

25. On 9 August 1847, in their house at Bermondsey, Maria and Frederick Manning (a lady of Swiss origin and a railway officer) killed Maria's secret lover Patrick O'Conner after a dinner together, burying his body under the floor. The trial (known as the 'Maria Manning Case') had a large public following because of its highly sensational tones, to the point that even Thomas Carlyle refers to it in his *Latter Day-Pamphlets* (1851) as his 'preferred murder'. For an analysis of famous murder cases, and of their influence on sensation novels, see Altick, *Victorian Studies in Scarlet* and *Deadly Encounters*.

26. Pamela K. Gilbert reflects upon the differences and the similarities between these two characters: 'Between the law as represented in the person of Robert Audley and the chaotic madness of Lady Audley lies only a difference of circumstance; their natures are the same' ('Madness and Civilization', p. 227). It is necessary to add here that Lady Audley shares her nephew's love of French novels.

27. Hopkins, *Giants of the Past*, p. 42.

28. Maudsley, *The Physiology and Pathology of Mind*, p. 205.

29. A few years later Braddon will refer in more explicit terms to hereditary madness in *Thou Art the Man* (1894), although on this occasion she will discard post-Darwinian theories on heredity and born criminals, replacing the term 'madness' with a more scientific reference to 'epilepsy'. Laurence Talairach-Vielmans asserts that 'this late-Victorian novel portrays women detecting male secrets, thus completely rewriting Braddon's older plots dealing with female criminality' ('Introduction', in Braddon, *Thou Art the Man*, p. x).

30. 'In any male-dominated society there is a special relationship between male homosocial (*including* homosexual) desire and the structures for maintaining and transmitting patriarchal power: a relationship founded on an inherent and potentially active structural congruence' (Sedgwick, *Between Men*, p. 25).

31. After Robert's meeting with Clara '[his] pursuit of Lady Audley receives an increased impetus, because the possibility of being forced to confront his own homoerotic responses is safely evaded' (Nemesvari, 'Robert Audley's Secret', p. 524).

32. On the 'disciplining' use of time, Michel Foucault says that '[the] principle that underlies the time-table in its traditional form was [. . .] the principle of non-idleness: it was forbidden to waste time [. . .] the time-table was to eliminate the danger of wasting it – a moral offence and an economic dishonesty. Discipline, on the other hand, arranges a positive economy; it poses a principle of a theoretically ever-growing use of time' (*Discipline and Punish*, p. 154).

33. 'Trials were changed from a scene dominated by witnesses to one dominated by lawyers, and from the cautious admission of anything other than direct testimony to the professional management of a mixture of evidence' (Welsh, *Strong Representations*, p. 95).

34. Qtd in Welsh, *George Eliot and Blackmail*, p. 100.

35. According to Natalie Schroeder and Ronald A. Schroeder, 'Robert's best option to contain Lucy is to keep her a secret. In a real sense, Lucy's secrets have become the Audley family's – at least the Audley males' – secrets, and now Lucy herself is the Audley secret. Ironically, Robert, who played amateur detective and strove to discover what Lucy was hiding, must now labour with equal diligence to keep her hidden' (*From Sensation to Society*, pp. 57–8).

36. The novel was first published in *The London Journal* with the title *The Outcasts* from 12 September 1863 to 24 March 1864. The original plot was rewritten and simplified (eliminating the reference to bigamy included in the first version), leaving space for two different texts: the first was *Henry Dunbar* in its final form, and the second was a long story entitled 'Lost and

Found' (serialised in *The London Journal* in 1864 as part of *The Outcasts*). All references to the novel will be taken from the first book edition, published in London by Maxwell in 1864.

37. In the words of Jennifer Carnell, 'Margaret is transformed from the amateur detective, a representative of the moral justice and authority the police will not use, to assisting a murderer and becoming herself a fugitive from justice' (*The Literary Lives*, p. 267). On the theme of heredity, associated in *Henry Dunbar* to 'filial affection', Lyn Pykett argues that '[the] sins of the father [. . .] lie at the root of the concealments of Margaret Wilmot/Wentworth in *Henry Dunbar*. Margaret not only bears the taint of her father's criminality and poverty, but is also implicated in his guilt through her dutifully filial concealment of his murder and impersonation of his former employer' (*The 'Improper' Feminine*, p. 85). The problematic relationship between fathers and daughters will occur in different forms in Braddon's macrotext, from sensation novels (*Eleanor's Victory*) to realistic fictions (*Joshua Haggard's Daughter*).

Chapter 5

Perception, Abduction, Disability: *Eleanor's Victory* and *The Trail of the Serpent*

Eleanor's Victory (1863) was one of the first novels to include a female detective as a leading character, although there had already been some sporadic examples in Catherine Crowe's *Susan Hopley* (1841), Wilkie Collins's short story 'The Story of Anne Rodway' (1856) and in *The Revelations of a Lady Detective* (1861) by W. S. Hayward. In just a few years female investigators became the narrative norm, whose success lay in 'novelty, dramatic effect', in their 'unorthodox method of detecting' and 'because noisiness – a fundamental requirement of the detective – [was] considered a feminine trait'.[1] However, while in the above-mentioned cases the activity of the detective represented an escape from the monotony of domestic life, in Braddon's Eleanor Vane (the main character in *Eleanor's Victory*) her investigation is motivated by a stubborn search for truth, vengeance and justice. Braddon's novel opens in August 1853, when fifteen-year-old Eleanor Vane arrives in Paris to live with her old father George, a decadent aristocrat who has squandered his money on gambling. In order to pay Eleanor's college fees George Vane decides to play his last game at cards with two mysterious characters. However, the loss of the card game drives him to suicide. He leaves only a torn and partially readable note, in which he accuses the two card players of having cheated. The day after, George Vane's body is found in the morgue by Richard Thornton, a young painter of theatrical backdrops, who convinces Eleanor to go back to London and to live with him and his aunt Eliza Piccirillo. After changing her name to 'Miss Vincent' so as not to be associated with her father's suicide, Eleanor succeeds in getting a post as a governess in Mrs Darrell's house at Hazelwood, in Berkshire, where she meets the lawyer Gilbert Monckton and the bohemian artist Launcelot Darrell, who has just come back from India, and who unsuccessfully proposes to her. Then, during a trip to London, Eleanor discovers that Launcelot was probably one of the two persons who were involved in her father's death in Paris. For this reason, she decides to become an amateur detective (with the help of Richard Thornton) and marries Gilbert Monckton to have the economic means to pursue her vengeance.[2] Eleanor discovers Launcelot's involvement in George Vane's death first by means of a drawing made by Launcelot and then with the help of Victor Bourbon, a reformed French villain who also took part in George Vane's final game at cards. At the end of the novel, she does not denounce Launcelot and obtains her most important victory: forgiveness.

Eleanor Vane's successful amateur detection can be juxtaposed with Henry Carter's disastrous investigation in *Henry Dunbar* and to John Faunce's initial failure in *Rough Justice*, as a demonstration that for Braddon 'liminal' characters such as Eleanor and Joseph Peters (in *The Trail of the Serpent*) have a more direct access to truth and a sharper perception of events than 'centralised' investigators. One of the peculiarities of Eleanor's detecting method lies in her ability to move from the private sphere (considered a context of female pertinence) to the public one (of male pertinence). Eleanor demonstrates that she possesses qualities such as adaptability and aggressiveness, which Richard Thornton and Mrs Piccirillo consider unwomanly. Eleanor's reply is emblematic: "'I don't know whether it is womanly or Christian-like," she said, "but I know that it is henceforward the purpose of my life, and that it is stronger than myself."'[3]

Observation represents a recurrent paradigm in *Eleanor's Victory*, since Eleanor is endowed with a visual and 'imaginative' ability which is a key element in her investigation. The first scene of the novel features Eleanor on board the steamer *Empress*, which is carrying her to France and, metaphorically, to an experience that will change her life. Her fixed look and her posture anticipate her firmness and determination to retrace a readable plot in the vast 'web of relations' surrounding her:

> The craggy cliffs of the Norman coast looked something like the terraced walls and turreted roofs of a ruined city in the hot afternoon sunshine, as the *Empress* steamer sped swiftly onward toward Dieppe. At least they looked thus in the eyes of a very young lady, who stood alone on the deck of the steam-packet, with yearning eyes fixed upon that foreign shore. (Chap. I, p. 1)[4]

Even the anonymous and chaotic mob of Paris, whose labyrinthine image had been recently revived by Eugène Sue's voluminous *Les Mystères de Paris* (1842–3), does not divert Eleanor from her research:

> Miss Vane's bright eyes were not closed once in that evening journey; and at last, when the train entered the great Parisian station, when all the trouble and confusion of arrival began [. . .] the young lady's head was thrust out

of the window, and her eager eyes wandered hither and thither amongst the faces of the crowd. (Chap. I, p. 6)

However, after her first meeting with her father George Vane, Eleanor's facing up to her problematic familial 'origins' will lead her to revise her belief in those Victorian moral principles upon which she previously relied.[5] Eleanor's visual skills are shown for the first time when she meets George Vane's mysterious friends. Despite the fact that she cannot clearly look at them, she immediately perceives their dangerous nature through her 'imaginative eye'. Eleanor will be engaged in reconstructing the memory of this event in order to discover the identity of these two people. This is why *Eleanor's Victory* is a novel where visuality plays a fundamental role in the narration:

> Eleanor *looked* at the two young men, wondering what new friends her father had made in Paris [. . .] Eleanor Vane *caught one passing glimpse* of this man's face as he turned sulkily away; but *she could see* the glimmer of a pair of bright restless eyes, black eyes under the shadow of his hat, and the fierce curve of a very thick black moustache, which completely concealed his mouth [. . .]
>
> She was *looking* at her father, Heaven knows how earnestly, for *she saw in his face*, in his nervous hesitating manner, *something that told her* there was some sinister influence to be dreaded from this garrulous eager Frenchman and his silent companion. (Chap. IV, pp. 36–7, my italics)[6]

Eleanor's Victory may be read as a reconstruction of George Vane's history and of Eleanor Vane's visual memory of her dangerous meeting. Finally, Eleanor's detection will take the form of a long auto analytic session through which a corrupted familial 'heritage' and 'heredity'[7] will start to emerge from the labyrinths of Paris, a metropolitan city the Victorians tended to associate with a topological and moral chaos:

> It was past twelve o'clock when the carriage drove away from the lights and splendour into the darkness of a *labyrinth of quiet streets* behind the Madeleine [. . .]
>
> Eleanor stopped suddenly, and looked at her companion. She had need to ask the question, for Richard Thornton was leading her into *a labyrinth of streets* in the direction of the Luxembourg, and he seemed to have very little notion whither he was going. (Chap. II, p. 9; Chap. VII, p. 55, my italics)

Because of the sense of alienation and anonymity they conveyed, cities such as Paris and London became the ideal settings for the crimes and the investigations of many detectives, including Braddon's (from *The Trail of the Serpent* to *Rough Justice* and *His Darling Sin*).[8] The Parisian world surrounding Eleanor resembles a Darwinian 'entangled bank', seemingly devoid of any meaningful pattern and whose design can be given an order only by the scientist/detective:

> Eleanor Vane shook her head hopelessly. The whole *fabric of the future* had been *shattered* by her father's desperate act. The simple dream of a life in which she was to have worked for that beloved father was over, and it seemed to Eleanor as if the future existed no longer [. . .]
>
>   The man whose treachery had destroyed George Vane had dropped into the *chaos of an over-crowded universe*, leaving no clue behind him by which he might be *traced*. (Chap. IX, p. 76; Chap. XV, p. 123, my italics)

The finding of George Vane's nameless body by Richard Thornton in the Parisian morgue is indicative of the intertextual influence of Edgar Allan Poe's 'Murders in the Rue Morgue' (1845), where detective Dupin makes his first appearance. Poe's depiction of Parisian streets, which was certainly on Braddon's mind when she was writing *Eleanor's Victory*, foregrounded their Babelic nature through the confusion of voices and reports related to the death of Madame L'Espanaye and of her daughter Camille. Their brutal murder (committed by an orangutan) seems to be a weird anticipation of Charles Darwin's studies on the descent of man.

Eleanor's methods of investigation, which mix her perceptive ability and her imaginative modality, juxtapose with Richard's providential and religious views, and imply a textual dialogue of an epistemological nature with the ideas and studies of many Victorian geologists and scientists. The climactic moment of this intertextual connection is represented by Eleanor's 'Lyellian' assertion that '[it] can only be from the discoveries I make in the present that I shall be able to trace my way back to the history of the past' (Chap. XXIII, p. 166). Given the lack of a complete documentation of her father's death – the fragment of a letter written by George before his suicide represents the only real clue – Eleanor appeals to her sharp observation of facts and to her imagination to fill in the empty spaces of this retroactive story. In another chapter, Eleanor defines the detective as a person who 'endeavour[s] to trace up the history of the past by those evidences which the progress of life can scarcely fail to leave behind' (Chap. XXXI, p. 215) and, during a discussion, Richard Thornton explicitly compares the detective's investigating strategy to that of the geologist:

> 'The science of detection, Mrs Monckton, lies in the observation of insignificant things. It is a species of *mental geology*. A geologist looks into the gravel pit, and tells you the history of the creation; a clever detective ransacks a man's carpet-bag, and convicts that man of a murder or a forgery.' (Chap. XXXI, p. 216, my italics)

Eleanor's Victory centres upon the interpretation of George Vane's fragmentary and incomplete letter as the only document possessed by Eleanor. Its deciphering will give her the opportunity to solve the mystery of her father's death, and to understand her present condition through a revision of the certainties of the past. The detective's *geological* reconstruction of the familial 'registers' will thus lead to a new awareness of her *genealogy*:

> It was a sheet of letter-paper, written upon in her father's hand, but a part of it had been torn away. Even had the whole of the letter been left, the writer's style was so wild and incoherent that it would have been no easy task to understand his meaning. In its torn and fragmentary style, this scrap of writing left by George Vane was only a scrabble of confused and broken sentences. The sheet of paper had been torn from the top to the bottom, so that the end of each line was missing. The [. . .] broken lines were therefore all that Eleanor could decipher, and in these the words were blotted and indistinct. (Chap. VIII, p. 70)

Eleanor's condition can be compared with that of the Lyellian scientist in *Principles of Geology*, in which he admitted that the 'natural registers' were lacunose and that the geologist's task consisted in their integration with a fictional reconstruction of the past. For Lyell, the language of the earth had to be imagined as an incomplete text. Its unreadable and partially erased words had to be deciphered by means of study and inferential imagination:

> The first and greatest difficulty, then, consists in our habitual unconsciousness that our position as observers is essentially unfavourable, when we endeavour to estimate the magnitude of the changes now in progress [. . .] We know, indeed, that new deposits are annually formed in seas and lakes, and that every year some new igneous rocks are produced in the bowels of the earth, but we cannot watch the progress of their formation; and, as they are only present to our minds by the aid of reflection, *it requires an effort both of the reason and the imagination to appreciate duly their importance.*[9]

At the end of the chapter entitled 'On the Imperfection of the Geological Record', included in *On the Origin of Species*, Darwin similarly compared geological records to incomplete documents, and scientists to creative readers of their blank spaces.[10] In this view, even the famous Darwinian diagram of the 'tree of life' (in which he illustrated in the chapter entitled 'Natural Selection' the connection between species, variations and descendants) represents a parodic reminder of the genealogical trees upon which many Victorian families built their own certainties and pride.

As with *Lady Audley's Secret*, *The Doctor's Wife*, *His Darling Sin* and many other novels, in *Eleanor's Victory* visual codes play a major role. Eleanor's perceptive ability turns her sight into a photographic plate upon which the most meaningful clues are metaphorically and literally 'impressed', as in the case of the 'photographic memory' of her casual meeting of two mysterious characters (Launcelot Darrell and Victor) before her father's death. During their investigations Eleanor and Richard come across a pencil sketch signed by 'Robert Lance' (Launcelot's pseudonym), which reproduces the suicide of Eleanor's father in almost photographic terms. Because of its richness in details and particulars, Launcelot's drawing can be compared to a colloidal print, a pre-photographic method which had replaced the daguerreotype and the collotype since 1851. Eleanor's 'photographic' perception is counterbalanced by Launcelot's 'pictorial' reproduction of George's suicide, which he partially alters and transfigures in his private scrapbook.

> [Richard Thornton] untied the strings of the loaded scrap-book, and flung it open. A chaotic mass of drawings lay before him [. . .] And, at last, a rough pencil sketch of a group in a small chamber at a *café*; an old man sat at a lamplit table playing *écarté* with a man whose face was hidden; an aristocratic-looking, shabby-genteel old man, whose nervous fingers seemed to clutch restlessly at a little pile of napoleons on the table before him. (Chap. XXXII, pp. 219–20; p. 222)[11]

Eleanor's investigation follows an analytical itinerary which rejects the limited parameters of male logic (represented by Richard and Monckton).[12] A voracious reader of French novels, she uses her imagination as a fundamental means of detection, to the point that her complex and mixed detecting strategy recalls mathematician Charles Sanders Peirce 'abductive' method of analysis and anticipates Sherlock Holmes's investigating principles. During a trip from Boston to New York on 20 June 1879 on the steamboat *Bristol* Charles Sanders Peirce turned into a detective in order to catch the thief who had stolen some valuable objects from him (including a Tiffany watch), succeeding where the Pinkerton investigating agency had failed. Peirce's backward reasoning helped him to solve this little mystery through what he will define as an 'abductive method'. Abduction, also described by Peirce as 'presumptive inference', 'retroduction' or the 'instinct to guess well' allows the scientist (and the detective) to collect intuitively all the clues available and to validate them through the discovery of real proofs. Preceded by induction and followed by deduction, the abductive practice represents for Charles Sanders Peirce, and later for Sherlock Holmes, the second and fundamental step in any inferential process:

I perform an abduction when I so much as express in a sentence anything I see. The truth is that the whole fabric of our knowledge is one matted felt of pure hypothesis confirmed and refined by induction. Not the smallest advance can be made in knowledge beyond the stage of vacant staring, without making an abduction at every step.[13]

Peirce's detection method will be joined by Doyle's most famous investigator, who will illustrate his 'abductive backward thinking' to Watson in the final pages of *A Study in Scarlet* (1888). Here Holmes asserts that in order to solve a case, 'the grand thing is to be able to reason backwards'. And then he adds: 'That is a very useful accomplishment, and a very easy one, but people do not practise it much. In the every-day affairs of life it is more useful to reason forwards, and so the other comes to be neglected.'[14]

Peirce's Darwinian-sounding term 'fabric' had already appeared in Braddon's *Eleanor's Victory* ('The whole fabric of the future had been shattered by her father's desperate act', p. 123) and, before it, in *Lady Audley's Secret*, where Robert Audley had dealt with the 'wonderful fabric which is built out of straws collected at every point of the compass' (p. 152). As Eleanor Vane's successful investigation of Launcelot Darrell demonstrates, abduction is not just a leap into improvisation and imprecision. Rather, the solution to an enigma is the most visible one: it was no other than the morally ambiguous Launcelot Darrell who led George Vane to death. Like many mysteries that will be solved by Holmes (whose deductions are the outcome of a long and complex detecting process), in *Eleanors' Victory* the discovery of Launcelot's involvement in George Vane's death emerges as an abductive epiphanic revelation:

> In that one moment – in the moment in which the pony-carriage, going at full speed, passed the young man – the thought which had flashed, so vague and indistinct, so transient and intangible, through the mind of Eleanor Vane that morning, took a new shape, and arose palpable and vivid in her brain.
> This man, Launcelot Darrell, was the sulky stranger who had stood on the Parisian boulevard, kicking the straws upon the kerbstone, and waiting to entrap her father to his ruin. (Chap. XX, p. 150)

Abandoning her role of unwomanly detective, Eleanor realises that everything she had fought for was, contrary to her hopes, a disquieting heredity. In her final transformation from avenging angel to angel of the house (which also entails a normalisation of her unwomanly assertiveness), she finally succeeds in pursuing her victory through a partial defeat, replacing vengeance with forgiveness.[15]

The most original element in *The Trail of the Serpent* (1861)[16] is not represented by its sensational plot but by its investigator, a dumb detective from the Gardenford police department named Joseph Peters. Although he is a representative of the law – a 'centralised' system of power and control – Peters is a 'liminal' character because of his lowly social origin, his reiterate mingling with people from the margins of society and, in particular, because of his physical disability. Most of the story takes place in the small provincial town of Slopperton-on-the-Sloshy, where the teacher Jabez North (a foundling) lives an apparently virtuous life. In fact, he is a greedy and unscrupulous man who, after poisoning one of his students, kills and robs Montague Hardin – who has just come back from India with enormous riches – and succeeds in having Hardin's nephew Richard Marwood blamed for the murder.[17] The only person who is sure of Richard's innocence is the dumb police detective Joseph Peters, who convinces Richard to avoid capital punishment by feigning madness. In the meantime a woman, who is the mother of Jabez's son and who now lives in poverty, is brutally rejected by Jabez; for this reason she throws herself and her baby in the Sloshy river. The baby is rescued by Peters, who decides to adopt him and to call him Sloshy. After killing a man named Jim Lomax who had a great resemblance to him and who he had chanced to meet one day in a poor suburb, Jabez (who is believed by everybody to be dead) moves to Paris with the new name of Raymond, Count de Marolles. Here he seduces the rich countess Valeria de Cervennes, convincing her to poison her husband Gaston de Lancy, a singer unjustly accused of adultery (who later on will reappear in one of the most sensational scenes of the novel). Braddon's decision to locate Jabez's 'second birth' (as Count de Marolles) in Paris – a city which Victorians associated with corruption – is not casual, since Jabez's criminal inclination to poison people suits the 'intoxicating' Parisian atmosphere.[18] Having escaped from the madhouse, Richard Marwood joins a group of amateur investigators named the 'Cherokees' (inspired by the 'Bow Street Runners'), which includes a pugilist and Sloshy.[19] Their aim is to catch Jabez North/Count de Marolles. In the meantime, Jabez North discovers that he is the son of the Marquis de Cervennes, the twin brother of Jim Lomax and Valeria's cousin. The final scenes are set on a boat sailing from Liverpool to America, where Jabez takes refuge in a coffin to escape the 'Cherokees'. After being arrested by Peters, who has collected a great amount of evidence against him, in order to avoid capital punishment Jabez North commits suicide and dies for the third, and last, time.

On the surface, *The Trail of the Serpent* is a detective story whose basic elements are represented by the discovery and persecution of the villain ('whodunit'). Nevertheless, the real innovation of this book lies in the detecting process aimed at understanding the motivations driving the criminal actions ('howdunit'). This 'vertical' investigation of the community living in Slopperton-on-the-Sloshy introduces in fact a 'horizontal' analysis of themes such as the hereditary nature of evil and the value of 'liminal' people, as opposed to the calls to order, sanity and morality of the citizens who are part of the Slopperton community. Apart from the intertextual influence of *The Mysteries of London* (1845) by G. W. M. Reynolds (inspired by Eugène Sue's *Les Mystères de Paris*), of Alexander Dumas's works (for the description of the Parisian setting), of detective Vidoq's *Memories* (1828) and of many other paraliterary texts such as the Newgate Novels,[20] the incipital section of *The Trail of the Serpent* is a tribute to Edward Bulwer Lytton's *Paul Clifford* (1830), and anticipates Dickens's *Our Mutual Friend* (1864).[21] Like the Thames, which for Dickens is a destructive as well as a rejuvenating natural force, the overflowing river Sloshy becomes a paradigm of the moral 'waste' emerging from its deep and of a Darwinian nature 'red in tooth and claw with ravine' (in Alfred Tennyson's words) which gives both life and death:

> I don't suppose it rained harder in the good town of Slopperton-on-the-Sloshy than it rained anywhere else. But it did rain. There was scarcely an umbrella in Slopperton that could hold its own against the rain that came pouring down that November afternoon, between the hours of four and five. Every gutter in High Street, Slopperton; every gutter in Broad Street (which was, of course, the narrowest street); in New Street (which by the same rule was the oldest street) [. . .] A bad, determined, black-minded November day. A day on which the fog shaped itself into a demon, and lurked behind men's shoulders, whispering into their ears, 'Cut your throat!' (Book 1, Chap. I, p. 5)

Braddon provides the Sloshy river with a metaphorical value, turning it into the novel's main narrative and diegetic chronotope, where either directly or indirectly all the events of the story take place: from Jabez North's rescue to the death of Sloshy's mother, up to the saving of Peters's adopted son and closest collaborator. The river and the other natural forces penetrate all the recesses ('gutters') of the Slopperton community without any distinction for rank, sex or culture, and make its most obscure truths emerge.[22] The Sloshy river represents the literal and metaphorical expression of a double evolutionary view of the natural world, described as unending energy which seems to be devoid of any theological and teleological meaning, but also endowed with a regenerating power. The river functions in *The Trail of the Serpent* as a semantic and topological aggregating centre in a way that is not dissimilar from George Eliot's 'Lyellian' descriptions of the Floss in her epilogue to *The Mill on the Floss* (1860).[23] If on the one hand the river brings destruction, on the other hand it gives new life to the foundling

Sloshy because of Joseph Peters's maternal saving presence. Despite the fact that Sloshy is Jabez North's biological son, Braddon in her novel negates many post-Darwinian theories dealing with the 'hereditariness' of evil. As Jennifer Carnell argues, '[With] Sloshy Braddon shows the son of a hardened murderer becoming a detective, and so [questions] the theories of inevitable heredity which were current at the time.'[24]

In another section of *The Trail of the Serpent*, where the river is described in anthropomorphic terms, the 'maternal' attributes of natural forces are reconfigured in an aggressive key, with a parodic inversion of the paradigms of womanliness, traditionally associated with watery images:

> The Sloshy is not a beautiful river, unless indeed mud is beautiful, for it is very muddy. The Sloshy is a disagreeable kind of compromise between a river and a canal [. . .] It has quite a knack of swelling and bursting, this Sloshy; it overflows its banks and swallows up a house or two, or takes an impromptu snack off a few overbuildings, once or twice a year. It is inimical to children, and has been known to *suck into its muddy bosom* the hopes of divers families; and has afterwards gone down to the distant sea, flaunting on its *breast* Billy's straw hat or Johnny's pinafore [. . .] It has been a soft pillow of rest, this *muddy breast* of the Sloshy; and weary heads have been known to sleep more soundly in that loathsome, dark, and slimy bed than on couches of down. (Book 1, Chap. V, p. 32, my italics)[25]

Jabez North, an 'assistant and usher' at Dr Tappenden's academy, is the first character to be introduced in *The Trail of the Serpent*. Jabez has been raised and nursed by the whole community of Slopperton after being rescued from the 'muddy' waters of the Sloshy river. Jabez North is repeatedly compared to a species bred by the Slopperton citizens according to a practice Darwin terms as 'domestication', and grotesquely describes in *On the Origin of Species*:

> Domestic races of the same species, also, often have a somewhat monstrous character; by which I mean, that, although different from each other, and from the other species of the same genus, in several trifling respects, they often differ in an extreme degree in some one part. (*On the Origin of Species*, p. 104)

Like Colonel Kurtz's community in Conrad's *Heart of Darkness*, the citizens of this small provincial town 'contributed to the creation' of Jabez North as the perfect specimen of the middle-class Victorian:

> Slopperton believed in Jabez North. Partly because Slopperton had in a manner created, clothed, and fed him, set him on his feet; patted him on his head, and reared him under the shadow of Sloppertonian wings, to be the good and worthy individual he was [. . .]

He was found in a Slopperton river by a Slopperton bargeman, resuscitated by a Slopperton society, and taken by the Slopperton beadle to the Slopperton workhouse; he therefore belonged to Slopperton. Sloppeton found him *a species of barnacle* rather difficult to shake off. (Book 1, Chap. I, pp. 7–8, my italics)

The sentence 'Slopperton found him *a species of barnacle* rather difficult to shake off' is an explicit allusion to Darwin's main object of interest before (or rather during) the elaboration of his theory of transmutation: 'cirripedia', also known as 'barnacles'. In October 1846, during his voyage along the Chilean coast he begun an eight-year study, which would evolve into a four-volume monograph (published in 1856) on a species which had been previously classified as molluscs and which he ascribed on the contrary to crustaceans. Cirripedia were for Darwin the example of a primitive organic being subject to evolution and adaptation. After the discovery of a barnacle affectionately called 'Mr Anthrobalanus' (because of the presence of small joints and articulations) Darwin would start collecting an enormous number of 'cirripedia' from all over the world, turning his interest in this small living form into an obsession that nearly killed him, but also into a blessing in disguise. As Rebecca Stott puts it, Darwin's *Monograph on the Sub-Class Cirripedia, with Figures of All Species* 'won him the Royal Society Medal in 1854 and established him as a scientist who had won his spurs. Without his barnacle spurs and his barnacle contacts, *On the Origin of Species by Natural Selection* would have been very differently received.'[26] Given this ironic reference to Darwin's first important scientific achievement, the comparison between Jabez and the grotesque barnacle in *The Trail of the Serpent* suggests that the echoes of Darwin's 'tiny' scientific obsession were still resonating in Braddon's ears. But Braddon's allusion has another ironic background: during the 1850s and 1860s the popularity of marine biology was at its height, and middle-class professionals used to collect small sea species for their fashionable drawing-room aquaria.

According to Darwin, the need to survive leads to the extermination of 'parent-species' or of species of the same genus. In *The Trail of the Serpent* Braddon translates these Darwinian assumptions into Slopperton's social context through the figure of Jabez North.[27] In his struggle for survival Jabez will not hesitate to kill his brother Jim Lomax and two of his fellow-citizens (his pupil and Montague Hardin) to achieve his ends. In this sense, Jabez's actions seem to replicate those described by Darwin:

The competition will generally be most severe [. . .] between the forms which are most like each other in all respects. Hence the improved and modified descendants of a species will generally cause the extermination of the parent-species; and if many new forms have been developed from any one species, the nearest ally of that species, *i.e.* the species of the same genus, will be the most liable to extermination. (*On the Origin of Species*, p. 294)

As far as Joseph Peters is concerned, Braddon was not the first Victorian writer to include a disabled character in a novel. Examples range amongst Dickens's deaf Baby Turveydrop in *Bleak House* (1854), the crippled Tiny Tim in *A Christmas Carol* (1843), the partially deformed 'Jenny Wren' in *Our Mutual Friend* (1864), the invalid Olive Rothesay in Dinah Craik's *Olive* (1850), the deaf and dumb Madonna Blyth in Wilkie Collins's *Hide and Seek* (1854), the blind Leonard in *The Dead Secret* (1857), and the blind Lidia Finch in *Poor Miss Finch* (1872), to the quintessential multidisabled Miserrimus Dexter in *The Law and the Lady* (1875).[28] The true innovation in Braddon's case lies in the fact that Joseph Peters is a successful detective and that his characterisation tends to avoid the 'melodramatic mode' that was usually associated with the depiction of invalidity in Victorian culture. For Martha Stoddard Holmes 'Victorian discourses of disability, and the texts that convey them, are overwhelmingly "melodramatic".' In this specific context the term 'melodramatic' 'invokes not only the recurrent use of disabled characters in stage melodramas, but more broadly the habitual association, in literary and other texts, between physical disability and emotional excess'.[29] Famous stage melodramas such as Thomas Holcroft's *A Tale of Mystery* (1802) and *Deaf and Dumb* (1809) paved the way for what would be one of the most successful theatrical pieces on disability in Victorian literature: B. F. Rayner's *The Dumb Man of Manchester. A Melodrama in Two Acts* (1837), a play Braddon probably knew. The title refers to Jane Wilton's brother Tom, wrongly accused of having killed his wealthy aunt Mrs Wilton. In truth, the real murderer is Edward Wilton (Jane's husband), who has recently come back after a five-year exile. In one of the most 'excessive' scenes of the play, Tom (who is also an orphan) tries to defend himself in front of the jury with a series of 'picturesque gestures' culminating in his melodramatic recognition and accusation of his brother-in-law Edward, who throws himself out of the window:

CHIEF JUSTICE: Advance. Examine attentively the countenance of all the present, and see if amongst them you can discover the assassin of your benefactress.

(Tom bows, and prepares to execute the order, his eye animated, his gestures raised [. . .] – when he comes to WILTON, R., *he starts with surprise, then examines him again, and makes a convulsive noise or sign of certainty. General movement – all eyes are fixed upon him.* TOM, *who returns to* WILTON, *points him out with extended arms.)*

CHIEF JUSTICE: That, then, is the murderer?
EDWARD: What! Dare to accuse me? My conduct has ever been that of an honourable man. I protest against a charge so foul. I murderer of my aunt! (Act III, scene ii)[30]

Even though *The Trail of the Serpent* almost certainly drew inspiration from *The Dumb Man of Manchester* for the trial scene and for the characterisation of Jabez North (a more 'refined' version of Edward Wilton), Joseph Peters's disability is not a melodramatic object of pity. Peters uses non-normative methods of investigation based on his peculiar bodily and emotional perceptions in order to read beyond the surfaces of middle-class respectability.[31] Moreover, Peters is always lucid and self-controlled, extremely rational and even endowed with the most important virtue for a potential detective: anonymity. Coming from a lower social class and working in the service of Gardenford detective Mr Jinks (who is totally wrong in laying the blame on Richard Marwood for the murder of his uncle Mr Hardin), Peters will be promoted thanks to his 'abilities' as a detective. Indeed, his physical impairment becomes an advantage to him.[32] People, including Jabez North, tend to speak without restraint in his presence because they erroneously think that he is both deaf and dumb. Moreover, his use of sign language and finger spelling (his 'dumb alphabet') helps him to communicate with those people who understand his code, without being intercepted.

It is also to be noticed that in her characterisation of a disabled detective Braddon does not avoid using stereotypes, and in portraying Peters's dumbness she depicts him in 'physiognomic' terms. Throughout *The Trail of the Serpent*, the narrator implies a strict relationship between the detective's peculiar facial features and his speech impairment (which is a non-immediately visible disability):

If you looked at his face for three hours together, you would in those three hours find only *one thing in that face that was any way out of the common* – that one thing was the expression of the mouth. It was a compressed mouth with thin lips, which tightened and drew themselves rigidly together when the man thought – and the man was almost always thinking: and this was not all, for when he thought most deeply *the mouth shifted in a palpable degree to the left side of his face.* This was *the only thing remarkable* about the man, except, indeed, that he was dumb but not deaf, having lost the use of his speech during a terrible illness which he had suffered in his youth. (Book 1, Chap. IV, pp. 28–9; my italics) not inserted.

The strange man seated himself at another table [. . .] *and his mouth, which was very much on one side, twitched now and then with a nervous action.* (Book 1, Chap. V, p. 37, my italics)

The translation and publication of Johann Kaspar Lavater's *Essays on Physiognomy: for the Promotion of the Knowledge and the Love of Mankind* (1789) represented the first important step in the anthropological study of the relationship between external and internal human traits, between body and mind and, as a consequence, between visible superficies and invisible/spiritual contents. In a way, Kaspar's assertion that the office of physiognomy is '[to] observe, to be attentive, to distinguish what is familiar, what dissimilar, to discover proportion and disproportion'[33] anticipates the classifying attitude of Darwinian-oriented studies in the fields of phrenology, criminology and eugenics. Indeed, the very concepts of norm and of normality are the invention of a society whose 'bio-power' and 'bio-politics' (in Michel Foucault's definition) are essential in the edification of the modern bourgeois state and of its medical, scientific, political and administrative apparatuses. Lennard Davis, one of the leading figures in Disability Studies, underlines the relationship between the notions of ability (and of 'middleness') and nineteenth-century cultural systems:

> [The] term that permeates our contemporary society – normal – is a configuration that arises in a particular historical moment. It is part of a notion of progress of industrialization, and of ideological consolidation, of the power of the bourgeoisie. The implications of the hegemony of normalcy are profound and extend into the very heart of cultural production.[34]

A contradictory representative of the Victorian frame of mind, Braddon could not refrain from using the discriminating idea of 'normativity' as a cornerstone to portray Peters's diversity. At the same time, she tends, however, to negotiate her tendency to search for a visible 'middleness' with a dismissal of the social implications of Charles Darwin and Herbert Spenser's ideas on the survival of the fittest, according to which the fittest is associated with healthy and 'able' species, and the unfit with weak and 'disabled' type. These scientific approaches suggested that the representatives of a potentially surviving species should correspond to upper-middle class educated citizens (like Jabez North) and the unfit to racially, socially, bodily or mentally defective people (like Joseph Peters). Nevertheless, as the plot of *The Trail of the Serpent* demonstrates, Braddon reverses these generalising assumptions, which will have terrible consequences in the years to come. Indeed, a decade after Braddon's novel was in print, Charles Darwin published *The Descent of Man* (1871), whose future misreading, from Francis Galton's eugenics to Nazism, would find scientific support in some of its most controversial pages, and in particular in the section dealing with the way savages and civilised species dispose of the mentally and bodily weak:

With savages, the weak in body and mind are soon eliminated; and those that survive commonly exhibit a vigorous state of health. We civilised men, on the other hand, do our utmost to check the process of elimination; we build asylums for the imbecile, the maimed, and the sick; we institute poor-laws; and our medical men exert their utmost skill to save the life of every one to the last moment [. . .] It is surprising how soon a want of care, or care wrongly directed, leads to the degeneration of a domestic race; but excepting in the case of man himself, hardly any one is so ignorant as to allow his worst animals to breed.[35]

In *The Trail of the Serpent* Braddon's attitude to negotiating (and questioning) Darwinian theories on the survival of the fittest emerges with reference to hereditary questions. Jabez North, for instance, possesses all the typical traits of the family de Cervennes and replicates his father's corrupted life. In the course of a dialogue, the novel's villain is described as follows:

'The de Cervennes have always taken care of themselves; it is *a family trait*.'

'[Jabez North] has proved himself worthy of that family, then. He was thrown into a river, but he did not sink; he was put into a workhouse and brought up as a pauper, but by the force of his own will and the help of his own brain he extricated himself, and won his way in the world. *He became what his father was before him*, a teacher in a school. He grew tired of that, *as his father did*, and left England for Paris. In Paris, *like his father before him*, he married a woman he did not love for the sake of her fortune.' (Book 6, Chap. II, p. 333, my italics)

This criminal 'heredity' will be brought to a halt by Peters, whose decision to adopt and raise Sloshy proves that individuals are not just the product of their past but also the result of the social, economic and cultural context in which they are 'bred'.[36] Despite Peters's role as defender of a 'centralised' and 'normative' institutional power, Braddon's novel repeatedly enhances his physical and cultural alterity, to the point that even in his description of his job as a police detective Peters introduces a significant 'variation' to the linguistic norm. When asked by another foundling named Kuppins about his business, Peters replies as follows:

Mr Peters presents remarks to the interested Kuppins, that he shall 'ederkate' – he is in some time deciding on the conflicting merits of a *c* or a *k* for his word – he shall 'ederkate the fondling, and bring him up to his own business'.

'Detecktive,' Mr Peters spells, embellishing the word with an extraneous *k*. (Book 1, Chap. 7, p. 49)

The embodiment of a normative society and, at the same time, a 'liminal' character because of his lowly social origin and his physical impairment, Peters is a new species of detec(k)tive, characterised by a physical, cultural and linguistic 'difference', and by a capacity to 'differ' from any stable definition. In the narrative and ideological economy of Braddon's text, Peters literally spells his *différance*, escaping from any form of 'logocentrism' and from the dominion of the written/spoken word through his politics of muteness.[37] Although Darwin in *On the Origin of Species* and *The Descent of Man* is quite explicit as far as the potential survival of weak or unfit species is concerned, in *The Trail of the Serpent* Joseph Peters's differing *k* represents a sort of non-normative genetic code which makes him a successful 'variation' on the species of the traditional Victorian detective. And, as Darwin repeatedly underlines in *On the Origin of Species*, only 'variations' are able to survive the struggle for life:

> From these remarks it will be seen that I look at the term species, as one arbitrarily given for the sake of convenience to a set of individuals closely resembling each other, and that does not necessarily differ from the term variety, which is given to *less distinct and more fluctuating forms*. (*On the Origin of Species*, p. 127, my italics)

> But if variations useful to any organic being do occur, assuredly individuals thus characterised will have the best chance of being preserved in the struggle for life; and from the strong principle of inheritance they will tend to produce offspring similarly characterised. (Ibid., p. 175)

Darwin's typically bourgeois background as the bedrock of his scientific theories (which basically followed a normative Victorian view of society) can be thus interpreted in an alternative key, proving that it is possible to reread *On the Origin of Species* against the grain of traditional approaches. As Jane Oppenheim observes, 'the chief reason for the ubiquity of evolutionary modes of thought lies in the capacity to appeal to all ideologies'.[38] In *The Trail of the Serpent* Peters's disability and his 'less distinct and more fluctuating' form do not condemn his detection to failure, but on the contrary turn his alterity into a winning 'variation' on the typical Victorian species. This is a further demonstration that Braddon's negotiation with evolutionary and Darwinian questions in *Eleanor's Victory* and in particular in *The Trail of the Serpent* reflected her complex and even contradictory view of nineteenth-century culture and epistemology. Because of their multiple approaches to the questions raised by evolutionary studies (in light of the increasing power attributed to socially normative figures such as detectives), these two novels represent an exemplary *trait d'union* between traditional sensational narratives and Braddon's future detective fictions.

Notes

1. Craig and Cadogan, *The Lady Investigates*, p. 13.
2. For Jan Davis Schipper 'Braddon [. . .] created fraudulent women – women who reinvented themselves as conventional domestic angels while their deceptive appearances permitted them to hide scandalous secrets or to perform unconventional actions' (*Becoming Frauds*, p. 4). In *Eleanor's Victory* Braddon negates the stereotype of many detective fictions, in which women were 'usually the victims, not the pursuers of criminals' (Bedell, 'Amateur and Professional Detectives', p. 21).
3. Braddon, *Eleanor's Victory*, Chap. X, p. 71; all further references will be from this edition. The novel was published in *Once a Week* from March to October 1863. 'Eleanor's unwomanly purposefulness results in other transgressions of the female ideal as well. To execute her plan of vengeance, she must turn detective, and in *Eleanor's Victory* Braddon complicates society's apprehensions about detectives with gender-based anxiety [. . .] Eleanor's actions [. . .] violate the sanctity of domestic space and threaten the security of the middle-class domicile' (Schroeder and Schroeder, *From Sensation to Society*, p. 139).
4. Laurie Garrison focuses on Eleanor's visual abilities as a means to acquire sexual power and assertiveness: 'Eleanor's "dilated" eyes take in and take over everything and everyone around her; the sense that she is consuming everything and everyone around her with her gaping pupils lends her a frightening power. Eleanor's power lies not only in taking in her surroundings through her eyes, but also in the transformation of her physical appearance' ('The Seduction of Seeing', p. 118).
5. Heidi H. Johnson deals with the influence of Electra's myth in *Eleanor's Victory*, concluding that the novel 'displays ambivalence about detection's multiple functions, since it serves as a corrective to father/daughter attachment [. . .] The truths she has learned about her father through the detecting process lead Eleanor to a less idealized vision of him' ('Electra-fying the Female Sleuth', p. 261).
6. While Simon Cooke focuses on the visual impact of the novel, illustrated by George du Maurier in the prestigious journal *Once a Week* ('George du Maurier's Illustrations'), Debrah Wynne reflects on the fact that the choice to publish *Eleanor's Victory* in *Once a Week* was an attempt to demonstrate Braddon's ability as a novelist to a different reading public (*The Sensation Novel and the Victorian Family Magazine*).
7. As far as the theme of heredity is concerned, it is interesting to read the following words: 'Richard Thornton spoke very seriously. He had never been able to speak of Eleanor's scheme of retribution without grief and regret. He recognised *the taint of her father's influence* in this vision of vengeance and destruction. All George Vane's notions of justice and honour had been rather the meretricious and flimsy ideas of a stage play, than the common-sense views of real life' (Chap. XIV, p. 115, my italics).
8. According to Walter Benjamin '[the] original social content of the detective story was the obliteration of the individual's traces in the big-city crowd' (*Charles Baudelaire*, p. 48).
9. Lyell, *Principles of Geology*, p. 31, my italics. Gideon Mantell – a great

populariser of geological studies and the author of *Wonders of Geology* (1838) – compared fossils to semantically labyrinthine geroglyphs: 'It is only by an acquaintance with the structure of the living forms around us, and by acquiring an intimate knowledge of their osseous frame-work or skeleton, that we can hope to *decipher the handwriting on the rock*, obtain a clue to guide us through the *labyrinth of fossil anatomy*, and conduct to those interesting results, which the genius of the immortal Cuvier first taught us how to acquire' (*The Wonders of Geology*, vol. 1, pp. 127–8).

10. 'For my part, following out Lyell's metaphor, I look at the natural geological record as a history of the world imperfectly kept, and written in a changing dialect; of this history we possess the last volume, only here and there a short chapter has been preserved; and of each page, only here and there a few lines' (Darwin, *On the Origin of Species*, p. 288).

11. This is an explicit tribute to Dickens's *Bleak House*, where the two portraits of Lady Dedlock help in solving the mystery related to the real identity of Esther's mother and of Turkinghorn's murderer. Indeed, Dickens's novel is a constant source of inspiration for Braddon, and a paradigmatic text as far as the dialogue between evolutionary issues and literature is concerned. In this respect, Gillian Beer argues that '[the] sense that everything is connected, though the connection may be obscure, gave urgency to the enterprise of uncovering such connections. This was a form of plotting crucial to Dickens's work [. . .] for example, in *Bleak House*, where the fifty-six named [. . .] characters all turn out to be related either by way of concealed descent (Esther and Lady Dedlock) or of economic dependency' (*Darwin's Plots*, p. 47).

12. Tamara S. Wagner reflects on Eleanor's use of unorthodox and irrational detecting practices ('Magnetic Clues to the Past').

13. Qtd in Sebeok and Umiker-Sebeok, '"You Know My Method"', p. 16. In Nancy Harrowitz's words, 'Peirce's construction of abduction essentially describes a process in which the subject is confronted with an observed fact which needs explaining and which seems important [. . .] Abduction is the step in between a fact and its origin; the instinctive, perceptual jump which allows the subject to guess an origin which can be tested out to prove or disprove the hypothesis. Abduction is a theory developed to explain a preexisting fact' ('The Body of the Detective Model', p. 182). Maurizio Ascari reflects upon the fusion of the scientist and the 'creative' artist in the figure of the detective, since the former's faults are counterbalanced by the 'abductive faculty' of the latter (*La leggibilità del male*, p. 128).

14. Doyle, *A Study in Scarlet*, in *The Adventures of Sherlock Holmes*, p. 61. In 'The Boscombe Valley Mystery' (1892) Sherlock Holmes suggests that sometimes the most obvious deductions are the product of complex investigations and the result of a long abductive practice: '"I am afraid," said [Watson], "that the facts are so obvious that you will find little credit to be gained out of this case." "There is nothing more deceptive than an obvious fact," [Holmes] answered, laughing' (*Adventures*, p. 161).

15. Commenting upon the novel's conciliating epilogue, Tamara S. Wagner suggests that 'the sudden reformulation of Eleanor's thereby redefined victory has a dual function: it undoes the woman detective's "unsexing"

and places the recapitulation, indeed the domestication, of the past firmly at the center of the detective plot' ('Magnetic Clues to the Past', p. 81).

16. *The Trail of the Serpent* is a revision of Braddon's first novel *Three Times Dead, or the Secret of the Hearth*, an artistically immature work published in 1860 by Empson which was neglected by critics and readers. In Braddon's affectionate memory, *Three Times Dead* was written 'with all the freedom of one who feared not the face of a critic [. . .] with a pen unchastened by experience' (Braddon, 'My First Novel', p. 25). The novel's title was changed and the text was republished in March 1861 to cash in on the success of *Lady Audley's Secret*. Our edition is Braddon, *The Trail of the Serpent*, ed. Willis.

17. *The Chambers's Edinburgh Journal*, co-edited by Robert Chambers (the author of the *Vestiges of the Natural History of Creation*), published in 1849 William Russell's 'Recollections of a Police Officer'. This text, collected in volume format as *Recollections of a Detective Police-Officer* (1856), featured detective Thomas Walters, and was a source of inspiration for Braddon. Like the lower-class detective Joseph Peters in *The Trail of the Serpent*, in the story entitled 'X. Y. Z.' detective Walters saves an innocent who was wrongly condemned. Walters's success is mainly due to his ability to collect clues, like a scientist who seeks evidence, meditates on it, and finds the missing link to a mystery.

18. The connection between French culture and poisoning was acquired data for the Victorians, as the opinions of critics, readers and journalists on famous trials featuring poisoning (such as the 'Madeleine Case' or the 'Adelaide Bartlett case') demonstrate. In her article dealing with the above-mentioned trials and with Braddon's *The Trail of the Serpent*, Randa Helfield points out that 'in all three cases the real poison was traced to a foreign source', adding that 'Valeria [de Cervennes]'s poisonous plots can be traced not only to a foreigner, but to the corrupting influence of foreign art, especially theatre' ('Poisonous Plots', p. 163; p. 177). For a detailed analysis of the 'Madeleine case', see Hartman, 'Murder for Respectability'.

19. 'The Bow Street Runners' was a group of constables founded in 1749 by the writer and journalist Henry Fielding, which at first included eight members. Unlike ordinary thief-takers, they worked in strict contact with the Magistrates' office at Bow Street. The activity of the 'Bow Street Runners' officially ended in 1839, first and foremost because of the institution in 1829 of the modern London police by Sir Robert Peel. See Kayman, *From Bow Street to Baker Street*.

20. The Newgate Novels, which fictionalised the lives of notorious criminals or invented fictional criminal biographies, included texts written by Edward Bulwer Lytton (*Paul Clifford*, 1830; *Eugene Aram*, 1832), by William Harrison Ainsworth (*Rockwood*, 1834; *Jack Sheppard*, 1840) and even by Charles Dickens (*Oliver Twist*, 1840). The debate that followed the creation of the Newgate Novel as a literary hybrid (headed by *The Athenaeum*) anticipated the critical attacks that in a few years would fall upon sensation fictions, which inherited many elements from it (see Introduction).

21. 'It was a dark and stormy night; the rain fell in torrents – except at occasional intervals, when it was checked by a violent gust of wind which swept up the streets (for it is in London that our scene lies), rattling along

the housetops, and fiercely agitating the scanty flame of the lamps that struggled against the darkness' (Bulwer Lytton, *Paul Clifford*, p. 13). Like *The Trail of the Serpent*, Charles Dickens's *Our Mutual Friend* features a symbolically-laden river, exchanges of identity, a feigned death (John Harmond), a murderous school teacher (Bradley Headsone) and also a foundling whose name (Sloppy) echoes Braddon's Sloshy.

22. In confirmation of the morally 'muddy' nature of Slopperton, it is necessary to add that in the first version of the novel the town was called 'Muddletown' (see Wolff, *Sensational Victorian*, p. 144). In his biography Wolff reports that Jabez North's former name was Ephraim East, of a clearly foreign (Jewish?) origin (p. 115).

23. The tragic flood that kills Tom and Maggie conveys a more tragic sense of instability than Braddon's more ambivalent and ironic treatment of the same image: 'Nature repairs her ravages – but not all. The up-torn trees are now rooted again; the parted hills are left scarred; if there is new growth, the trees are not the same as the old, and the hills underneath their green vesture bear the marks of the past rending. To the eyes that have dwelt on the past, there is no thorough repair' (Eliot, *The Mill on the Floss*, p. 535).

24. Carnell, *The Literary Lives*, p. 241. Sloshy's story is reminiscent of Thames Darrell's in W. H. Ainsworth's *Jack Sheppard* (1840), since in that case as well the baby was saved from the Thames and was given the name of the river. In her 'Calendar of Mary Braddon's Theatrical Career' (Ibid., pp. 287–375), Jennifer Carnell reports that Braddon played the role of Thames during her dramatic apprenticeship. In turn, the character of Sloshy inspired Wilkie Collins for the creation of Octavius Guy (nicknamed 'Gooseberry' because of his large and bulging eyes) in *The Moonstone*.

25. In his study on the codification of the image of the mother (who was perceived as both caring and murderous) in Victorian medical and fictional texts, Andrew Mangham argues that '[this] Dickensian description employs the period's ideas on the demonic potential of the maternal role. Its characterisation of the Sloshy as overflowing, bursting and swelling, for example, echoes the period's preoccupations with child mortality and infanticide. Its allusions to the river's "muddy bosom" and "breast", plus references to sucking, invoke the image of breast-feeding' (*Violent Women and Sensation Fiction*, p. 105).

26. Stott, *Darwin and the Barnacle*, p. xx. For a further discussion on the theme, see Stott, 'Darwin's Barnacles'. In a letter to Thomas Huxley dated 11 April 1853 Darwin admits that 'I have become a man of one idea – cirripedes morning and night' (*Charles Darwin's Letters*, pp. 127–8).

27. Braddon's cultural dialogue with pseudosciences such as phrenology emerges, in particular, with reference to Jabez North: 'A professor of phrenology, lecturing at Slopperton, had declared Jabez North to be singularly wanting in [conscientiousness]; and had even gone so far as to hint that he had never met with a parallel case of deficiency in the entire moral region, except in the skull of a very distinguished criminal, who invited a friend to dinner and murdered him on the kitchen stairs while the first course was being dished' (Book 1, Chap. I, p. 7); '[That] absurd professor of phrenology had declared that both the head and face of Jabez bespoke a marvellous power of secretiveness' (Book 2, Chap. I, p. 73). Despite the

fact that neither the organ of 'conscientiousness' nor that of 'secretiveness' is included in Franz Joseph Gall's twenty-seven brain organs described in *The Anatomy and Physiology of the Nervous System* (1819), Braddon demonstrates that even the most abstruse pseudo-scientific theories cannot be simply dismissed and derided but can give unexpected results, as in Jabez North's case.

28. For an analysis of Collins's disabled characters, see Flint, 'Disability and Difference', and Costantini, *Venturing into Unknown Waters* (in particular Chaps 10 and 11).

29. Stoddard Holmes, *Fictions of Affliction*, p. 4. Stoddard's notion of melodrama derives from Peter Brooks's *The Melodramatic Imagination* (1976), according to which the 'melodramatic mode' is to be intended as the visual representation of inner feelings. *Fictions of Affliction* remains the most complete treatment of disability in Victorian literature, although Stoddard tends to focus on female disability.

30. Rayner, *The Dumb Man of Manchester*, p. 29.

31. In Christine Ferguson's opinion, '[In] the world of *The Trail of the Serpent* the meaning of visual signs is never self-evident, nor can such signs be read statically [. . .] Peters first suspects North's guilt [. . .] through the hardness of expression and the coldness of speech he directs towards his former lover', and then realises Richard Marwood's innocence 'not in the regularity of his facial features, but in his spontaneous nervous reaction to the news of his uncle's murder' ('Sensational Dependence', p. 10).

32. For Chris Willis, Peters remains 'what is arguably one of the most positive portrayals of a disabled person in Victorian fiction. Peters is unable to speak because of a childhood illness, but, paradoxically, this supposed disability gives him an extra level of ability' ('Afterword', in Braddon, *The Trail of the Serpent*, p. 411). Peters's successful career recalls the experience of John Kitto, whose biography *The Memoirs of John Kitto* (1856) was still having an enormous success at the time Braddon was writing this novel.

33. Lavater, *Essays on Physiognomy*, vol. 1, p. 119. Victorian physiognomist Charles Bell explained that 'the expressions, attitudes, and movements of the human figure are the characters of his language, adapted to convey the effect of historical narration, as well as to show the working of human passion' (*The Anatomy and Physiology of Expression*, p. 2). Lucy Hartley opens her study on nineteenth-century physiognomy asserting that '[physiognomic] practice assumes the picture it draws of an individual is truthful because it is derived from what the external appearance of an individual tells us about the interior nature, even though the latter is conceptualized within strict codes' (*Physiognomy and the Meaning of Expression*, p. 3).

34. Davis, *Enforcing Normalcy*, p. 49. Michel Foucault's definitions of 'bio-power' and 'bio-politics' are included in *The History of Sexuality*.

35. Darwin, *The Descent of Man*, vol. 1, pp. 168–9. Karl Pearson, a famous expert on statistics who had a strong interest in eugenics, and who was also a great friend of Francis Galton, defines the 'unfit' as '[the] habitual criminal, the professional tramp, the tuberculous, the insane, the mentally defective, the alcoholic, the diseased from birth or from excess' (qtd in Kavles, *In the Name of Eugenics*, p. 33). For Adolf Hitler 'the struggle for

daily livelihood leaves behind, in the ruck, everything that is weak, diseased or wavering' (Hitler, *Mein Kampf*, 1925, qtd in Blaker, *Eugenics*, p. 143).

36. The fact that Peters – who does not have a female companion and lives a chaste life – is an adoptive father rather than a biological one for Sloshy proves Braddon's partial sharing of contemporary opinions on the unhealthy results of mixed marriages. In *Memoir Upon the Formation of a Deaf Variety of the Human Race* (1883), statistician, scientist and eugenicist Alexander Graham Bell warned against the dangers of intermarriages in Darwinian terms, defining the eventual 'formation of a deaf variety of the human race' as 'a great calamity' (Bell, *Memoir*, p. 217).

37. For Jacques Derrida the 'logocentric' system 'has necessarily dominated the history of the world during an entire epoch, and has even produced the idea of the world, the idea of world origin' (*Of Grammatology*, p. 8). Applying Derrida's ideas on logocentrism to disability and sign language, H.-Dirksen L. Bauman says that 'the constitutive role of the voice results from the self-presence created by hearing-oneself-speak. One's own voice is completely interior, fully present to the speaker; it is the source of self-identity, of self-presence. Meaning constituted within this full-presence then becomes the standard for notions of identity, precipitating a metaphysics based on the full-presence of self, meaning, and identity' ('Towards a Poetics of Vision, Space, and the Body', p. 356).

38. Oppenheim, *The Other World*, p. 268. George Levine in *Darwin Loves You* has assessed Darwin's ideas in a new perspective. Levine focuses in particular on Darwin's sense of 'enchantment' and on his capacity to convey an enthusiastic feeling for nature to his readers. According to Levine, Darwin's non-theistic world is a universe 'in motion' where nothing stands and where everything changes, and Darwin's view of nature is based upon exceptions rather than upon rules, upon violations rather than upon fixed laws. Gillian Beer comments that Darwin 'viewed extinction as inevitable in evolutionary process. But he emphasized also that *survival depends upon variability*, and that *diversity is essential* to the island of the world' ('Introduction', in Darwin, *The Origin of Species*, p. xxviii).

Chapter 6

John Faunce's Normalising Investigations in *Rough Justice* and *His Darling Sin*

Rough Justice (1898) is Braddon's explicit tribute to the modern detective novel, where the influence of Dickens's Inspector Bucket, of Collins's Sergeant Cuff and, above all, of Baker Street's private detective Holmes emerges in the creation of the 'inevitable detective' (in the definition coined by the *Spectator*)[1] John Faunce, the chief inspector of the London Bow Street Division. Set in the late eighties, *Rough Justice* opens with our introduction to Arnold Wentworth, who left England to find his fortune in the African diamond mines and who has just returned. After a casual meeting with Mary Freeman (a childhood friend) on a steamer, Arnold is accused of the brutal murder of his former wife Lisa Rayner, whom he abandoned to earn his fortune abroad. These charges are based upon the fact that a handkerchief with the initials 'A. W.' and some African banknotes, which seem to confirm Arnold's responsibility, were found on the crime scene. Due to these coincidences police detective John Faunce is sure of Arnold's guilt, although the man is finally released for lack of firm proof. The most important thing for Arnold is to demonstrate his innocence to Mary Freeman, whom he loves. For this reason he privately employs Faunce (who has retired from the police department to devote himself to gardening at his home – Hawthorn Lodge, Putney Hill) to discover the identity of the real murderer. The criminal is none other than Oliver Greswold, a philanthropist and skilful radical orator of socialist ideas, who killed Lisa to stop her inheriting a large fortune. At the end of the novel Oliver is forced by Arnold to write a confession which is first read by Mary and then burnt to avoid a scandal involving the wealthy Lady Violet, recently married to Oliver. From a narrative point of view, Braddon takes inspiration from Collins's 'multivocal' novels (a technique she had already introduced in *Henry Dunbar*), experimenting with a mixture of omniscient narration, free indirect speech and first-person accounts to give her novel a more dynamic rhythm.

In *Rough Justice* the socio-political context plays a fundamental role both in creating the premises of crime and in informing Faunce's methods of investigation, which are reminiscent of Sherlock Holmes's detecting strategies. Like Conan Doyle's fictions (from *The Sign of Four* to 'The Adventure of the Yellow Face'), Braddon's treatment of the investigative process relates to late-Victorian fears of menaces to national stability coming from inside and outside England.[2] After having replaced national police as a more acceptable and 'humanised' form of power, in late-Victorian Britain and in particular soon after Queen Victoria's crowning as Empress of India detectives embodied in the public imagination one of the most effective means to detect and combat any form of alien threat to British familial, social and political institutions. For Ronald R. Thomas:

> In a period when the middle-class saw itself as menaced by subversive elements from the outside and inside alike, national identity became increasingly exclusivist, defensive and conservative, revising the earlier nineteenth-century concept of the nation as the spirit of the people to a more modern conception of the nation as a state apparatus.[3]

The opening of Braddon's novel centres upon Arnold's physical 'Africanisation' and the fear of his 'going native' as two indications of his potential criminality. However, these bodily signs are put alongside his typical Anglo-Saxon racial traits:

> He was tall, dark with sun and weather, but originally of the fair Anglo-Saxon type, as witnessed by large, bold blue eyes and crisp, light-brown hair; age about thirty, powerful frame, and easy movements – a man who had lived mostly in the open, and had looked the sun in the face, like the eagles. (vol. 1, p. 8)

A man whose temper is inherited from his mother (who admits that 'heredity accounts for everything; and you always took after my people'; vol. 1, p. 103), and who has been hardened by his experiences in the African diamond mines, Arnold embodies for John Faunce the quintessential criminal species. For this reason, he is accused of having brutally shot his wife Lisa in the head. Arnold's African experience in contact with the 'dark races' (as Robert Knox defined them), along with other evidence against him found in Lisa's room and on Lisa's body, mislead Faunce. Compared to the detective in *The Trial of the Serpent*, Faunce is not properly the antithesis of Joseph Peters but rather a more disciplined evolution of some of the former's traits. Like Peters, who is Sloshy's surrogate father *and* mother, Faunce displays a 'feminine' side in his love of gardening (reminiscent of Sergeant Cuff's love of roses in *The*

Moonstone), in his tenderness to his wife and in his refined international literary tastes which include Scott, Dickens, Bulwer Lytton, Collins, Dumas, Gaboriau and Balzac, whom he considers 'a born detective' (vol. 1, p. 154). At the same time, his physical 'normativity' puts him on the side of order and discipline, as he demonstrates during his investigation on the crime scene. Through his 'evolutionary' interest in searching for the 'links that were wanting' in his 'chain of evidence' (vol. 1, p. 178) Faunce inspects, and, so to speak, violates Lisa's dead body not just with his 'scrutinising' eyes but also with his hands. In this case, his examination of the woman's body is the first step of a more complex and disquieting investigation into the nation's social body:

> The story told by [Lisa's] corpse was brief and conclusive. The story told by the room was of the baldest. Faunce's keen eyes *scrutinised* every object in that room; and his deft fingers *touched and turned* over everything movable. The story was of abject poverty, but not of abject vice [. . .] The two men knelt down, handling the dead form very gently, and Faunce found a pocket in the thin black gown [. . .] He *unhooked* the front of the bodice, spattered and stained so dreadfully that even the Chief Inspector's strong nerves, hardened amid scenes of horror, thrilled as he *touched* that murdered form. (vol. 1, p. 133; p. 135, my italics)

Faunce's policing attitude, his knowledge of and trust in Lombrosian criminology, are counterbalanced by his homely and domestic traits. This coexistence of contradictory elements had already been introduced in Sherlock Holmes, who mixed easily with people of all social classes, who played the violin to lull Watson to sleep, and who was fragile to the point of being prey to fits of melancholy (which he usually cured with opium). Despite these unorthodox traits, Doyle's Holmes remained 'the most perfect reasoning and observing machine that the world has ever seen' and 'occupied his immense faculties and extraordinary powers of observation in following out those clues, and clearing up those mysteries, which had been abandoned as hopeless by the official police'.[4] On the contrary, Braddon proves with her professional and amateur investigators that their exercise of power is far from being solid and that her detectives represent 'a site of profound cultural struggle over the meaning of English authority'.[5]

As Braddon's novel demonstrates, late-Victorian attempts to normalise cultural, moral, ideological and racial 'otherness' are the symptoms of *internal* discontents and fears. The 'alien' is a cultural creation rather than an essence, so that the desire to categorise and even destroy the 'other' is basically a projection of terrors rooted *within* the geographic and cultural boundaries of Britain and of Western countries. In this respect, Edward Said points out:

Along with other peoples variously designated as backward, degenerate, uncivilized, and retarded, the Orientals were viewed in a framework constructed out of biological determinism and moral-political admonishment. The Oriental was linked thus to elements in Western society (delinquents, the insane, women, the poor) having in common an identity best described as lamentably other.[6]

In studying the alien as the dark side of European civilisation and culture, evolutionary thought was sometimes used to classify outsiders and to justify practices of discrimination. It is thus significant that during the late nineties, post-Darwinian studies on heredity, eugenics, criminal anthropology and forensic science tended to approach racial issues (outside Britain) and political questions (inside Britain) using the same language and a commonly shared vocabulary.[7]

In *Rough Justice* Faunce repeatedly alludes to the idea of the 'born criminal' first introduced by Cesare Lombroso, whose *L'uomo criminale* was translated into English in 1876. Havelock Ellis, who contributed to the spread of Lombrosian ideas in Britain, published in 1890 an essay entitled 'The Criminal' that formally opened the era of criminal anthropology. These studies, which mixed sociological analyses and anthropological reflections, made use of Darwinian researches and of Herbert Spencer's 'social' approach to evolutionism in an often racist and class-conscious way. Moreover, during those years Darwin's half-cousin Francis Galton was working on eugenics, a science which claimed superior strains of races could be demonstrated through analysis of hereditary traits. Against the grain of these studies, *Rough Justice* shows that Arnold Wentworth's compromising experience in contact with the African 'dark race' negates the ideas about the criminal man in which Faunce firmly believes.[8] Like Lady Audley, who bore no signs of madness, Arnold similarly bears 'no mark' of criminality in his actions and behaviour:

> And yet I could but own to mystery that this man was a remarkable specimen of that class of villain from whom nobody would take for a villain. From head to foot I could see upon him *no mark of the criminal character*. His erect form and easy bearing, the straight and steady look of his well-opened blue eyes, the firm yet kindly mouth, the broad forehead and finely modelled chin would have made a favourable impression anywhere and upon anybody. (vol. 1, p. 252, my italics)

Detective Faunce's opinions can be compared here with those of Havelock Ellis, who represents (together with Lombroso) the detective's source of inspiration. Ellis identified the somatic traits of 'undeveloped' races, of foreigners or of people living on the margins of society with those of criminals:

[In] general born criminals have projecting ears, thick hair, a thin beard, projecting frontal eminences, enormous jaws, a square and projecting chin, large cheek bones and frequent gesticulation. It is, in short, a type resembling the Mongolian, or sometimes the Negroid [. . .] Perhaps the most general statement to be made is that criminals present a far larger proportion of anatomical abnormalities than the ordinary European population.[9]

Braddon's introduction of 'liminal' and non-normative detectives such as a lazy reader of French novels (Robert Audley), a woman who marries only to achieve her aims (Eleanor Vane) or a lower-class disabled investigator who mingles with criminals (Joseph Peters), proves her complex negotiation with Darwinian and post-Darwinian ideas, alternately rejected and incorporated, contested and approved.

If Volume 1 of *Rough Justice* concludes with Faunce's defeat and with his leaving the Bow Street Division to live a retired life as a gardener, Volume 2 shows Braddon's partial debunking of the previous assumptions about the direct or indirect influence of corrupting colonies. Privately employed by Arnold, Faunce now relocates the crime *within* the geographic boundaries of Englishness and uses his knowledge of criminal anthropology against a new form of 'internal' menace represented by radical and socialist ideas, identified in the figure of Oliver Greswold. Braddon's novel was published soon after the violent strikes and protests of factory workers in 1887 and is strongly connected to late-Victorian debates on Karl Marx's ideas (see Part III, Chapter 9). Indeed, the first 'link' in the long 'chain of evidence' against Greswold is a piece of paper containing a socialist speech, found by Faunce in Lisa's house:

> The fragment of essay or speech found in the lodging-house had not been traced to its source, in spite of Faunce's efforts. He had enlisted the sub-editor and reporters of a city paper in the search; but the most careful examination of files of newspapers had been barren of result. Faunce's friend the sub-editor opined that the fragment was part of a lecture. A few sentences had the bluntness and strong ring of language intended for oral delivery.
>
> '*The man who wrote these lines is a Socialist*, but not a member of the working classes,' said the Editor. (vol. 2, pp. 28–9, my italics)

Along with Lombroso and Ellis's studies on the criminal man, those were the years which witnessed the advance and success of degeneration theories, beginning with the publication of Bénédict Augustin Morel's *Traité des dégénérescences physiques, intellectuelles et morales de l'espèce humaine* in 1857. Evolutionary scientists and criminal anthropologists 'confronted themselves with the apparent paradox that civilization, science and economic progress might be the catalyst of, as much as the defence against, physical and social pathology'.[10] Among the causes of *dégénérescence* were included heterogeneous factors such as rapid technological progress, decadent literary and artistic tendencies, the insalubrious life in big towns, a sense of physical and psychological 'fatigue' connected with the modern rhythms of life (according to Max Nordau in *Degeneration*), and finally the spread of anarchism, feminism, radicalism and socialism. An interesting case in point is alienist Henry Maudsley, who couples his reflections on heredity and disease with his attacks against socialism, described as a symptom, but also a cause, of degeneration. In a lecture published in *The Lancet* in April 1870, Maudsley asserts that '[certain] unfavourable conditions of life tend unquestionably to produce degeneracy of the individual [. . .] and thus is formed a morbid variety of the human kind, which is incapable of being a link in the line of progress of humanity'. More than a decade after, in *Body and Will* (1883) Maudsley would point out that '[in] scattered and recurring manifestations there is ample evidence of a deep feeling of revolt in the working-classes against the domination of capitalism', with 'a crop of self-prising and self-deceiving demagogues' ready to exploit 'the selfish passions and ignorant prejudices of the mob who put them in power'.[11]

Oliver Greswold, the ambitious socialist orator who is Lisa's murderer, represents in *Rough Justice* the updated villain of late-nineteenth-century imperial England, as well as the embodiment of all those 'degenerate' social tendencies John Faunce wishes to detect and to normalise. From a historical point of view, the late nineteen-eighties were characterised by the spread of socialism, nihilism and anarchism on the one hand and by the sensation caused by terrorist attacks (especially in Russia) on the other, which contributed to create the complex and heterogeneous myth of the political dissident. Maurizio Ascari is thus right when he refers to the Victorian mixture of fascination and repulsion for the figure of the nihilist. His image as 'fallen angel' had an implicit melodramatic quality, which both seduced and terrified people.[12] Furthermore, in those years the Rose Street Club in London became a famous meeting point for international and English anarchists (headed by Johann Most from 1878), along with a plethora of reviews such as *The Anarchist* (1885–8), *The Revolutionary Review* (1889), *Freedom* (1886) and *The Herald of Anarchy* (1890–2) which nourished public terrors. Therefore, in describing Greswold, the omniscient narrator of *Rough Justice* makes use of all the Victorian fears and stereotypes associated with ultra-radicalism and socialism:

[Greswold] was among the ultra-Radicals, the men who want to abolish almost everything that makes up old-fashioned people's idea of England, and to create a new England, without an established Church, or a House of Peers, or a great Capitalist, and possibly without a beer-shop along ten miles of dusty highroad. (vol. 2, p. 160)

The fatherless son of a 'vain, weak-brained mother' who spent his boyhood 'under the gloomiest conditions' (vol. 2, p. 207), Greswold is the product of the biological, social and moral degeneration of the times. Despite Braddon's overtly critical view of his socialist ideas and of his violent radicalism, the origin of Greswold's crimes seems to be the outcome of his negative experiences and of his unhealthy family life, as with Lady Audley.[13] *Rough Justice* repeatedly alludes to the fact that even his political opinions are not the expression of a firm belief but rather a means to acquire power and to satisfy his hedonism. It is thus significant that in one of Oliver Greswold's public speeches Arnold finds an important link that connects him to Lisa's violent death, discovering that the words of the socialist orator are the same as those written on a shorthand note left by the murderer in Lisa's poor lodging-house in Bloomsbury. Greswold's socialist views thus become the real proof, and implicitly the cause, of his criminal actions:

> This Greswold was an accomplished public speaker – a man who had made oratory a fine art. The low quiet voice in which he begun penetrated to the furthest corner of the room [. . .] Suddenly a phrase – a word – struck [Arnold's] ear as if a gun had been fired close beside him [. . .] Word for word – sentence for sentence – he heard the words and phrases copied from the shorthand notes found in the Dynevor Street lodging-house. Every syllable was engraved upon his memory. (vol. 2, pp. 51–4)

Greswold is modelled upon many contemporary figures, including Simon Webb, Henry George and Oscar Wilde, whose scandalous life and trial would inspire Braddon in the creation of Daniel Lester in *The Rose of Life* (1905), although in that case she had to replace Wilde's charge of sodomy with one of fraud. Like Greswold's, Wilde's ideas were considered another expression of his hedonism, because he found 'in roaring Democracies, reigns of Terror, and great Anarchies congenial images of his own wildness'.[14]

Although set in a different historical and cultural context, *Rough Justice* pays direct and indirect tributes to Braddon's most famous sensation novel. Along with the theme of marital abandonment, allusions to *Lady Audley's Secret* include the initial scene, similarly set on board a steamer called *The Saxon* (vol. 1, p. 7), the news on Lisa's death casually read by Arnold on the pages of *The Times* (vol. 1, p. 123) and, finally, the concealment of the truth regarding Lisa's tragic destiny. Indeed, Greswold's written confession of his crime will be read in front of Mary and then buried in order to save the reputation of Lady Violet, an independently rich woman who had just married him. Like the investigation of Robert Audley (and Clement Austin), the detection of John Faunce and Arnold Wentworth is a counter-detection which aims at saving appearances and social reputation.

His Darling Sin (1899) features many themes already included in *Rough Justice* and reintroduces detective John Faunce, whose task is to save a lady's reputation.[15] The story is centred upon a scandal involving the aristocratic widow Lady Perivale, falsely accused of having spent the winter holidays in Algiers, Corsica and Sardinia with Colonel Richard Rannock, while going by the name of 'Mrs Randall'. Braddon informs her readers that Lady Perivale had refused Rannock's marriage proposal the year before. Snubbed by high society and unable to defend herself from these rumours, Lady Perivale employs private investigator John Faunce. Through the help of a series of photographs, Faunce discovers that the real 'Mrs Randall' is in truth Kate Dalmaine, an actress who bears a close resemblance to Lady Perivale, and who is Rannock's lover. Readers are then told that, during a fight, Kate's violent husband James Bolisco (an ex-pugilist who blackmailed her) kills Colonel Rannock, whose mysterious disappearance engages Faunce in a parallel investigation. Faunce finally saves Kate, who is the only witness to the homicide and to Rannock's attempt to raise a vengeful scandal involving Lady Perivale. After a public trial which rehabilitates her, Lady Perivale finally decides to marry the writer Arthur Haldane and Faunce helps Kate to find a peaceful retreat at Ventnor, where she can live out her life.

Because of his gentlemanliness and education, John Faunce enters the private lives and houses of the wealthy classes and, through his professional skills, penetrates the upper-class world of which Lady Perivale is a part. Faunce's 'normalising' detection is typical of a society which testifies, in Foucault's opinion, to an evolution from the punishment of crimes to their control, 'from the exposition of the facts or the confession to the slow process of discovery; from the execution to the investigation; from the physical confrontation to the intellectual struggle between criminal and investigator'.[16] Unlike other Braddonian detectives, Faunce is not only an avid reader of international literature ranging from Scott to Balzac, but he is also of upper-middle class origin. His social position allows him to be a more acceptable version of authoritarian power and, as Jennifer Carnell argues, 'to work among the upper classes. There is no possibility of Faunce entering one of those homes as an ambiguous mix of policeman and potential criminal'.[17] In this sense, Braddon's novel enhances the newly acquired position of the detective, who changes from an unwelcome intruder of familial spaces into a persecutor of crimes. Faunce's most recognisable quality is thus his reassuring 'middleness':

> 'Mr Faunce,' said the butler; and a serious-looking, *middle-aged* man of *medium height* and strong frame, with broad, high forehead, *kindly* black eyes and short, close-cut black whiskers, came into the room.
>
> There was a *pleasant* shrewdness in his countenance, and his manner was *easy without being familiar.* (p. 38, my italics)

In *His Darling Sin* Colonel Rannock represents a more disquieting example of degeneration, because he comes neither from the lower classes nor from the margins of Empire. As a conversation between Lady Perivale and her friend Miss Sue Rodney suggests, despite his respectable 'origin' Rannock is inclined to criminal actions:

> 'As for Colonel Rannock, he may be dissipated, and a spendthrift; but he is well-born, and he ought to be a gentleman.'
>
> 'Who said he was ill-born? Surely you know that there are good races and bad. Who can tell when the bad blood came in, and the character of the race began to degenerate? Under the Plantagenets, perhaps. Colonel Rannock comes from a bad race – everybody knows that. His grandfather, Lord Kirkmichael, was notorious in the Regency.' (p. 8)

The setting of *His Darling Sin* (London high society) and the presence of a series of photographs at the centre of the investigation has a strong resemblance to Conan Doyle's 'A Scandal in Bohemia' (1892), which also includes these elements. Although in Braddon's novel the photos are the main detecting means that help save Lady Perivale's reputation, in Conan Doyle they are the detected object that Irene Adler uses to blackmail the hereditary king of Bohemia before his marriage.[18] Like Lady Audley's pre-Raphaelite picture and Launcelot Darrell's self-accusing drawing in *Eleanor's Victory*, in *His Darling Sin* the visual and, in this case, photographic reproduction of the characters' features is an important element in the narration and in the detecting process. Faunce's investigation centres upon a series of cabinet photographs of Lady Perivale, Kate Dalmaine and Colonel Rannock (given to Faunce by his mother), through which the detective identifies doubles (Perivale and Dalmaine) as well as corpses (Rannock), in order to juxtapose the codes of truth with those of falsity and deceit. Here photography represents a realistic narrative paradigm and a material allusion to contemporary late-Victorian society, where photographs were used as an instrument to recognise and be recognised in a world based upon the primacy of visuality and upon the proliferation of mass-produced images. While on the one hand in *His Darling Sin* the three characters' cabinet photographs perfectly suit Faunce's archival needs, on the other hand they also become a metaphor of his scientific methods of detection, since 'in the eyes of the gifted literary detective – as if through the telescopic lens of a camera – neither the "truth itself" nor the guilty culprit could escape, and the true nature of things was recaptured and re-presented to the reader for more careful and accurate scrutiny'.[19] In Lady Perivale's case, Faunce will not use her photograph as proof of her criminal immoral-ity but, on the contrary, as an instrument to save her reputation. As for Kate Dalmaine, Faunce asks her to give him 'one of [her] photographs – one that, in [her] opinion, does [her] most justice'. Recalling the times in which she was 'in the market' as a London beauty immortalised by photographs, like Lesbia Haselden in *Phantom Fortune* (see Part III, Chapter 9), Kate confesses that '[the] photographers were the plague of [her] life when [she] was on the boards' (p. 78). After having selected two of her photographs, Faunce concludes his interview with Kate with a sort of comprehensive 'photographic study' which integrates Kate's physical features to her moral traits: 'He had studied the woman intently during the quarter of an hour's tête-à-tête, and he did not think that she was a bad woman, from the criminal point of view. He did not think she was treacherous or cruel' (p. 79).[20]

Faunce's criminologically oriented use of cabinet photographs reflects the importance they had in late-Victorian policing practices, in par-ticular after Alphonse Bertillon's introduction of the *portrait parlé* of renowned criminals. Since the 1840s (with the creation of the modern police system) 'mug shots' had already been used to identify criminals and to create collections of criminal portraits. American police inspec-tor Thomas Byrnes of the New York Police Department had published an illustrated book entitled *Professional Criminals of America* in 1886, which included a large number of photographs sometimes forcibly taken. However, it is thanks to Bertillon that a new archival system, based on the association between Lombrosian facial measurements and photographic identification, was introduced. A former police inspec-tor in Paris and an expert in biometrics, Alphonse Bertillon created in 1882 the pseudoscience called anthropometrics (also known as *Bertillonage*), based upon the 'biometrical' data he collected at the Santé Prison in Paris, such as for instance the distance between the eyes, the shape of the nose, the height of the forehead and hairline. These data were integrated in a 'disciplined' system for photographing criminals, which prescribed the use of a standard lens, a pre-defined posture and distance from the camera as well as the use of two-sided images. His ideas would later be summarised and illustrated in *The Identification of Criminal Cases by the Anthropometrical Method* (1889). Bertillon's studies also contributed to reinforce Francis Galton's researches on eugenics, which found in anthropometrical measurements a scientific support and an ideological encouragement. There were, however, some basic differences between Galton's and Bertillon's approaches. Galton in *Inquiries into Human Faculty and its Development* (1883) looked for a typological classification of criminals and even devised a photographic technique called 'composite portrait', where he superimposed on a single photographic plate the faces of various criminals who had some common features, in order to create the photograph of the quintessential outlaw.[21] Unlike Galton's search for the perfect Lombrosian 'born criminal', Bertillon's aim was to 'individualise' (rather than to 'typify') criminals and to show that each person had his/her own peculiar facial and anthropometrical features. In *His Darling Sin* John Faunce's 'archival' attitude towards collecting photos of detected people moves halfway between the Galtonian desire to find a criminal 'type', frustrated and contradicted by the fact that Kate Dalmaine is strikingly similar to the aristocratic Lady Perivale, and the need to retrace any difference between the woman who has employed him and her double. *His Darling Sin* recapitulates many assumptions already introduced in *Lady Audley's Secret* about social permeability, although in the former case it is a photograph (which is actually a 'copy' from nature) that helps discriminate between 'originals', that is between a lady and an actress. This paradox can be explained in light of the epistemological revolution introduced by the spread of photography not only in Victorian culture but also in the reproduction of visual reality, given that, as Nancy Armstrong argues, 'photography, as a method of reading, reversed the priorities between object over image, so that the image usurped the position of the individual body as the basis for legibility'.[22]

Despite Faunce's 'normalising' criminological attitude, Braddon in *His Darling Sin* alternately shares and challenges traditional detection practices and detecting roles, in particular as far as female figures are concerned. While for instance Sherlock Holmes has a misanthropic attitude towards women (with the notable exception of Irene Adler), Faunce enjoys his married life and chooses his wife as his best collaborator. Differently from *Rough Justice*, where the detective's wife is only a secondary character, in *His Darling Sin* she plays a primary role by collecting in a scrapbook all the information on the latest crimes that will be useful for the solution of the enigma.

> Mrs Faunce's book was a large folio bound in red leather, and containing newspaper cuttings, pasted in by the lady's careful hands, and indexed and classified with neatness and intelligence [. . .] It contained the reports of coroner's inquests upon all manner of mysterious deaths, the unexplained cases which might have been murder, the 'found drowned', the nameless corpses

discovered in empty houses, in lodging-house garrets, on desolate heaths and waste places; a dismal calendar of tragic destinies, the record of hard fate or of undiscovered crime. (p. 110)

It is thanks to Mrs Faunce's 'neat' and 'intelligent' classification that Faunce will be able to give the nameless corpse discovered at Redbridge the identity of Colonel Rannock. The decision to introduce Faunce's wife as an indispensable helper proves Braddon's interest in asserting that behind the success of male professionals there are liminal female figures.

The novel ends with the 'containment' of Lady Perivale's dangerous double, Kate, who is sent by Faunce to Ventnor Island to end her life peacefully in the same place where, many years and many novels before, Helen Talboys was buried in order to give birth to her double Lucy Graham/Lady Audley. In a sort of literary *déjà-vu*, the novel's epilogue projects the narration to other stories and to other Lady Audleys:

> Faunce engaged Betsy, the good-natured lodging-house drudge, to take care of Mrs Randall, and took them to cottage lodgings at Ventnor, not far from the Consumption Hospital, and in that lovely spot, facing the blue water, Kate Dalmaine lived through the Summer and Autumn after Bolisco's execution. (p. 126)

Lady Audley's Secret, Henry Dunbar, Eleanor's Victory, The Trail of the Serpent, Rough Justice and *His Darling Sin* deal with disquieting detections, because they show unexpected fractures in the solid familial edifices of Victorian society. The leap back to the geological origins of a nebulous present will lead Braddon's readers to an even more tragic awareness of the unacceptable genealogical relationships that bind together the members of the Victorian community. The investigations of Victorian families by Robert Audley and Henry Carter, of the paternal figure by Eleanor Vane, of the whole community of Slopperton-on-the-Sloshy by Joseph Peters and of London high society by Faunce are basically 'retrograde' analyses on the origins of crime and on its endemic nature in nineteenth-century England. The geological and genealogical unearthing of criminality reflects a Victorian 'political unconscious', as well as Braddon's complex negotiation with Darwinian studies. In this view, sensation fictions – a sort of generic 'variation' on the 'type' of realist novels – succeeded not only in portraying many of the censored aspects of Victorian society but also in creating new literary species, such as the detective novel. Braddon's evolution from mid-century sensation novelist to writer of traditional detective fictions, exemplified in particular by *Rough Justice* and *His Darling Sin*, does not represent a complete break with the 'novel with a secret' (in Kathleen Tillotson's definition) and a dismissal of the Lady Audley paradigm, but its natural evolution. In the words of Alastair Fowler, who discusses the adaptation and survival (rather than the erasure) of literary genres and 'kinds' using a recognisable Darwinian code, '[A] kind's last stage by no means ends in mere extinction. For it may have generated modal transformations of other kinds. Then, even after the adaptive possibilities of the "fixed" kind have been played out, its corresponding mode may remain lively.'[23] Indeed, the Lady Audley species will continue to be evoked in Braddon's future narration, and her ghost will continue to haunt other writers as well. It is thus significant that, in a short story entitled 'Greenshaw's Folly' (1961), Agatha Christie paid her literary homage to Mary Elizabeth Braddon by including an explicit tribute to her sensational blockbuster *Lady Audley's Secret*, in whose pages old Miss Greenshaw conceals her own secret testament before being murdered:

> She moved across the bookcase and stood looking at them uncertainly, then she opened a glass door, took out a book and slipped the folded parchment inside.
>
> 'I've my own places for keeping things,' she said.
>
> '*Lady Audley's Secret*,' Raymond West remarked, catching sight of the title as she replaced the book [. . .]
>
> 'Best-seller in its day,' she remarked. 'Not like your books, eh?'
>
> She gave Raymond a sudden friendly nudge in the ribs [. . .][24]

Notes

1. [Anonym.], 'His Darling Sin', p. 662. *Rough Justice* was first published with the title *A Shadowed Life* in the *Sheffield Weekly Telegraph* in nineteen weekly instalments from 19 January to 22 May 1897 and then in book format by London, Simpkin and Marshall in 1898. Our edition is the one issued by Bernhard Tauchnitz in two volumes (Leipzig, 1898).
2. According to Caroline Reitz, the creation of the domestic police and the creation of the British Empire 'are the twin stories at the heart of the detective narrative' (*Detecting the Nation*, p. xvi).
3. Thomas, 'The Fingerprint of the Foreigner', pp. 679–80. 'In seeking a substitute for organic, paternalistic community control and the Providential eye, what was needed was a master who embodied an acceptable *image of surveillance*, ideologically as rigorous but also *benign* as the eye of God' (Kayman, *From Bow Street to Baker Street*, p. 83, my italics).
4. Doyle, 'A Scandal in Bohemia' (1891), in *The Adventures of Sherlock Holmes*, p. 117.
5. Reitz, *Detecting the Nation*, p. xxi.
6. Said, *Orientalism*, p. 207.
7. In his study on degeneration, Daniel Pick asserts that '[evolutionary] anthropology functioned not only to differentiate the colonised overseas

from the imperial race, but also to scrutinise portions of the population at home: the 'other' was outside and inside' (*Faces of Degeneration*, p. 39).

8. For Ronald R. Thomas, 'Darwin provided the theoretical justification and method by which Lombroso elaborated the notion [of the criminal as human variety], and evolutionary theory encouraged him to identify the physical characteristics of the criminal with earlier incarnations of the human species, which he invariably associated with the nonwhite races of Asia and Africa' ('*The Moonstone*, Detective Fiction and Forensic Science', p. 73).

9. Ellis, *The Criminal*, pp. 90–1; p. 258. In *The Criminal Man* (1876) Cesare Lombroso said that '[if] we examine a number of criminals, we shall find that they exhibit numerous anomalies in the face, skeleton, and various psychic and sensitive functions, so that they strongly resemble primitive races' (qtd in Otis (ed.), *Literature and Science in the Nineteenth Century*, p. 517).

10. Pick, *Faces of Degeneration*, p. 11. Despite the Darwinian background of degeneration theories, Charles Darwin was uneasy about their implications. In a letter to Anton Dohr, a friend of Sir Edwin Lancaster (the author of *Degeneration. A Chapter in Darwinism*, published in 1880), Darwin says: 'I venture to advise you not to carry the degradation principle too far' (letter dated 24 May 1875, qtd in Ibid., p. 192n).

11. Maudsley, 'Galstonian Lecture II', pp. 609–10; Maudsley, *Body and Will* (1883), qtd in Pick, *Faces of Degeneration*, p. 211. Maudsley's fears of the threat of socialist ideas were already introduced in his book on mental pathologies: 'Destroy the social structure of a nation, as in the French Revolution, and then behold what monsters of apish deformity and tigerish ferocity the individuals are capable of becoming' (*The Physiology and Pathology of Mind*, p. 2).

12. Ascari, *La leggibilità del male*, p. 195.

13. 'Despite her savage critical touches, MEB's portrait of the megalomaniac philanthropist, the totalitarian liberal, was completely convincing, especially since [. . .] she took pain to give him a plausible childhood stimulus for his later beliefs and behaviour' (Wolff, *Sensational Victorian*, pp. 385–6).

14. Ellmann, *Oscar Wilde*, p. 115.

15. *His Darling Sin* was Braddon's first attempt to write a 'one volume novel'. Our edition is the one issued by the Sensation Press in 2001. Robert Lee Wolff describes it as a 'sophisticated story of hard boiled society people' (*Sensational Victorian*, pp. 386–7).

16. Foucault, *Discipline and Punish*, p. 69.

17. Carnell, *The Literary Lives*, p. 250.

18. Holmes is praised by Watson for his tactful attitude with people of the upper classes: 'Your recent services to one of the Royal Houses of Europe have shown that you are one who may be safely trusted with matters which are of an importance which can hardly be exaggerated' (Doyle, 'A Scandal in Bohemia', in *The Adventures of Sherlock Holmes*, p. 119).

19. Thomas, *Detective Fiction*, p. 112. According to Thomas, '[The] immediate adaptation of photography to the bureaucratic procedures of personal documentation and identification in police work seemed as natural as its

rapid rise to popularity among the middle classes as an inexpensive form of personal portraiture' (Ibid., p. 113).

20. Faunce's brief interview with pugilist Bolisco (Rannock's murderer and Kate's violent husband) suffices to classify him as a criminal: 'The evening's talk was mostly of the Turf and the prize-ring, and it furnished Faunce with no direct answers to his questions; but it enabled him to turn the full light of his psychological science upon Bolisco's character and temperament. "A wild beast on two legs," was Faunce's summing up of the pugilist, as he strolled away from the sporting tavern' (p. 116).

21. 'These ideal faces have a surprising air of reality [. . .] Nobody who glanced at one of them for the first time would doubt it being the likeness of a living person, yet, as I have said, it is no such thing; it is the portrait of the type and not of an individual [. . .] A composite portrait represents the picture that would rise before the mind's eye of a man who had the gift of pictorial imagination in an exalted degree' (Galton, *Inquiries into Human Faculty*, pp. 222–4).

22. Armstrong, *Fiction in the Age of Photography*, p. 19. For Armstrong '[the] new sciences of identity – by which I mean the human sciences, as well as physiognomy, phrenology and criminology – invariably used photographic technology to make the body legible' (Ibid., p. 17).

23. Fowler, *Kinds of Literature*, p. 267.

24. Christie, 'Greenshaw's Folly', p. 127.

Part III

Victorian Realisms

This question of realism, let it then be clearly understood, regards not in the least degree the fundamental truth, but only the technical method, of a work of art. Be as ideal or as abstract as you please, you will be none the less veracious; but if you be weak, you run the risk of being tedious and inexpressive; and if you be very strong and honest, you may chance upon masterpiece.

Robert Louis Stevenson, *'A Note on Realism'*, 1883[1]

Chapter 7

'So Like and Yet So Unlike': Reality Effects, Sensational Letters and Pre-Raphaelite Portraits in *Lady Audley's Secret*

'Realism' is a very slippery concept, because it often refers to a supposed identification between reality and its narrative, painterly, photographic or cinematographic transposition. However, as far as realism in the novel is concerned, it may be more useful to take into consideration multiple notions of 'realism' rather than a single, unified idea. Look at the difference, for instance, between English and French approaches to the representation of 'reality', or even between contradicting definitions of the same term *within* Victorian Britain, as the following statements by Anthony Trollope, Charles Dickens and Mary Elizabeth Braddon suggest:

> Among English novels of the present day, and among English novelists, a great division is made. There are sensational novels and anti-sensational, sensational novelists and anti-sensational; sensational readers and anti-sensational. The novelists who are considered to be anti-sensational are generally called realistic. I am realistic. My friend Wilkie Collins is supposed to be sensational. The readers who prefer the one are supposed to take delight in the elucidation of character. They who hold by the other are charmed by the construction and the gradual development of the plot. All is, I think a mistake, – which mistake arises from the inability of the imperfect artist to be at the same time realistic and sensational. A good novel should be both, and both in the highest degree. If a novel fails in either, there is a failure in art.

> It does not seem to me to be enough to say of any description that it is the exact truth. The exact truth must be there; but the merit or art in the narrator, is the manner of stating the truth. As to which thing in literature, it always seems to me that there is a world to be done.

> English realism seems to me the deification of the commonplace. Your English realist [i.e. Anthony Trollope] lacks the grim grandeur of Balzac, who can impart an awful sublimity to the bruizes [sic] of a persecuted servant girl

– or the senile sorrows of Pere Goriot. Except George Eliot there is no realist writer I care to read – & she seems to me above all criticism.[2]

In the first excerpt, in trying to compare realist and sensation novels, Trollope concentrates upon the narrative predominance of plot over characterisation in sensation fictions. Then, he suggests ways to 'contaminate' realistic plots with sensational elements to give a dynamic twist to their monotony, and vice versa to engraft sensation novels with realistic elements in order to make them more credible and less abstruse. From a more polemical perspective, Dickens poses some important questions on narrative form (on which 'there is a world to be done') which Braddon seems to share. Dickens has the impression that the language of the English realist novel has been, in a way, defaced by ages of careless usage, as Joseph Conrad will say in a few years. Braddon's literary career (from *Lady Audley's Secret* onwards) could be described as a textual quest for an original narrative form free from the limits imposed by sensational plotting. Despite their faults and limits, her realistically-oriented attempts at experimentation (from *The Doctor's Wife* and *The Lady's Mile* to *Joshua Haggard's Daughter*, *Vixen* and *Phantom Fortune*) are the signs of her desire to renew the genre she contributed to creating. While for an 'imperfect artist' such as Trollope sensation writing represents a sort of beneficial virus which has to infect realistic novels to make them more 'charming', on the contrary for Braddon realism and realistic characterisation are used as a means to defeat the sensational (and Audleian) ghosts which haunted, and will continue to haunt, her fictions. This is the reason she revered French writers, whom she considered models of narration.

The first neat difference between the schools of British and French 'realism' consisted in the fact that the Victorian aspiration to 'truthfulness' was generally related to the acceptance of institutionalised moral codes. George Eliot's Ruskinian association between 'truth' and 'beauty', established by means of a 'humble and faithful study of nature', as well as George Henry Lewes's reflections on art as an instrument to show reality in a mediated form (he juxtaposed 'Realism' with 'Falsism') can be considered the manifestos of the implicit moral lesson at the basis of English realism.[3] Indeed, the morally-oriented approach of English realism was in sharp contrast with the ideas of Honoré de Balzac and Gustave Flaubert, whose novels Braddon appreciated, imitated and even plagiarised on some occasions. Although Braddon's French masters Balzac and Flaubert (later joined by Zola) depicted nineteenth-century bourgeois society from a cynical and amoral perspective that Braddon partially despised, she took them as models of novel-writing. On the other hand, the traditional mid-Victorian realistic novel (which included a heterogeneous group of writers such as Anthony Trollope, W. M. Thackeray, Charles Dickens, George Eliot and Elizabeth Gaskell) considered the identification of a stark difference between truth and morality as a solution to the problems raised by a world from which God seemed to have gradually disappeared. From a narrative point of view, this spiritual void was replaced by the construction of plots leading credible characters towards a happy ending.[4]

Despite its differences from traditional realistic novels, sensation fiction contributed to the evolution and modernisation of the Victorian literary genres (including the realistic novels) in many ways. First, it anticipated issues that would be raised by French naturalists such as Émile Zola, and then introduced narrative strategies later developed by Sir Arthur Conan Doyle in his detective stories (see Part II). Because of its evident success in the mass-literary market, the sensation novel not only became a large-scale phenomenon but also raised important questions about (narrative) procrastination regarding uncomfortable truths. Feeding upon a more and more demanding audience, sensation novels indulged in what many critics considered a pernicious dialogue with readers from all social levels. This dialogue was guaranteed by their inclusion in circulating libraries and by their availability in cheap serials. The publication of a sensation story at accessible prices gave readers the possibility of following the actions and crimes of its dark heroes and heroines almost daily. From a narratological point of view, on many occasions the weaving of, and the solution to, an entangled plot was achieved through documents which denied or confirmed the actions of the characters involved. It is thus easy to understand why many intellectuals and journalists such as Margaret Oliphant, Rev. Henry Longueville Mansel and Frances Rae regarded sensation novelists and Braddon's congruity to everyday reality as the most dangerous crime of sensationalism. If reality had to be founded on moral principles, the negative criticism attributed to Braddon's and others' novels consisted in the fact that they were labelled as 'unrealistic' and romance-like narrations, although formally they seemed to be the opposite. The contrast between the categories of truth/moral order and falsehood/moral disorder became one of the leading analytical filters through which many Victorian literary critics and journalists judged these fictions. By excluding sensation fictions from the nineteenth-century literary canon and by attributing to their narrated events a lack of factual credibility, Victorian cultural institutions wanted to prove their lack of compatibility with the didactic aspirations of the English realistic novel. They even rejected and negated their Englishness, comparing these novels to the works imported from the 'corrupted' French culture, and in particular from scandalous writers such as George Sand, Honoré de Balzac and Gustave Flaubert. In his article entitled 'Sensation Novels', published in the *Quarterly Review* (113, April 1863, pp. 483–91), Henry Longueville Mansel defines the sensation mania as the expression of a 'widespread corruption' in morality, as well as a pathological (another term for 'altered' and 'unnatural') expression of nineteenth-century values. For him the moral incongruities of sensation fictions affected these novels on a formal and narrative ground. Reverend Mansel foregrounds the lack of realism in Braddon's sensational blockbuster *Lady Audley's Secret* and describes the 'improbability of the incidents, superhuman wickedness of the principal character and the incongruity of the others'. His opinions are shared by W. Frances Rae in her article published in the *North British Review* (September 1865), where she asserts that, '[with] the exception of [. . .] the lady's maid [Phoebe Marks], not a single personage has any resemblance to the people we meet with in the flesh'.[5] This long series of accusations culminated in a review attributed to Margaret Oliphant and published in the *Blackwood's Edinburgh Magazine* in September 1867. Oliphant describes the tradition of the English novel (juxtaposed with 'the French school of fiction') as marked by 'a certain sanity, wholesomeness, and cleanliness'. In another article, also dealing with sensationalism, Oliphant criticises the deleterious teachings of those novels that feature '*unseemly* references and exhibitions of forbidden knowledge'.[6] According to the traditional division of artistic works in high culture and low culture products, Braddon's sensation school would undoubtedly find its place in the second group, among the so-called 'penny dreadfuls' and the novels with little artistic value but high sales.

These opinions reflect the commonly-shared ideas of many Victorian intellectuals and journalists, and underscore some of the structural premises of Braddon's most famous novel *Lady Audley's Secret* in the form of 'public epitexts'.[7] Braddon knew well the negative views critics had expressed and would continue to express to discredit her novels. From the beginning of her literary career, she had to construct her own style upon notions of 'truth' and 'reality' which often clashed and contrasted with the approach offered by realistic novels. At the same time, she had to introduce deliberately 'realistic' features into her texts to make their provocative topics as convincing as possible. Among the various realistically oriented strategies Braddon included in *Lady Audley's Secret*, her use of letters and her peculiar treatment of picturesque visuality (in the form of a Pre-Raphaelite painting) represent her most remarkable attempts at pursuing what Roland Barthes calls 'a reality effect':

Semiotically, the 'concrete detail' is constituted by the *direct* collusion of a referent and a signifier; the signified is expelled from the sign [. . .] This is what might be called the referential illusion. The truth behind this illusion is this: eliminated from the realist utterance as a signified by denotation, the 'real' slips back as a signified of connotation, for, at the very moment when these details are supposed to denote reality directly, all they do, tacitly, is to signify it [. . .] in other words, the very absence of the signified, to the advantage of the referent, standing alone, becomes the true signifier of realism. An *effect de réel* (a reality effect) is produced, which is the basis of that [. . .] 'vraisemblance' which forms the aesthetics of all the standard works of modernity.[8]

In Braddon's case, while on the one hand the inclusion of epistolary documents is a stylistic strategy based on the explicit 'collusion of a referent' (letters in real life) and a 'signifier' (letters in the novel), on the other hand the presence of a minutely-described Pre-Raphaelite portrait is a narrative and descriptive means 'to signify reality', which introduces the reader to Lady Audley's nature by way of an explicit allusion to an artistic school that was famous at the time, and whose figurative traits would be easily recognised by any reader. Both choices can be read as a useful key to understanding Braddon's realistically-aimed aspirations as a sensation novelist. Moreover, they highlight the importance she gave to writing as a textually engaging activity, despite her difficulty in reconciling quality with quantity or, as she says in one of her letters to Lytton, wanting 'to serve two masters'.[9]

The choice to reduce in a deliberate way the gnosiological status of the narrator, which is typical of many sensation fictions, is the expression of the crisis of an unerring and commonly-shared notion of 'truth', dispersed in the various documentary items that are disseminated in the text. As a consequence, the reader is directly involved as co-operator in the solution of the 'mystery' and in the unfolding of the original story (from the *sjužet* back to the *fabula*, as Tzvetan Todorov suggests).[10] Since reality is not approached in sensation fiction according to a morally stable point of view, this precarious narrative voice – at least compared to the omniscient perspective of many realist novels – does nothing but reorder the documents to try and make sense of the maze of events described in the text. This stylistic strategy gives a first-rate value to any textual fragment through which the narrator and the reader try to reach the same conclusions, in a sense both partaking in the development of the story. This fact justifies Wilkie Collins, Mary Braddon or Charles Reade's insistent inclusion of letters, bills, even scraps of papers, newspaper articles and whatever could have been useful to give the narration a formally 'realistic' and a potentially sensational impact. In the case of letters, the author/narrator manifests the desire to conform to a realistic reproduction of events, first of all because the time spent reading epistles in novels generally corresponds to the time spent reading ordinary letters in everyday life. Even their paratextual features (the reference to dates, the ritual *formulae* of salutation and closing) are based on rules shared by readers and fictional characters; besides, through letters the plot seems to be written in the 'present tense'.[11] Letters also offer the audience a detailed social and psychological portrait of their creator, because they reveal the identity, social status, culture, feelings and even little obsessions of the writer, which can be retraced by the implied reader in the form of specific lexical repetitions or peculiar choices in the register. The presence of an epistolary fragment determines the diegetic reliability of the narration, because it testifies to the connection between causes and effects in the evolution of the plot.

The use of epistles in Mary Elizabeth Braddon's *Lady Audley's Secret* is not just a secondary textual strategy intended to vary or to interrupt the course of events but plays a fundamental role in the semantic organisation of her novel. Since letters guarantee a realistic 'imprint' to events, Braddon's choice to give them such a primary value in *Lady Audley's Secret* proves her efforts to create a novel as dangerously plausible as possible. Apart from Braddon's attempts to question the moral standards of Victorian novels through her scandalous heroine, she also decided to reconfigure the teachings of the Victorian realistic school with a subversive intent. Basically, Braddon wanted to demonstrate that behind the façade of quiet English country estates (which for Victorians were the icons of political, social and moral stability) there lurked unspeakable mysteries. If letters are manipulated by Lady Audley to construct a parallel life that originates in falsehood, Robert Audley's investigations lead to the discovery of those very lies. Victorians considered falsity 'as a fundamental form of resistance to social control, as a way to recognise the presence and the force of desire, and [. . .] as a way to rethink the distribution of power across lines of social and sexual difference'.[12] For Lady Audley and for Victorian women from all social classes, whose opportunities to move freely were limited and strictly disciplined, words were propaedeutic to actions or, better, words *became* actions. The paradox lies in the fact that Lady Audley can aspire to individual independence only by using letters, in the double meaning of linguistic acts and epistolary documents, to tell lies in order to construct a deceitful, but satisfactory existence as the wife of the wealthy old aristocrat Michael Audley. In Braddon's text writing becomes a negation of the content because the search for a mimetic reproduction of events clashes with the subversive and uncanny value of the lies told in the novel. The discovery of the Lady's secret is thus strictly related to the interception, destruction or possession of texts such as letters, telegrams, scraps of blotted paper or calligraphic traces. Moreover, letters in *Lady Audley's Secret* become important written and bodily traces of the main dramatis personae and reveal their writers' identity as the expression of an 'ideologeme', of a word becoming a whole world.[13] Epistles possess a dynamic quality because, as intrinsically 'dialogic' texts, they determine and delimit the condition of the fictional addresser, and function as the primary instruments of his/her communication with the audience inside and outside the narrative boundaries of the novel. Unlike diaries, which are basically self-referential documents, letters carry out an informative and a performative task, both in the fictional heterocosm of the text and in the readers' world. In the case of the sensation novel in particular, letters set many of its narrative mechanisms in motion.

The first reference to epistles in *Lady Audley's Secret* is made by George Talboys, the former husband of Helen Talboys (the future Lucy Graham/Lady Audley) who was forced to emigrate to Australia because of financial problems, leaving his wife and only son alone and economically unprotected. On coming back from Sydney to Liverpool on board the *Argus* (a name that bears an ironic Homeric echo, reminding the reader of Ulysses's faithful dog at Ithaca), George tells his tragic personal experience to a stranger:

> 'My pretty little wife! My gentle, innocent, loving little wife! Do you know, Miss Morley,' he said with all his old hopefulness of manner, 'that I left my little girl asleep, with her baby in her arms, and with *nothing but a few blotted lines* to tell her why her faithful husband had deserted her?'[14]

Talboys's letter is the first documented reason for Helen's future escape from a life of misery, and reproduces in its very form ('few blotted lines') his conflicting feelings, connecting the causes of the past to their future effects.

Another allusion to letters – this time *in absentia* – appears during the meeting between George Talboys and Robert Audley, an old friend of his and Michael Audley's nephew. Back from Australia, George is waiting in vain for a written reply from his wife in a Westminster coffee-house. But this much-awaited private document turns into the tragic news of his wife's death, casually read in *The Times*:

> He did not want much – only a bottle of soda water, and to know if there was a letter at the bar directed to George Talboys [. . .] No; there was no letter for that name [. . .] By-and-by George looked up, and mechanically taking a greasy *Times* newspaper of the day before from a heap of journals, stared vacantly at the first page [. . .] and with an awful calmness in his manner, he pointed with his finger to a line which ran thus: –

'On the 24th inst, at Ventnor, Isle of Wight, Helen Talboys, aged twenty-two'. (Book 1, Chap. 4, pp. 75–6)

In this passage the value of the document is transferred from a private sphere (letter) to a public one (the newspaper), so that the *absence* of Helen's epistle corresponds to the *presence* of the news on her false death. From a paradigmatic point of view, this is a further hint at the impossibility of distinguishing truth from falsehood in any printed document. In this case, the 'translation' of private information into a public text alters its condition and reinforces its plausibility. Here Braddon suggests how thin the line separating reality and fiction, morality and immorality, right and wrong, can be. Writing does not become the assertion of an unchanging truth but a means to narrate fragmented stories and incomplete biographies.

Another passage, which describes Robert Audley's opinions on Lady Audley's handwriting, foregrounds the function of the act of writing as a synecdoche for the writer's personality. In this case, the physical representation of an individual conveyed by the letter can be compared to the Pre-Raphaelite 'portrait of a Lady' hanging in Lucy Audley's rooms:

'What a pretty hand she writes!' said Robert, as his cousin folded the note [. . .] 'It is the prettiest, most coquettish little hand I ever saw [. . .] but upon my word I think that if I had never seen your aunt, I should know what she was like by this slip of paper. Yes, here it all is – the feathery, gold-shot, flaxen curls, the pencilled eyebrows, the tiny straight nose, the winning childish smile, all to be guessed in these few graceful up-strokes and down-strokes.' (Book 1, Chap. 8, p. 101)

In order to escape safely from Audley Court and to avoid meeting her first husband George, Lady Audley orders her maid Phoebe to send her a message (dictated by her) with the false news of Mrs Vincent's illness, who 'implored her pupil to go and see her' (Book 1, Chap. 7, pp. 95–7). Lady Audley astutely decides to convert this simple note into a 'telegraphic message' to avoid its potential effects as a written document: namely, the slowness with which its content would be transferred to the receiver (Lady Audley), and the possibility of deciphering its sender's handwriting. This artifice testifies to the intersemiotic dialogue Braddon creates between the literary and socio-cultural context of her narration. Structurally and formally different from epistolary documents, telegrams were considered during the Victorian age as a new sensational means of communication in an era characterised by other technological innovations such as photography (see next chapter) and railways (see Part I, Chapter 2). Although the graphic sign is here totally absent, or better deliberately negated to achieve a specific purpose, the use of the telegram proves Lady Audley's scriptural leadership.

But epistles in Braddon's novel are not only important for what they *are* but also for what they *represent*. For instance, after a long and difficult investigation at Wildernsea, Robert Audley succeeds in discovering Helen Talboys's farewell letter (sent to her father on 16 August 1854) as another 'picture' – in this case of Helen's past – juxtaposed with Lady Audley's Pre-Raphaelite present:

> I am weary of my life here, and wish, if I can, to find a new one. I go out into the world, dissevered from every link which binds me to the hateful past, to seek another home and another fortune. Forgive me if I have been fretful, capricious, changeable. You should forgive me, for you know *why* I have been so. You know the *secret* which is the key to my life. (Book 2, Chap. 9, p. 267)

As this letter demonstrates, the secret that connects the identities of Helen and Lucy is not simply the Lady's inherited and intermittent madness, but rather her dangerous female assertiveness, which (as Rosina Wheeler's emblematic case demonstrates) must be clinically domesticated. This document sums up the whole course of Lady Audley's existence by focusing on the reasons for her choice (in the past: 'I am weary of my life here'), her change of identity (in the present: 'another home and another fortune'), and the final revelation of her mystery (in the future: 'You know the *secret* which is the key to my life'). A neutral sign and a form without substance, this farewell letter acquires semantic weight for Robert because of its material existence, which gives evidence of Lucy Audley's real identity:

> The lines were written in a hand that Robert Audley knew only too well.
> He sat for a long time pondering silently over the letter written by Helen Talboys.
> What was the meaning of those two last sentences – 'You should forgive me, for you know *why* I have been so. You know the *secret* which is the key to my life'? (Book 2, Chap. 9, p. 268)

Because of its implications, here the epistolary text negates its own meaning and becomes – in Jacques Lacan's definition – a pure signifier endowed with a physical existence based on absence.[15] Despite the fact that the farewell letter exists only as an 'empty space', its content (Lady Audley's story) will be filled up both by Robert Audley and by readers, whose knowledge of the events provide what her letter only hints at. In Robert Audley's diachronic perception, the idea of separation and distance in Helen's letter (suggested by expressions such as 'I go out into the world' and 'dissevered from every link') clashes with the isotopy of proximity ('knew only too well'). In his Darwinian 'retrograde investigation', the amateur detective Robert will fill in the gaps between past and present through a gradual assimilation of the unknown Helen to the well-known aunt Lady Audley.

The disappearance of any reference to Lady Audley's activity as a writer anticipates her obliteration as an individual, which culminates in her final change of identity in the *maison de santé* of Villebrumeuse, where 'Madame Taylor' will be condemned to a physical and textual death. The end of Lady Audley's scriptural presence will be introduced in another letter sent by the Belgian doctor Val, who had cured (or tried to domesticate) her.[16] The black edge of the letter functions as another pure signifier whose content is contextual rather than textual. This last 'black-edged letter' is deliberately concealed from the reader, who can only infer the woman's slow decay and silent consumption:

> It is more than a year since a black-edged letter, written upon foreign paper, came to Robert Audley, to announce the death of a certain Madame Taylor, who has expired peacefully at Villebrumeuse, dying after a long illness, which Monsieur Val describes as *maladie de langueur*. (Book 3, Chap. 10, p. 445)

On more than one occasion Lady Audley's handwriting replicates her bodily traits and her moral principles: 'the feathery, gold-shot, flaxen curls, the pencilled eyebrows, the tiny straight nose, the winning childish smile, all to be guessed in these few graceful up-strokes and down-strokes' (p. 101). This scriptural and epistolary characterisation foregrounds the way she will be reproduced in painterly terms in the famous Pre-Raphaelite portrait included in the novel. Figurative art has a profound value in Braddon's novels[17] because it is not only a way to give her narration a 'reality effect' (in her allusions to real painters or painting schools) but, above all, because it serves as a means to deal with questions related to realistic visual representation. It is not accidental that in discussing her own and other writers' styles Braddon usually borrows images and examples from painting. In many of her letters to Edward Bulwer Lytton, she reconfigures and translates the figurative language of the Pre-Raphaelites in narrative terms to underline the influence of Flaubert's and Balzac's descriptive techniques on the 'realistic' style she was looking for during the composition of *The Doctor's Wife*:

> Have you read anything of Gustave Flaubert's, & do you like the extraordinary Pre-Raphaelite style. I have been wonderfully fascinated by it, but I suppose that unvarnished realism is the very reverse of poetry. (Letter dated 17 January, 1864)

> The idea of the Doctor's Wife *is* founded on 'Madame Bovary', the style of which book struck me immensely despite it's [sic] *hideous* immorality. There

seems an extraordinary Pre-Raphaelite power of description – a power to make manifest a scene and an atmosphere in a few lines – almost a few words – that very few writers possess – & a grim kind of humour equal to Balzac in its way. (Letter dated Summer 1864)[18]

Braddon was not the only Victorian writer and intellectual who used painting as an instrument to deal with issues of representation. The debates on the realistic novel and on figurative art often intersected and influenced each other in light of the importance visuality had, in particular, in bourgeois society, interested in the (re)production of material reality. That is why, according to Peter Brooks, '[T]he very premise of realism is that one cannot understand human beings outside the context of the things that surround them, and knowing these things is a matter of viewing them, detailing them, and describing the concrete milieux in which men and woman enact their destinies.'[19] Among the many Victorian writers who focused on these questions, George Eliot's reflections on Dutch painting included in *Adam Bede* (1859) are exemplary illustrations of her narrative technique and of her ideological aspirations. However, while for Eliot the term 'realism' stood for a depiction of humble realities that aimed at inspiring sympathy in readers, for Braddon it would acquire a totally different Pre-Raphaelite meaning:

> So I am content to tell my simple story, without trying to make things seem better than they were; dreading nothing, indeed, but falsity, which, in spite of one's best efforts, there is reason to dread. Falsehood is so easy, truth so difficult [. . .] It is for this rare, precious quality of truthfulness that I delight in many Dutch paintings, which lofty-minded people despise. I find a source of delicious sympathy in these faithful pictures of a monotonous homely existence, which has been the fate of so many more among my fellow-mortals than a life of pomp, or of absolute indigence, of tragic suffering or of world-stirring actions.[20]

In his reflections on the necessity of avoiding any kind of improvisation in art, John Ruskin did not call for a revival of 'imitation' but suggested (from *Modern Painters* to *The Stones of Venice*) the creation – through the mediation of the object – of a new relationship between the observing artist and the observed world. The purpose of the Ruskinian artist and of the realist writer was thus to be able to reach a truth that went beyond the image, although the attention to particulars remained the fundamental premise to this renewed form of revelation. For Ruskin, truthful works of art 'have no pretence, no hypocrisy [. . .] there is nothing to be found out, or sifted, or surprised in them; they bear their message simply and clearly; and it is that message which the mind takes from them and dwells upon, regardless of the language in which it is delivered'.[21] This justifies the choices of many Pre-Raphaelites (most notably Dante Gabriel Rossetti, William Holman Hunt and John Everett Millais), who relied on Ruskin's ideas on art and on his technical advice as a common ground for the creation of an anti-academic movement that privileged the ultra-detailed depiction of ordinary, historical and literary subjects. In this sense, they deliberately juxtaposed their pictorial experiments with the 'panoramic' view supported by Joshua Reynolds in his *Discourse on Art* (1769–90) and defended by the Royal Academy of Arts as the officially respected figurative practice for many years. According to Reynolds, beauty is produced only by attending to the general ideas of nature. In his words, the interest in 'minute particularities' leads to aesthetic 'pollution' and 'deformity'. Contrarily, the Pre-Raphaelite interest in detailed representation of subjects did not have a formal value only, and it also implicated questions of gender. Indeed, the revolutionary outcome of their attention to visual details was in fact related to the interest they had in female subjects. As Naomi Schor puts it:

> The story of the rise of detail is, of course, inseparable from the all too familiar story of the demise of classicism and the birth of realism, but it should not, indeed cannot be reduced to that story, for to retell the story from the perspective of the detail is inevitably to tell *another* story [. . .] The detail does not occupy a conceptual space beyond the laws of sexual difference: the detail is gendered and doubly gendered as feminine.[22]

Lady Audley's Secret demonstrates that the narration of the story of a sexually and socially 'marginal' character who aspires to ascend the social scale can shed new light on the mechanisms of power in nineteenth-century cultural systems. Moreover, the decision to include a Pre-Raphaelite portrait in Braddon's novel proves her ambivalent use of a Ruskinian approach to visual reproduction. Her detailed description of Lady Audley's physical features through a sensualised Pre-Raphaelite figurative code anticipates, in some ways, what many Pre-Raphaelites will do in the so-called 'second phase' of this artistic movement, characterised by the interest in minutely-portrayed images of seductive women and summarised by Rossetti's *Astarte Syriaca* (1875–7). Many of Lady Audley's physical traits described in the portrait are reminiscent of Rossetti's *Bocca Baciata* (1859) while, as far as her dangerous female qualities are concerned, Braddon had in mind Edward Burne-Jones's painting entitled *Sidonia Von Bork* (1860), inspired by Wilhelm Meinhold's novel *Sidonia von Bork, die Klosterhexe* (1847–8; translated into English by Lady Wilde in 1849).[23] The choice of a Pre-Raphaelite painter as the author of Lady Audley's portrait is indicative of Braddon's desire to render in detail the complexity of her female character. Braddon creates an association between the Pre-Raphaelite cult of peripheral 'minute particularities' and the woman's nature as liminal creature. From both an aesthetic and an ideological point of view, the Lady's portrait (thanks to which George Talboys discovers the real identity of Lucy Audley) introduces her complex condition as victim and villain, delicate creature and femme fatale, ordinary woman and monster:

> My lady's portrait stood on an easel covered with a green baize in the centre of the octagonal chamber. It had been a fancy of the artist to paint her stand-ing in this very room, and to make his background a faithful reproduction of the pictured walls. I am afraid the young man belonged to the pre-Raphaelite brotherhood, for he had spent a most unconscious time upon the accessories of this picture – upon my lady's crispy ringlets and the heavy folds of her crimson velvet dress [. . .]
>
> 'There are our friend's eternal white horses,' said Robert, stopping before a Wouvermans. 'Nicholas Poussin – Salvator – ha – hum! Now for the portrait!'.
>
> He paused with his hand on the baize, and solemnly addressed his friend.
>
> 'George Talboys,' he said, 'we have between us only one wax candle, a very inadequate light with which to look at a painting' [. . .]
>
> When he turned round he saw that Robert had arranged the easel very con-veniently, and that he had seated himself on a chair before it for the purpose of contemplating the painting at his leisure.
>
> He rose as George turned round.
>
> 'Now, then, for your turn, Talboys,' he said. 'It's an extraordinary picture'.
>
> He took George's place at the window, and George seated himself in the chair before the easel. (Book 1, Chap. 10, pp. 105–6)

The narration is focused on the two men's desire to read and interpret the Lady's portrait in order to enter her mysteries through a voyeuristic practice that recalls Phoebe's and Luke Marks's incursion into the Lady's boudoir. The two men are sitting in front of the painting, illuminated by a candle, with the intention of contemplating it 'at [their] leisure'. Given the differences between George and Robert (and their respective expectations), the outcomes of their readings diverge. For Talboys this portrait turns into a striking revelation of his wife's survival and bigamy, while for Robert it is a further sign of his aunt's moral ambivalence. For both men Lady Audley is an assertive woman who needs to be contained, controlled and 'framed' within a portrait which hints at her assertive-ness and that, at the same time, becomes her cage.[24] The background of the portrait does not reproduce an 'idealised' naturalistic scene but the Lady's chamber ('a faithful reproduction of the pictured walls'), as if to underline the fact that she is a product of her times, of her social status and of her condition as a Victorian woman. This dangerous figural and chronological proximity has an implicit polemical meaning related to the realistic representation of truth, intensified 'by its sharp contrast with mainstream art [by Wouvermans, Poussin and Rosa] ornamenting the antechamber leading to Lady Audley's boudoir'.[25]

The description of the portrait is delegated to Robert Audley, whose point of view identifies with the narrator's free indirect speech. An embodiment of the rising middle classes, Robert Audley will later be involved in the detection of the Lady's traces, so that his 'internally-focalised'[26] perspective on the painting anticipates his future enquiry on Lady Audley's identity:

> Yes, the painter must have been a pre-Raphaelite. No one but a pre-Raphaelite would have painted, hair by hair, those feathery masses of ring-lets with every glimmer of gold, and every shadow of pale brown. No one but a pre-Raphaelite would have exaggerated every attribute of that delicate face as to give a lurid lightness to the blonde complexion, and a strange, sinister light to the deep blue eyes. No one but a pre-Raphaelite could have given to that pretty pouting mouth the hard and almost wicked look it had in the portrait.
>
> It was like and yet so unlike; it was as if you had burned strange coloured fires before my lady's face, and by their influence brought out new lines and new expressions never seen in it before. The perfection of feature, the brilliancy of colouring, were there; but I suppose the painter had copied quaint mediaeval monstrosities until his brain had grown bewildered, for my lady, in his portrait of her, had something of the aspect of a beautiful fiend. (Book 1, Chap. 10, p. 107)

The choice to introduce the verbal description of a visual work of art (an 'ekphrasis')[27] via an intra-diegetic narration suggests that Braddon wanted Robert to embody a commonly-shared male opinion not only on women but, in particular, on the realistic representation of women in art. Robert's words 'like and yet so unlike' sum up Victorian readers' expectations and the betrayal of those very expectations. An important element is here represented by the aesthetic and cultural antithesis between what is considered as 'like' (a truthful and morally acceptable image, according to Victorian canons of representation) and what is 'unlike', immoral and artistically improper. The expression 'beautiful fiend' becomes in this sense a perfect expression of Lady Audley's two-sided aesthetic description and of *Lady Audley's Secret* as oxymoronic fictional narration, where sensational themes are contaminated by realistic descriptions (paintings) and stylistic strategies (letters):[28]

LIKE	UNLIKE
delicate face	exaggerated [. . .] attribute
deep blue eyes	strange sinister light
blonde complexion	lurid lightness
pretty pouting mouth	hard and almost wicked look

The term 'exaggeration' (in all of its lexical variations) is repeated throughout the passage, as if to emphasise the fact that this word is the pervasive filter of Robert's description. His perception of the Lady's physical and implicitly moral features is made more upsetting because of the co-existence of normative and non-normative aesthetic attributes. This mixture of realistic ('like') and non-realistic ('unlike') features can be read in a wider perspective, connecting it to questions of figural and literary representation. Victorian writers referred to pictorial art also to try and bridge questions of realistic 'reproducibility'. By using figural allusions novelists invoked a 'non-literary mode of description and representation' in order to be 'exempted from the impossible task of describing the real world in all its complexity'. Therefore, according to Alison Byerly, these 'references to painting [. . .] authorise the work of art through reference to other works of art, thereby eliding the question of the work's relation to reality'.[29] In this view, it is interesting to compare this 'ekphrastic' description with a scene from Elizabeth Gaskell's unfinished novel *Wives and Daughters* (1864–6), featuring Molly Gibson talking to Mrs Hamley in front of the sketches of her two boys. In Gaskell's case Molly will be able to get a faithful idea of the two characters (who are now adults) from a truthful crayon sketch:

> Molly turned round, and saw one of the crayon sketches – representing the two boys, in the most youthful kind of jackets and trousers, and falling collars. The elder was sitting down, reading intently. The younger was standing by him, and evidently trying to call the attention of the reader off to some object out of doors [. . .] 'Tell me just what you think of them, my dear; it will amuse me *to compare your impressions with what they really are*.'[30]

Despite the fact that Braddon's and Gaskell's inclusion of 'ekphrastic' descriptions is based upon their interest to picture reality as it is (or as it should be), these two writers embody antithetical views on the relationship between figurative art and literature. While both novels are focused on questions of truth and reality, they represent the sometimes opposite ways in which Victorian writers engaged with questions of mimetic reproduction.[31] In contrast with Gaskell's figural reproduction of truth, for Robert Audley (as well as for many contemporary readers and critics) the 'effect' of this unusual combination between likeness and unlikeness is not 'an agreeable one' (p. 107). Robert's words are significantly counterbalanced by Alicia's, who suggests that painters and implicitly writers are able to see 'through the normal expression of the face, another expression that is equally part of it, though not to be perceived by common eyes. *We* have never seen my lady look as she does in that picture; but I think that she *could* look so' (p. 108). Alicia's opinions seem to echo, in a paradoxical form, Ruskin's ideas on the importance of the artist's peculiar perception of reality. Finally, the fact that Braddon leaves the Lady's portrait 'unfinished' implies the intervention of potential and implied readers, to whom she offers her picture as a (limited) representation of reality which has to be completed. Figurative art thus becomes an instrument Braddon uses to describe in a captivating, involving and credible way the physical features of her characters, as well as a metaphor to discuss questions of representation in an age 'fascinated with the act of seeing, with the question of reliability'.[32]

The references to painting, however, are far from episodic in Braddon's macrotext, and will be an instrument to convey her changing approach to narration in the course of her whole career. In *The Lady's Mile* (1866), dedicated to the painter Edward Landseer, Braddon refers to pictorial art as a vehicle to deal with the problems artists have to face (in their constant battles to assert their own ideas against hostile criticism), and with the limits and possibilities of artistic creation.[33] Through the characters of the three-decker novelist Sigismund Smythe (already introduced in *The Doctor's Wife* with the name of Sigismund Smith), the 'academic' painter William Crawford and his young Turneresque pupil Philip Fowley, Braddon constructs a realistic 'novel of manners' which turns the aesthetic premises of *Lady Audley's Secret* upside down. Here she replaces its Pre-Raphaelite pictorial style with an institutional one. Braddon's words lurk behind William Crawford's opinions, in particular when the painter laments that his ambivalent relationship with success and with money clashes with his aspirations to create pure art. Like Braddon (see letter to Bulwer Lytton dated May 1863), Crawford also admits to serving 'two masters': 'The real artist should care for nothing but his art. This is the doctrine which William Crawford had preached and practised for fifteen years of life; but in these latter days he was false to his own teachings, and *tried to serve two masters*.'[34]

The fact that this novel privileges an evidently realistic approach to narration and to figurative representation by way of constant allusion to classical, or at least academic, art (Crawford's projected masterpiece *Dido and Aeneas* is inspired by Nicholas Poussin and Rubens) is indicative of Braddon's desire to experiment with stylistic and narrative strategies that differed from those which granted her enormous success. This oscillation between artistic aspirations and economic necessities will continue to haunt Braddon, as another proof of her uneven attempt to disengage herself from the Lady Audley paradigm.

Notes

1. Stevenson, 'A Note on Realism', in *R. L. Stevenson on Fiction*, p. 222.
2. Trollope, *An Autobiography*, pp. 226–7; Dickens, letter to John Forster, qtd in Forster, *The Life of Charles Dickens*, p. 279; Braddon, letter to Edward Bulwer Lytton dated March 1866, in Wolff, '"Devoted Disciple"', p. 134. Braddon is alluding to Trollope's novel *Miss Mackenzie*.
3. Eliot, *George Eliot, A Writer's Notebook*, p. 273 (George Eliot's words are drawn from her review of John Ruskin's *Modern Painters III*, published in the *Westminster Review* in April 1856). For G. H. Lewes, '[Art] is a Representation of Reality [. . .] Art always aims at the representation of Reality, i.e. of Truth; and no departures from truth are permissible, except such as inevitably lies in the nature of the medium itself. Realism is thus the basis of all Art, and its antithesis is not Idealism, but Falsism ('Realism in Art', p. 493). According to John P. McGowan, '[The] Victorians' penchant to locate spiritual or moral truths as the most fundamental reality marks their distance from the realism found in France during the same period' (*Representation and Revelation*, p. 1).
4. For a reflection on the teleological nature of plot and 'plotting' in Victorian culture and in nineteenth-century novels, see Brooks, *Reading for the Plot*. Katherine Kearns argues that '[the] realist author articulates multiple obligations: a duty to the faithful representation, a duty to the truthful treatment of material, a duty to the everyday and the ordinary, and so on. But that author speaks these obligations into a discursive field felt as both enriched and disorderly, a place where ideal containers – words as well as concepts – have begun to burgeon with fitful, multiplicative, and contradictory particulars' (*Nineteenth-century Literary Realism*, p. 3).
5. Rae, 'Sensation Novelists: Miss Braddon', p. 186. Alfred Austin, in 'Our Novels: the Sensational School', admonishes his readers that sensation novels 'represent life neither as it is nor as it ought to be' (p. 94). On the relationship between novel-reading habits and social behaviour, R. C. Terry states that there was a 'commonly shared assumption about the general moral efficacy of novels' (*Victorian Popular Fiction*, p. 5).
6. Oliphant, 'Novels', p. 257; Oliphant, 'Our Female Sensational Novelists', p. 209, my italics.
7. The term 'epitext' refers to elements outside the bound volume, such as interviews, reviews, correspondence, diaries etc. On the notion of 'epitext', see Genette, *Seuils*.
8. Barthes, 'The Reality Effect', p. 17.
9. 'I want to serve two masters. I want to be artistic & to please you. I want to be sensational, & to please Mudie's subscribers' (letter dated May 1863, in Wolff, '"Devoted Disciple"', p. 14).
10. See Todorov, 'The Typology of the Detective Fiction'.

11. See Rousset, *Forme et Signification*, especially Chapter 4.
12. Kucich, *The Power of Lies*, p. 15.
13. 'The fundamental condition, that which makes a novel a novel, that which is responsible for its stylistic uniqueness, is *the speaking person and his discourse* [. . .] The speaking person in the novel is always, to one degree or another, an *ideologue*, and his words are always *ideologemes*. A particular language in a novel is always a particular way of viewing the world, one that strives for social significance' (Bakhtin, *The Dialogic Imagination*, pp. 332–3, my italics).
14. Braddon, *Lady Audley's Secret*, ed. Houston, Book 1, Chap. 2, p. 59, my italics. All further quotations will be from this edition.
15. See Lacan, 'Le séminaire sur *La Lettre volée*', in *Écrits*, pp. 11–61.
16. On the use of asylums as instruments of moral education for 'fallen women' see Showalter, *The Female Malady*. For Shoshana Felman behind the term 'madness' lies the fear of what she calls 'feminine difference' ('Women and Madness: the Critical Fallacy', p. 6).
17. Apart from Launcelot Darrell's drawing in *Eleanor's Victory* (Part II, Chapter 5) and Michael Kerstall's painting of the 'real' Henry Dunbar in the eponymous novel, many other texts by Braddon allude to painting to convey the nature of a certain character. In *Sir Jasper's Tenant* (1864), for instance, elderly sir Jasper gives a 'painterly' appreciation of women. *The Lady's Mile* (1865) is centred on figurative art, and in *Phantom Fortune* (1883) the main female characters Lesbia and Mary are described according to antithetical artistic codes (see Part III, Chapter 9). *Circe*, a novel evidently plagiarising Octave Feuillet's *Dalila* (published in 1867 under the pseudonym of Babington White), features a love-obsessed young painter named Laurence Bell.
18. Wolff, '"Devoted Disciple"', p. 19; p. 22.
19. Brooks, *Body Work*, p. 88. Brooks opens his book entitled *The Realist Vision* with the assertion that 'realist literature is attached to the visual, to looking at things, registering their presence in the world through sight' (p. 3).
20. Eliot, *Adam Bede*, pp. 222–3.
21. Ruskin, *Modern Painters* (1846), in *The Complete Works of John Ruskin*, vol. 3, p. 108.
22. Schor, *Reading in Detail*, p. xlii. Joshua Reynolds's quotations are taken from *The Literary Works of Sir Joshua Reynolds*, vol. 2, p. 135. Tim Barringer asserts that the Pre-Raphaelites' cult of detail 'belongs to the nineteenth century, to the era of photography, of empirical science and of botanical classification. It is unmistakably modern, a variety of realism specific to the historical period which produced art' (*The Pre-Raphaelites*, p. 8).
23. Meinhold's text is a Gothic romance set in Pomerania, and deals with the story of a seducing and criminal lady, accused of witchcraft and finally condemned to death in 1620. Sophia Andres, who retraces the origins of Lady Audley's portrait in Rossetti's *Bocca Baciata* (1859) and Edward Burne-Jones's *Sidonia Von Bork* (1860), demonstrates that through her use of Pre-Raphaelite sources Braddon tries to start a discussion on sexual and cultural transgression 'outside the arena of fiction' ('Mary

Elizabeth Braddon's Ambivalent Pre-Raphaelite Ekphrasis'). For Chris Willis, Braddon draws inspiration exclusively from Edward Burne-Jones's picture ('Braddon and Burne-Jones'). Pamela Didlake Brewer suggests that Rossetti, in turn, took inspiration from Braddon for his painting entitled *Lady Lilith* and for its companion poem 'Body's Beauty' ('Pre-Raphaelitism in *Lady Audley's Secret*', p. 8).

24. 'Braddon's presentation of the portrait comprises a multivalent critique: it protests the power and authority of the male gaze [. . .] and it raises questions about the construction of women and their sexuality in Victorian society. While titillating, and perhaps even satisfying, male gazers, Braddon's portrait also functions to screen a more profound feminist statement about Victorian patriarchy's relation to women and heterosexuality' (Felber, 'The Literary Portrait as Centerfold', p. 473).

25. Andres, *The Pre-Raphaelite Art of the Victorian Novel*, p. 1.

26. See Genette, 'Mood', in *Narrative Discourse*, pp. 161–211.

27. See Heffernan, *Museum of Words*. In narratological terms, this '[set-piece] description is seen by narratologists as the paradigm example of narrative pause, in the semi technical sense of a passage at the level of narrative to which nothing corresponds at the level of story. The plot does not advance, but something is described' (Fowler, 'Narrate and Describe: the Problem of Ekphrasis', pp. 25–6).

28. According to Brian Donnelly, who deals with Braddon's complex relationship with Rossetti's changing notion of Pre-Raphaelitism, in *Lady Audley's Secret* she 'problematises the perceived distance between realism and sensationalism [. . .] through the appearance of the portrait. In doing so, she articulates the contemporary shift between the realism characteristic of early Pre-Raphaelite art and Dante Gabriel Rossetti's later distortion of it' ('Sensational Bodies', p. 69).

29. Byerly, *Realism, Representation and the Arts*, p. 6; p. 17. In *Fictional Truth*, Riffaterre argues that these non-narrative forms function as a 'metalanguage' and that artistic metaphors can be defined as 'fictional indices' and tropes that 'presuppose the real' (p. 52).

30. Gaskell, *Wives and Daughters*, pp. 64–5, my italics.

31. For George Levine realism 'defines itself against the excesses, both stylistic and narrative, of various kinds of romantic, exotic, or sensational literature' (*The Realistic Imagination*, p. 5).

32. Flint, *The Victorians and the Visual Imagination*, p. 1.

33. During the year in which she wrote *The Lady's Mile* Braddon intensified her acquaintance with William Powell Frith, who had painted her first portrait in 1865, and who jocosely used to call her 'Aurora', 'Lady Audley' or 'The Doctor's Wife'.

34. Braddon, *The Lady's Mile*, vol. 2, p. 147, my italics.

Chapter 8

Reading Sensation/Writing Realism: Photographic Strategies in *The Doctor's Wife*

To misquote from Jane Austen's *Pride and Prejudice*, it is a truth universally acknowledged that Mary Elizabeth Braddon is recognised as the author of a great number of novels and short stories generally labelled under the name of 'sensation'. But for those who do not like stereotypes, it is a far more relevant truth that she was something more than a talented plot maker, the creator of immoral intrigues, a peculiar anti-conformist and a sharp witness of her times. Braddon was, first of all, a self-conscious novelist always dissatisfied with the final result of her works and eager to learn from 'eminent Victorians' such as Edward Bulwer Lytton, her literary mentor. In a letter in which she deals with *Aurora Floyd*, Braddon admits:

> I know that my writing teams with errors, absurdities, contradictions and inconsistancies [sic]; but I have never written a line that has not been written against time – sometimes with the printer waiting outside the door. I have written as conscientiously as I could; but more with a view to the interests of my publishers than with any great regard to my own reputation.[1]

In this letter Braddon confesses to having lost her battle to limit herself to serious writing, a battle which had George Eliot among its most strenuous advocates. In 'Silly Novels by Lady Novelists' (1856), Eliot stated that 'the most mischievous form of feminine silliness is the literary form, because it tends to confirm the popular prejudice against the more solid education of women', concluding her article on the necessity for women to have 'patient diligence, a sense of responsibility involved in publication, and an appreciation of the sacredness of the writer's art'.[2] Like many other Victorian writers, Braddon tried to negotiate her economic necessities and her belief in what Eliot calls 'the sacredness of the writer's art', with mixed results. Like George Eliot, Dickens, Collins and, later, Gissing, Braddon was both attracted by and estranged from the Victorian literary world, in particular because of the haunting presence of Lady Audley's narrative ghost.[3] Therefore, Braddon always sought a double form of emancipation: first as a successful woman of letters in a market still dominated by patriarchal attitudes, and then as a writer who experimented in a wide range of fictional genres ranging from historical texts to novels of manners, dramas and even poetry, in a way trying to follow in the footsteps of her master Edward Bulwer Lytton. As many of her letters to Lytton testify, Braddon's increasing interest in French literature suggests that she was aiming at replacing sensation plots with a new kind of characterisation. The result of her efforts was *The Doctor's Wife*, a rewriting of Gustave Flaubert's *Madame Bovary* (1857) intended as a reply to the most recurrent critical attacks against her writing style:

> I have thought very much of what you said in your last letter with regard to a novel in which the story arises naturally out of the characters of the actors in it [. . .] I venture to think you will like my new story 'The Doctor's Wife' (this is not a title of my own choosing) better than anything I have yet done, because I am going in a little for the subjective [. . .] Have you read anything of Gustave Flaubert's, & do you like the extraordinary Pre-Raphaelite style. I have been wonderfully fascinated by it, but I suppose that unvarnished realism is the very reverse of poetry [. . .]
>
> The idea of 'The Doctor's Wife' *is* founded on 'Madame Bovary', the style of which book struck me immensely in spite of it's [sic] *hideous* immorality. There seems an extraordinary Pre-Raphaelite power of description – a power to make manifest a scene and an atmosphere in a few lines – almost a few words – that very few writers possess – & a grim kind of humour equal to Balzac in its way.[4]

The Doctor's Wife is the story of George Gilbert, a middle-class country doctor who is a friend of Sigismund Smith, a sensation novelist living in London. When the pragmatic George meets the beautiful and dreamy Isabel Sleaford he immediately falls in love with this eighteen-year-old girl who loves reading romances and wishes her life was like the books she reads. At the end of George's stay, the Sleafords suddenly pack up and leave home. Isabel's father, who has pretended to be a barrister (and whose characterisation is indebted to Braddon's autobio-graphic memories of her own father), is accused of forgery and has to flee to avoid the law. Some months later, when George is plodding along with his country practice, he learns that Isabel is working as a governess for Mr Raymond, a philanthropist and amateur phrenologist who lives eleven miles away. Sigismund visits his friend and the two men begin to spend a lot of time with Isabel and Mr Raymond. Then George proposes to Isabel, though there are many indications that she is not the quiet, domestic wife he is looking for. Isabel, who has grown weary of being a governess, accepts his proposal. On their honeymoon, Isabel realises that George is not what she expected him to be and begins to regret marrying him. In an attempt to escape from her boredom, Isabel returns to her reading and makes the acquaintance of Roland Lansdell, an aristocratic neighbour who is the author of a volume of poetry written under a pseudonym ('The Alien'). Roland embodies the ideal romantic hero she has been looking for. They fall in love, meet secretly, exchange books but never engage in a sexual affair. When Raymond realises the nature of the relationship between Isabel and Roland, he advises him to leave the country. Roland follows his friend's advice, while Isabel contemplates suicide. After a few weeks, Roland returns and begs Isabel to run away with him, but she refuses. Despite her doubts about her married life, Isabel admits that she never meant to be unfaithful to her husband. Roland begins to suspect Isabel after she borrows some money from him and after he sees her talking to a mysterious stranger who is actually her father Mr Sleaford, now a fugitive from justice. Mr Sleaford recognises Lansdell as the man whose testimony had sent him to jail and beats him to death. At the end of the novel George Gilbert catches typhoid fever and dies, while Isabel inherits Lansdell's fortune and is left to a life of charitable works.

As Braddon repeatedly admitted, in *The Doctor's Wife* she drew inspiration from Flaubert's much debated novel for its peculiarly realistic style rather than for its plot and themes, which she partially altered and even 'moralised' about at the end. In Braddon's novel, for instance, there is more explicit reference to social difference than in Flaubert's (the other doctor living at Graybridge on the Wayverne, called Mr Pawlkatt, cures only aristocratic patients). Moreover, in *Madame Bovary* Charles was previously married to a widow for economical reasons and even the decision to marry Emma is prompted by the fact that she is the daughter of a rich landowner, while on the contrary Isabel's father is a forger and a murderer. The character of Roland Lansdell is a fusion of the young and inexperienced Léon Dupin (who works as a practitioner for a notary and loves art, poetry and music) and the skilful Rodolphe Boulanger de la Huchette. The characters of Mr Charles Raymond and of the sensation writer Sigismund Smith are Braddon's original creations. But the more evident contrast is related to the main characters' behaviour: Isabel Sleaford does not betray her husband (she refuses her only lover's proposal to flee with him); on the contrary, in *Madame Bovary* Emma Rouault is repeatedly unfaithful to Charles and uses her passion for books as a means rather than an end (as in Isabel's case). Even the two epilogues are antithetical, because Emma commits suicide by poisoning herself with arsenic and Isabel spends the last part of her

life repenting for her 'reading' sins, giving the money she has inherited to
the poor. Moreover, Braddon's decision to write *The Doctor's Wife* as a
morally edifying version of Flaubert's text emerges from the novel's lack
of any form of eroticism (Gilbert and Isabel's matrimonial life seems
totally sexless). One of the reasons behind Braddon's censored version
of Flaubert lies in the fact that she did not want to be recognised as the
writer of another scandalous novel, and wished to be treated by critics
as a serious artist.[5] These legitimate motivations must be integrated with
Braddon's wish to prove that sensation or romance reading does not
necessarily lead to moral corruption. Had she followed Flaubert's steps
scrupulously, she would have betrayed, in a sense, the ideological premises upon which *The Doctor's Wife* was founded. Despite the fact that
this novel cannot be considered Braddon's literary masterpiece, and was
not greeted favourably by many Victorian critics, it represents an interesting metaliterary reflection on fictional writing and reading, written in
an innovative style. *The Doctor's Wife* testifies to Braddon's attempts to
write a realistic novel that also turns into a novel on novel-writing (and
reading), the narrative intersected with metanarrative levels through the
characters of Isabel and Sigismund Smith, Braddon's fictional alter-ego.
The realistic narration of Isabel's dreamy nature and love of novels (as
well as her unsatisfactory life as a 'doctor's wife') is put alongside the
opinions of Sigismund Smith on his 'dirty job' as penny fiction writer. In
this way, Braddon wanted to indicate that the two experiences of consuming literature (Isabel Sleaford) and producing literature (Sigismund
Smith) are mutually dependent.

Braddon's novel is a heterogeneous assemblage of different literary
genres: the English realistic novels of George Eliot, Charles Dickens and
Anthony Trollope (in their accurate description of the social context),
the French realistic novels of Honoré de Balzac, George Sand and
Gustave Flaubert (for their detailed portrait of human vices and virtues),
the sentimental novels of Rhoda Broughton, Ouida and Charlotte
Yonge (in the characterisation of positive female values), and finally
sensation novels (in the episode of the murder committed by Isabel's
father).[6] Moreover, Braddon engrafts the parodic lesson of Charlotte
Lennox's *The Female Quixote* (1752) and Jane Austen's *Northanger
Abbey* (1798/1803) in the didactic tradition of conduct books and
advice manuals on reading. In her attempt to create a new literary style
she deconstructs the typical tendency of traditional Victorian literature,
which often proposed a 'monologic' reading and approach to reality in
the form of a reassuring plot and an unproblematic perception of the
world. As Bakhtin underlines, 'Parodic stylizations of canonized genres
and styles occupy an essential place in the novel [. . .] Throughout its

entire history there is a consistent parodying or travestying of dominant or fashionable novels that attempt to become models for the genre [. . .] This ability of the novel to criticise itself is a remarkable feature of this ever-developing genre.'[7] These parodic aspects are also enhanced by the presence of the autobiographical character of Sigismund Smith, an ironic version of Braddon's submission to and position as a victim of her Audleyan ghost, particularly in her unofficial serial publications (such as *The Black Band, or the Mysteries of Midnight*, written under the pseudonym of Lady Caroline Lascelles). Sigismund Smith epitomises two of the many facets of Braddon's literary apprenticeship, since he is a male version of Mary Elizabeth Braddon's aspirations as a writer and of Babington White/Lady Lascelles's dissipated gifts as contributor of highly sensational fictions. Like Braddon, Smith will acquire a respectable position in the literary market in a few years, turning, in *The Lady's Mile* (1866), into a three-volume author (with the name of Smythe), whose works are included in circulating libraries. From a biographical point of view Isabel's naivety and innocent love of reading recalls Braddon's experiences as a girl living in a quiet Camberwell house 'before the knowledge of evil' (the title of her unfinished autobiography), and before she was forced to move with her family and start a career as an actress after her father's sudden departure.

The first indirect reference to Isabel is included in the first pages of the novel, in the course of the description of George Gilbert's acceptance of the dull quiet life at Graybridge, contrasted with Isabel's intolerance for its suffocating atmosphere. Rather than simply describing the Midland setting, this passage alludes to Victorian women's condition as physically, culturally, socially and morally secluded subjects:

> There are prisoners and prisoners. There are some who grow flowers in the windows of their cells, who make themselves comfortable, who invent all manner of ingenious contrivances whereby to render their narrow chambers pleasant, who eat and drink and sleep, placidly indifferent to all the world outside the cruel walls that shut them in. There are other captives who sit at their barred windows staring for ever at one patch of distant sky – that lovely sky, which covers a free world and slowly consume themselves with the fire of their own souls.[8]

Images of imprisonment and suffocation are put alongside parodic references to Gothic literature, which privileged the role of women as undefended victims of male villains. The presence of words such as 'prisoners', 'cells', 'narrow chambers', 'cruel walls', 'shut them', 'captives' and 'barred windows' is to be noted.

Isabel Sleaford's only vice is that of reading too many romantic stories. Like a sort of new 'Mariana in the Moated Grange' (a Tennysonian image that is continually evoked in the novel), Isabel lives in a modest Camberwell country house, waiting for her dreams of love to come true. Her belief that life and fiction are mutually dependent is constantly alluded to in the novel, usually with a mixture of irony and seriousness in referring to the causes of her book-related dysfunction: 'She wanted her life to be like her books; she wanted to be a heroine, – unhappy, perhaps, and dying early' (p. 28). In the course of a dialogue between Sigismund and Isabel, during which they deal with the unhealthy effects of the books written by writers of sentimental stories, Braddon's novel significantly addresses questions related to female reading habits, comparing them to a form of drug addiction:

> '[Algernon Mountfort's] books are so beautiful,' she said.
> 'Dangerously beautiful, I'm afraid, Isabel,' the young man said gravely, 'beautiful sweet-meats, with *opium inside the sugar*. These books don't make you happy, do they Lizzie?'
> 'No, they make me unhappy; but' – she hesitated a little, and then blushed as she said – 'I like that sort of unhappiness. It's better than eating and drinking and sleeping, and being happy that way.' (p. 24, my italics)

Ironically, Sigismund's words seem to echo the opinions of many detractors of the sensation genre, who compared the consumption of printed material to the consumption of food, blaming the effects that the 'indigestion' of dangerous products may have on the bodily, spiritual and moral equilibrium of the female 'eater'.[9]

In another passage, through the words of the omniscient narrator, Braddon creates a direct connection between Isabel's excessive love of reading and the lack of interest and activity in the life of many middle-class Victorian women. In this way, Braddon partially justifies the reasons behind Isabel's novelistic opium-like addiction:

> Poor Lizzie's life was altogether vulgar and commonplace, and she could not extract one ray of romance out of it, twist it as she would [. . .] Alas, alas! She looked north and south and east and west, and the sky was all dark, so she was obliged to go back to the intellectual *opium-eating*, and become a *dreamer of dreams*. (p. 29, my italics)

> [Isabel] was satisfied as an *opium-reader* is satisfied with the common every-day world; which is only the frame that holds together all manner of splendid and ever-changing pictures. She was content with a life in which she had ample leisure to *dream* of a different existence. (p. 118, my italics)

Nevertheless, in *The Doctor's Wife* reading is seen neither as a purely corrupting practice nor as a balm to sentimental problems, but rather as a mirror reflecting the cultural, social and historical context in which Victorian women readers lived. The relationship between Isabel and

Sigismund Smith is reiterated throughout the novel, in order to under-
line the bond that linked the consumers to the producers of literature:
'To say that George did not understand his wife is to say very little.
Nobody, except perhaps Sigismund Smith, had ever yet understood
Isabel' (p. 116).

Isabel's unromantic honeymoon and marriage to Dr Gilbert seem
even more intolerable than her previous boring life as a governess.
Consequently, her married life becomes the beginning (and not the end,
as was the case in traditional Victorian novels) of an increasing dissatisfaction. The meeting with Roland Lansdell, a decadent aristocratic
who writes poems that are 'a sort of mixture of Tennyson and Alfred de
Musset' (p. 130), projects her into a new romantic dimension. Roland
Lansdell's Warncliffe Castle in Mordred Priory stands for the ideal
romantic *locus* contrasted with George Gilbert's realistically and ordi-
narily dull mansion at Graybridge. In this sense, the narrator's repeated
comments on Isabel's tendency to blur the distinctions between reality
and imagination hint at her condition of 'undefended' woman reader:

> Isabel was not a woman of the world. She had read novels while other people
> perused the Sunday papers; and of a world out of a three-volume romance she
> had no more idea than a baby. She believed in a phantasmal universe, created
> out of the pages of poets and romancers. (p. 253)

Assertions like these are reminiscent of *The Female Quixote* and
Northanger Abbey, two novels with which *The Doctor's Wife* has much
in common. Lennox's and Austen's texts were primarily concerned with
the dangers of romance-reading to young untrained minds. But they also
became an implicit illustration of the values represented by the rising
bourgeois society, whose principles coincided with a 'realistic' perception of events. In Lennox's novel, Arabella juxtaposes her female textual
locus (romance) with the male *locus* of empirical narration, while in
the last part of the story she accepts her destiny as a wife, admitting
'the absurdity of her past behaviour, and the contempt and ridicule to
which she now saw plainly she had exposed herself'.[10] Even Catherine
Morland's realisation that the world is not a Radcliffean novel becomes
a self-revelation, and an introspective experience as well. The underly-
ing message in *Northanger Abbey* does not consist of a condemnation
of novel-reading *per se*, but of the conditions which lead women to
be treated as 'imbeciles' (to use John Stuart Mill's expression in *The
Subjection of Women*):

> The visions of romance were over. Catherine was completely awakened.
> Henry's address, short as it had been, had more thoroughly opened her eyes

to the extravagance of her late fancies than all their several disappointments had done. Most grievously was she humbled. Most bitterly did she cry.[11]

Following John Locke's opinions – who in *An Essay Concerning Human Understanding* (1690) warned of the dangers of reading – Victorian debates concerning readers and reading centred on female subjects, considered as naturally weaker and more easily influenced by extreme narrative stimuli. Along with evangelical trust in the importance of the Scriptural word as a way to enlighten life (whose effect was the widespread presence not only of the Bible but also of a huge mass of literature meant for religious guidance), there was a growing suspicion of fictive literature and of romances in particular, which was also of an evangelical origin. The author who signs himself/herself 'A. A.' admonishes on the pages of *The Christian Observer* that the most dangerous quality of many novels is their 'continual feeding of the imagination [. . .] which, once deceived, becomes itself the deceiver; and instead of embellishing life, as it is falsely represented to do, it heightens only imaginative and unattainable enjoyments'.[12] Lennox's, Austen's and Braddon's novels are thus part of a long debate concerning the status of women readers in their relationship with patriarchal controlling practices over their reading choices and tastes. Women were the main targets of advice manuals, informative works and didactic articles, which largely aimed at reaching middle-class girls in their mid-to-late teens, forming a specific literary genre written for women either by men or by women. At their basis there was the circulation and dissemination of a shared paradigm of domesticity, according to which women had to accept their role as 'rulers of the house'. Along with Sarah Stickney Ellis's exemplary domestic manuals entitled *The Women of England* (1838), *The Daughters of England* (1842), *The Mothers of England* (1843) and *The Wives of England* (1843), John Ruskin's reflection on the moral value of the home helps us to understand Victorian women's condition as reading subjects. The Victorian home is described by Ruskin as 'a sacred place, a vestal temple, a temple of the hearth watched by the Household Gods'[13] which women cannot abandon or even *imagine* abandoning.

As Foucault argues in the first volume of his *Histoire de la sexualité*, the most apparent effect of the presence of controlling practices in a society is the abundance of 'discourses' (whether scientific, political, cultural or literary) on a particular topic. The proliferation of a (para)literature written 'for women's sake' must be necessarily approached as the expression of a patriarchal attempt at surveying female subjects in the most complete way possible. Not only did women's reading have to be checked with reference to its moral content, but sometimes even the mere reading of fictional works became a vice because it distracted women from their duties as wives and mothers. The writer who signs himself 'Doubledale' [Alfred Ainger] in 'Books and their Uses' (*Macmillan's Magazine*, I, 1859) considered the craving for books a real 'disease' and condemned the reading of fashionable publications. Only four months later, Francis Palgrave (in 'On Readers in 1760 and 1860', *Macmillan's Magazine*, I, 1860) claimed that reading for reading's sake (that is, the reading of books that were neither scientific nor written for professionals) could be compared to gossiping and in the long run could be dangerous, especially for women. Matilda Pullan in *Maternal Counsels to a Daughter* (1855) suggested a literary diet for those women who had a morbid appetite for fiction, and Lady Laura Ridding in her article 'What Should Women Read?' (in *Women at Home*, 36, 1896) adopted the traditional metaphor of consumption to describe the consequences of the unrestrained love of novels. Along with these publications on the moral consequences of reading, there was a proliferation of scientific (or para-scientific) books dealing with the physical and psychological effects of reading. Of course, the general reading supervisor in all situations had to be the father/husband or his substitute in the medical field, the doctor. Although *The Doctor's Wife* presupposes an intertextual dialogue with this advisory literature, it finally demonstrates that the heroine is not a potentially corrupted woman. Indeed, Braddon's novel contradicts its paratextual premises and deflates the readers' sensational expectations in a way that is not too different from what happens in a later 'Austenian' novel entitled *Vixen* (1879).[14] Rather than being 'poisoned to death' by her readings (like Emma Bovary), Isabel Sleaford survives and triumphs from a moral, social and economic point of view. In this view, *The Doctor's Wife* is not simply a revised English version of *Madame Bovary*, but an articulated interrogation on the relationships between what can be considered as reassuringly 'real' and what is not; between what readers want and what life offers them.[15]

This discussion on novel-reading leads inevitably to the producers of novels as well, embodied in Braddon's text by the sensation writer Sigismund Smith, George Gilbert's old college friend. Given that the connection between these two characters is tinged with irony, Braddon implies that illness (Sigismund) and cure (Gilbert) are more closely related than people would normally imagine. At the beginning of the novel, Sigismund is associated with darkness and dirt, as if to reinforce the critical prejudice surrounding his job as a writer who prostitutes his art:

It was in the most *obscure* corner of the dingiest court in the Temple that George Gilbert found his name. He climbed a very *dirty* staircase, thumping at the end of his portmanteau upon every stair as he went up, until he came to a landing [. . .]

George Gilbert stopped to take breath; and he had scarcely done so, when he was terrified by the apparition of a very *dirty* boy, who slid suddenly down the baluster between the floor above and the landing, and alighted face to face with the young surgeon. The boy's face was very *black* [. . .]

George Gilbert went up, and knocked at the door above. It was a *black* door, and the names of Mr Andrew Morgan and Mr Sigismund Smith were painted upon it in white letters as upon the door-post below.

A pale-faced young man, with a *smudge of ink* upon the end of his nose, and very *dirty* wrist-bands, opened the door. (pp. 9–10, my italics)

In *The Doctor's Wife* Braddon parodies public opinion on sensation writers and reverses it, describing Sigismund as an ordinary person doing an ordinary job. This assertion is reinforced in another chapter (entitled 'A Sensation Author'), devoted to the description of Sigismund's activity. Although the narratorial intrusions and comments are self-ironic, there is a final reflection on the alienation of artists, sometimes forced to sell themselves to the tastes of a voracious public:

Mr Sigismund Smith was a sensation author [. . .] Sigismund Smith was the author of about half a dozen highly-spiced fictions, which enjoyed an immense popularity among the classes who like their literature as they like their tobacco – very strong. Sigismund had never in his life presented himself before the public in a complete form; he appeared in weekly numbers at a penny, and was always so appearing [. . .] He was well paid for his work, and he was contented. He had his ambition, which was to write a great novel and the archetype of this *magnum opus* was the dream which he carried about with him wherever he went, and fondly nursed by night and day. In the mean time he wrote for his public, which was a public that bought its literature in the same manner as its pudding – in penny slices. (pp. 11–12)[16]

Via Sigismund Smith, Braddon pays her literary debt to Balzac, the other French writer she admired (in a letter she refers to her novel's 'grim kind of humour equal to Balzac in its way'), who in *Les illusions perdues* (1837/1843) described the gradual unveiling of truth behind the literary dreams cultivated by Lucien Chardon. Lucien is destroyed by the laws of that bourgeois society of which Paris was an emblem, where fame – according to the unscrupulous bookseller and publisher Dauriat – could be defined as the possibility of earning 'twelve thousand francs in reviews and a thousand more for dinners'.[17] Moreover, in *The Doctor's Wife* Braddon anticipates many of the themes George Gissing will treat in *New Grub Street* (1891), and contradicts George Henry Frazer's idealising mid-century view that '[literature] should be a profession, not a trade. It should be a profession, just lucrative enough to furnish a decent subsistence to its members, but in no way lucrative enough to tempt speculators.'[18] A former student of law, Sigismund Smith is working on his next novel entitled *The Smuggler's Bride* (a title which ironically echoes Braddon's own titles), when George Gilbert enters his room. Like a proto-postmodern narration, on this occasion Braddon is letting her readers enter the sensation writer's workshop. Sigismund is here dramatising the cutting of a throat with a bone paper-knife, which he will include in his novel:

> 'I'm only trying whether a man would cut his throat from right to left, or left to right,' Mr Smith said, in answer to his friend's look of terror; 'it's as well to be true to nature; or as true as one can be, for a pound a page.' (p. 12)

In this scene Braddon suggests that sensation writers are not different from realistic ones, and that the notion of truthfulness can be a matter of individual perspective rather than a question of thematic choice. According to Sigismund Smith, the only difference between a more respected three-volume novel and a sensation serial does not lie in its content but in the number of missing, disappeared or dead bodies. While talking about *The Mystery of Mowbray Manor*, a projected three-volume novel with all the story centred on one single murder, he suggests that it could be easily turned into a penny serial, 'for in penny numbers one body leads on to another, and you never know, when you begin, how far you may be obliged to go' (p. 194). One of the most intriguing narratorial intrusions in *The Doctor's Wife* is inserted after the 'sensational' episode of the vengeance of Isabel's father on Lansdell (who accused him and helped get him condemned for forgery). Notwithstanding the presence of sensational codes (a secret, a villain, a murder, a helpless victim, an apparently peaceful country setting and finally two melodramatic deathbed scenes featuring Lansdell and George Gilbert), the narrator will try to persuade readers that '[this] is not a sensation novel', adding 'I write here what I know to be the truth.' This sentence paradoxically collides with the nature of Braddon's novel as a rewriting of *Madame Bovary* and, therefore, a doubly imaginary fictional text in which she plays with the categories of reality and fiction. It follows that in *The Doctor's Wife* Braddon wanted to suggest that sensation novels helped to look at reality through a new fictional lens, which questioned the foundations of Victorian literary genres.[19]

One of the formal peculiarities of *The Doctor's Wife* is represented by its 'Pre-Raphaelite' style and by its descriptive strategy, which (like French realistic novels) can be also read under the lens of the increasing influence of photography as a new means of depicting reality. During the Victorian age photography influenced not just the way truth was conveyed in terms of its 'reproducibility' by artists and intellectuals, but also determined a total revolution in the relationship between reality and image, original and copy. The advance of photography played a crucial role in changing the perception of events and people, becoming a new kind of hyper-realistic strategy to codify reality according to new visual paradigms. Even though the role of photography was at first to reproduce familial images or at least to record in the most faithful way what happened in the world, it gradually acquired a more complex status. Along with the Pre-Raphaelite views on the detailed reproduction of 'nature' (see Chapter 7), mediated by John Ruskin's reflections on the 'detached eye',[20] Victorian photography testified to a more articulated development of the ways in which reality was subjectively and objectively experienced, perceived and filtered. Photography was not limited to the reproduction of reality, but, from its first appearance in Victorian artistic discourses, began to influence the modalities through which reality was narrated and fictionalised by writers such as Lewis Carroll (in his activity as a photographer and in many of his short stories), Thomas Hardy (for instance in his short story entitled 'An Imaginative Woman' or in *A Laodicean*), William M. Thackeray (whose 'mirror-like narrations' have been compared with photographer Fox Talbot's 'permanent mirrors') and Nathaniel Hawthorne (whose novel *The House of the Seven Gables* features a daguerreotypist depicted as a wizard and a scientist).[21] This relationship between literary and 'photographic' realism, and between textual practices and mechanical reproduction of events, determined a totally new approach to empirical reality. In the words of Nancy Armstrong, in Victorian literature the image 'supplanted writing as the grounding of fiction', and 'the kind of visual description we associate with literary realism refers not to things, but to visual representations of things'.[22]

In this view, *The Doctor's Wife* enhances its metafictional and self-referential nature through its peculiar style and the use of a 'photographic' narrative construction. Braddon's novel echoes Victorian debates concerning the status of realism and the status of photography, especially in view of the changing notion of what their referential object was. If realism in literature was the consensual way in which reality could be perceived by writers and readers, the presence of a constant exchange in Braddon's novel between what is 'truth' and what is 'human creation' (which centres on the consumer and the producer of literature, respectively Isabel and Sigismund) owes a lot to the problems in figural reproduction raised by photography. If on the one hand Braddon's controversial attempt to be realistic in narrating a second-hand story based on Flaubert's *Madame Bovary* is part of the nineteenth-century epistemological debate on representation, on the other through her realistic narrative technique she shows her desire to cultivate an interest in a new form of narration (in which subjective characterisation prevails over plot-making) which is indebted to the lesson of Ruskin's 'detached eye', and to photography as well. Her desire to move the narrator out of the narrating scene, to use visual perception as a guiding principle for character analysis, and her interest in describing the intersection between the 'ideal' and the 'real' are the most recurring elements of her novel. It is thus significant that, in order to illustrate her idea of literary inspiration and creation during the composition of *The Doctor's Wife*, Braddon makes use of a photographic metaphor in one of her letters:

> There he goes gliding through the turbid waters of the brain, such a beautiful shining *rainbow-hued creature*. You try to grasp him, and Lo he is gone [. . .] not so much as a quarter of an inch of his *silvery tail* remains. If some new Dirks & Pepper would only invent an *intellectual photographic apparatus* – by means of which the ghost of the Ideal could be siezed [sic] upon.[23]

Instead of using photography as a documentary instrument to capture everyday reality, Braddon associates it with 'the ghost of the Ideal', deautomatising its power to reproduce only visible experiences. She connects photography with subjective visual control ('siezed [sic] upon'), technology ('apparatus') and individual knowledge ('intellectual').[24] Braddon's idea of style seems to integrate Pre-Raphaelite and French-oriented narrative approaches to the renewed visual paradigms introduced by the latest optical devices (daguerreotypes, stereoscopes and photographic apparatuses), which altered the relation between realism and realistic technique. Indeed, the traditional mimetic association between 'copy' and 'original' was revised (and altered) the moment Louis Daguerre and Fox Talbot replaced the old camera obscura with a totally different visual representation of reality, according to which the connection between 'copy' and 'original' was not linear any more. Moreover, if the artistic drive towards accuracy and empirical truth was seemingly validated by refinements in optical instruments (culminating in photography), its consequences were problematic because '[even] though they provide access to the "real", they make no claim that the real is anything other than a mechanical production. The optical experiences they manufacture are clearly disjunct from the images used in the device.'[25]

On many occasions Braddon uses photographic paradigms to convey the desire (shared by almost all of the male characters of the story) to survey Isabel not only through their control over her as a female reading subject, but also through their male 'archival' gaze. If control is first and foremost exercised through knowledge and classification, the more organised and scientifically structured are these two activities, the more efficacious are the results. As the example of many Victorian medical and criminal institutions proves, this 'archival desire'[26] found a perfect application on 'improper females', mad people and criminals. In late-Victorian Britain this explosion of interest in visuality will lead to a sci-entific textualisation of the photographic image. Phrenological studies, Cesare Lombroso's researches on *l'uomo criminale* and Alphonse Bertillon's anthropometrical science (largely employed by the police) will make extensive use of photos as a means of classifying, in order to justify their own methods both to the general public and to the courts of justice (see Part II, Chapter 6). With the notable exception of Sigismund Smith – who shares Isabel's precarious condition as liminal subject – the male characters in Braddon's *The Doctor's Wife* dramatise the wish to control Isabel Sleaford's desires through a peculiarly photographic approach to her female body. Indeed, Isabel's first appearance in the novel resembles a typical Victorian photo, which portrays a woman reader framed in a bucolic context, scrutinised by the male gaze of her husband. The description of events by the omniscient narrator, whose indirect speech shifts slowly into free indirect speech, suggests that the angle of perception can be identified with George Gilbert's, who is inter-ested in 'framing' Isabel's image in order to control her:

> She was sitting in a basket-chair under one of the pear trees when Sigismund Smith and [George Gilbert] went into the garden to look for her. She was lolling in a low basket chair, with a book on her lap and her chin resting on the palm of her hand, so absorbed by the interest of the page before her she did not even lift her eyes when the two young men went up close to her. She wore a muslin dress, a good deal tumbled and not too clean, and a strip of black velvet was tied round her long throat. Her hair was almost as black as her brother's, and was rolled up in a great loose knot, from which a long untidy curl fell straggling on her white throat – her throat was very white, with the dead, yellowish whiteness of ivory. (p. 23)

Gilbert's interest in visualising Isabel as an object ('to look for her', 'went up close to her') to be 'taken' and contained within a photo-graphic frame is included in a passage characterised by the use of terms associated with death and killing, which enhance the male character's desire to possess her and to turn her into a dead art object ('black velvet tied round her long throat', 'straggling on her white throat', and 'dead yellowish whiteness of ivory').[27]

Even Roland Lansdell, although he is a more sensible and refined man than George Gilbert, will try to control Isabel by turning her into another visual object to be kept under scrutiny. In Lansdell's description there is a large presence of verbs that refer to optical perception:

But he always listened to her, and he always *looked at her* from a *certain position* which he had elected for himself in relation to her. She was a beautiful child; and he, a man of the world, very much tired and worn out by the ordinary men and women of the world, was self-amused, half interested, by her simplicity and sentimentality [. . .] There was no harm, so long as he *held firmly to the position* he had chosen for himself; so long as he *contemplated* this young gushing creature from across all the *width* of his own wasted youth and useless days, so long as he *looked* at her as a bright unapproachable being. (p. 195, my italics)

The Doctor's Wife includes many references to phrenology through the character of Charles Raymond. Like Gilbert and Lansdell, Charles's individual angle of perception makes Isabel a perfect species to be 'photographically' classified. Lamenting Isabel's tendency to read too much and dream too much, Raymond applies a phrenological approach to her deviant behaviour:

> He was thinking that, after all, these bright faculties might not be the best gifts for a woman. It would have been better, perhaps, for Isabel, to have possessed the organ of pudding-making and stocking-darning, if those useful accomplishments are represented by an organ. (p. 83)[28]

The premises of Braddon's text turn into the conclusions of Austen's *Pride and Prejudice*, since marriage in *The Doctor's Wife* is not the end of the story (the last words in Austen's text are 'uniting them') but only its beginning. Braddon's female heroine escapes both its intertextual model (Emma Bovary) and the attempts to classify her as a beautifully-dangerous and potentially-corrupted species of woman reader. *The Doctor's Wife* thus becomes a complex reflection on Victorian novel writing and reading and on the relationship between imagination and reality; between what books offer as fictional truths and what reality is (or appears to be). Braddon's continual questioning on the difficulty of separating the antithetical paradigms of truth and imagination is coherent with her attitude as a writer interested in demystifying binary oppositions of good/bad, male/female, angel/demon and, speaking of literary genres, realism/sensation. In *The Doctor's Wife* she shows her readers that everyday reality can be both reliable and evanescent, like an old Victorian photograph, and that, at the same time, she was continuing her struggle to escape her Audleyan Nemesis.

Notes

1. Letter dated Dec. 1862, in Wolff, '"Devoted Disciple"', p. 10.
2. Eliot, 'Silly Novels by Lady Novelists', p. 454; p. 460. George Eliot's letter

to John Blackwood (dated 11 September 1866) can be taken as an exemplary illustration of her opinions about Braddon: 'And yet I sicken again with despondency under the sense that the most carefully written books lie, both outside and inside people's minds, deep undermost in a heap of trash. I suppose the reason my 6/- editions are never on the railway stalls is [that they] are not so attractive to the majority as "The Trail of the Serpent"; still a minority might sometimes buy them if they were there' (*The George Eliot Letters*, pp. 309–10).

3. For Patrick Brantlinger, Charles Dickens and George Gissing embody two opposite examples of confidence with and isolation from the public and from editors (Brantlinger, *The Reading Lesson*, p. 13). In *Literature, Money and the Market*, Paul Delany notices the strong relationship between 'market forces' and literary activity, adding that '[since] at least the sixteenth century English literature – especially drama and the novel – has been shaped by market forces' (p. 13).

4. Wolff, '"Devoted Disciple"', pp. 19–20; p. 22.

5. Catherine J. Golden argues that '[in] *The Doctor's Wife*, Braddon bowdlerized Gustave Flaubert [. . .] and, in effect, censored her own sensational writing style to be conventional enough to appease her harshest critics' ('Censoring her Sensationalism', p. 30). *The Doctor's Wife* is as much derivative as it is influencing. Many critics agree that it became the source for the creation of George Eliot's Dorothea Brooke in *Middlemarch* (1871), of Thomas Hardy's Eustacia Vye in *The Return of the Native* (1878) and of the assertive heroines depicted by George Moore, who in turn adapted Flaubert's novel in his two short stories 'Emma Bovary' and 'Priscilla and Emily Lofft' (dated 1902 and 1922). Furthermore, the heroine of Moore's *A Midsummer's Wife* (1885) is an avid reader of Braddon's novel (Heilmann, 'Emma Bovary's Sisters'; see also Heywood's 'Miss Braddon's *The Doctor's Wife*' and 'A Source for *Middlemarch*').

6. Tabitha Sparks offers a detailed analysis of the intertextual dialogue between Braddon and Victorian literary genres, concluding that in her desire to gain a credible critical reputation and '[in] the interest of pleasing her public, Braddon attempted to meet the requirements of three incompatible fictional genres' ('Fiction Becomes Her', p. 208).

7. Bakhtin, *The Dialogic Imagination*, p. 6. According to M. A. Rose, '[From] being regarded as a mirror to other texts [. . .] parody has progressed (by its own ability to transform dialectically from which it itself comes) to become a way to an "archaeology of the text", to a self-reflexive mirror of a discourse, to a critique of itself, and, so, too, an analysis [. . .] of concepts of reflection and representation' (*Parody/Metafiction*, p. 187).

8. Braddon, *The Doctor's Wife*, ed. Pykett, p. 7; all quotations will be from this edition. This passage was omitted from the edition of the novel published by Ward, Lock and Tyles (and then by Maxwell, Spencer Blackett and Simpkin and Marshall), and it was included in the serial version (published from January to December 1864 in *Temple Bar*) and in the first three-volume edition, published by Maxwell and Company in 1864.

9. In Margaret Beetham's opinion, '[The] analogy of the consumption of food and the consumption of print [. . .] was endemic in nineteenth-century discourses of reading, particularly female reading [. . .] It was linked to

In Lady Audley's Shadow

another persistent metaphor of reading, particularly the reading of novels, as addictive' ('Women and the Consumption of Print', p. 70). For Henry Longueville Mansel, 'As excitement [. . .] cannot be continually produced without becoming morbid in degree, works of this class manifest themselves as belonging [. . .] to the morbid phenomena of literature [. . .] called into existence to supply the cravings of a diseased appetite, and contributing themselves to foster the disease, and to stimulate the want which they supply' ('Sensation Novels', pp. 482–3).

10. Lennox, *The Female Quixote*, p. 383.

11. Austen, *Northanger Abbey*, p. 159. On the connections between Charlotte Lennox's novel and Austen's *Northanger Abbey* see Kauvar, 'Jane Austen and *The Female Quixote*'.

12. A. A., *The Christian Observer*, p. 512. According to Richard D. Altick, '[Along] with the evangelicals' deep faith in the efficacy of print, however, went an equally profound distrust. Rightly used, books could make men wiser, purer, and more devout; but misapplied, they could prove a snare of the devil' (*The English Common Reader*, pp. 108–9).

13. Ruskin, 'Of Queen's Gardens' (1864), in *Selected Writings*, p. 159. In another passage Ruskin argues that '[the] best romance becomes dangerous if, by its excitement, it renders the ordinary course of life uninteresting, and increases the morbid thirst for useless acquaintance with scenes in which we shall never be called upon to act [. . .] *Keep the modern magazine and novel out of your poor girl's way*: turn her loose into the old library every wet day, and let her alone' (Ibid., p. 164, my italics).

14. Its heroine Violet Tempest is always faithful to her only true love Roderick Vawdrey, despite the fact that her physical traits are typical of the sensual woman (slim figure, red hair and assertive behaviour) of sensation fictions. Ellen Miller Casey notices that '[after] 1870, Braddon moved in accordance with the popular taste from the sensation novel to the domestic one [. . .] With its wealth of detail about the manners and mores of the times, *Vixen* is probably more representative of Braddon's natural taste than the earlier sensation novels' ('"Other's People Prudery"', p. 74). Like *The Doctor's Wife*, *Vixen* 'is a novel that teases readers with sensational expectation, but in the end Braddon reveals that generic fashions have changed or at least should be questioned' (Sears, 'Mary Elizabeth Braddon and the "Combination Novel"', p. 50).

15. According to Kate Flint, in *The Doctor's Wife* 'we meet with the most sustained investigation of reading in relation to sensation fiction' (*The Woman Reader*, p. 288).

16. In one of her letters to Edward Bulwer Lytton, written during the composition of *The Doctor's Wife*, Braddon refers to her long-time planned masterpiece in similar terms: 'This unwritten novel always seems to me destined to become my magnum opus [. . .] I can see the scenes. I compose the dialogue [. . .] I can never write anything half as good, for that Archetype is a perfect eel in the matter of slipperiness' (19 September 1863, qtd Wolff, '"Devoted Disciple"', p. 18). As far as the image of literature as consumable product is concerned, in another letter to Edward Bulwer Lytton (dated May 1863) Braddon admits she has learnt 'to look at everything in a mercantile sense, & to write solely for the circulating library reader, whose palette [sic]

requires strong meat, & is not very particular as to the quality thereof' (Ibid., p. 14).

17. Georg Lukàcs asserts that in *Lost Illusions* Balzac dramatises the transformation of literature into a commodity: 'From the writer's ideas, emotions and convictions to the paper on which he writes them down, everything is turned into a commodity that can be bought and sold. Nor is Balzac content merely to register in general terms the ideological consequences of the rule of capitalism – he uncovers every stage (the periodical press, the theatre, the publishing industry, etc. . . .) together with all the factors governing the process' (*Studies in European Realism*, p. 49).

18. Frazer, 'The Condition of Authors in England', p. 285.

19. For Marlene Tromp, 'sensation both derived and revised realist fiction', and 'we might read sensation as a mimetic reformation of the master text of realism' (*The Private Rod*, p. 3; p. 104). If, according to Patrick Brantlinger, '[the] development of the sensation novel marks a crisis in the history of literary realism, in part because of its challenge to the naive empiricism or observation that serves such realism as its epistemology' (*The Reading Lesson*, p. 161), for Richard Nemesvari '[by] learning what sensation fiction was, Victorian readers learned what realist fiction was (and vice versa), and could thus partake in constructing the horizon of expectation required' ('"Judged by a Purely Literary Standard"', p. 19).

20. 'The moment [the artist] can make us think that he has done nothing, that nature has done all, that moment he becomes ennobled, he proves himself great. As long as we remember him, we cannot respect him. We honour him most when we most forget him. He becomes great when he becomes invisible' (Ruskin, *The Complete Works of John Ruskin*, vol. 3, p. 170). On the influence of photography on Pre-Raphaelitism, see Smith, *Victorian Photography* and Bartram, *The Pre-Raphaelite Camera*.

21. For an analysis of the intersemiotic dialogue between photography and Victorian literature, see Mavor, *Pleasures Taken*; Jackson, 'Photography as Style'; Lodge, 'Thomas Hardy and Cinematographic Form'; and Spiegel, *Fiction and the Camera Eye*.

22. Armstrong, *Fiction in the Age of Photography*, p. 3. According to Jennifer Green-Lewis '[photography] itself slides precipitously in writing and conversation from noun to verb – a photograph, to photograph – from image to praxis, from viewer to view and back again to the eye of the lens. This tendency dates from the mid-nineteenth century, when photography became useful as a site for the discussion of topics beyond itself' (*Framing the Victorians*, p. 19).

23. Letter to Bulwer Lytton, dated 19 September 1863, qtd in Wolff, '"Devoted Disciple"', p. 18. Henry Dirks (1806–73) invented an apparatus for creating optical illusions and illustrated Charles Dickens's short story 'The Haunted Man' (1848).

24. For Roland Barthes photography is denotative and connotative, an image and the code of that image, in a paradoxical co-existence of 'two messages, the one without a code (the photographic analogue), the other with a code (the "art", or the treatment, or the "writing", or the rhetoric, of the photograph)' ('The Photographic Message', p. 19).

25. Crary, *Techniques of the Observer*, p. 132.

26. For a Foucaultian reading of the 'archival' use of photography, see Sekula, 'The Body and the Archive' and Tagg, 'Power and Photography'.

27. George describes his dreams of loving Isabel not as a human being but more as a pictured image, a photo to be contemplated: 'He was thinking of another face, which he had only seen for a few brief hours, and which he was perhaps never again to look upon; a pale girlish countenance, *framed* with dense black hair; a pale face, out of which there looked large solemn eyes, like stars that glimmer faintly through the twilight shadows' (pp. 50–1, my italics).

28. Later in the novel, Raymond will continue to refer to Isabel in phrenological terms, saying that 'her head is a good one, though by no means so well-balanced as it might be' (p. 341).

Chapter 9

'All That is Solid Melts into Air': *Phantom Fortune* and the Ghosts of Capitalism

A spectre is haunting the pages of Mary Elizabeth Braddon's *Phantom Fortune* (1883) – the spectre of Karl Marx. Although this misquotation from *The Manifesto of the Communist Party* (1848) seems paradoxical when applied to a Victorian novelist who was far from being a Socialist,[1] Marx's rhetoric (on a textual level) and Marx's 'political unconscious' (on an ideological level) haunt Braddon's novel in unpredictable ways and define its themes, as well as its context of discussion. *Phantom Fortune* is another attempt to move beyond the Lady Audley paradigm, in order to invigorate Braddon's narrative through the influence of French realism and the interest in new social questions. Apart from the intertextual dialogue with novelists such as Émile Zola and Honoré de Balzac in the critical depiction of London society, Braddon's novel dramatises the (traumatic) transition from a world economically dependent upon a 'material' notion of wealth in a rigid social context to a modern capitalistic society, in which the 'phantom-like' nature of money and of 'fetishised' commodities reflect the changing epistemology and the social permeability of late-Victorian England.

Phantom Fortune opens during the late thirties with the description of Lord Maulevrier's social fall. Accused of various crimes as former governor of the Madras Presidency in India, Lord Maulevrier dies in the course of his journey to his voluntary exile in the Grasmere Vale, accompanied by his wife and the *factotum* James Steadman. With a chronological shift, the novel reopens forty years after in the isolated familial setting of Fellside Manor near Windermere (not far from William Wordsworth's tomb), where old Lady Maulevrier lives with her two nieces Mary Haselden (intelligent and independent) and Lesbia Haselden (beautiful and spoiled), along with the young and impulsive nephew Maulevrier and the trustful Steadman. Things start to change when John Hammond, a friend of young Maulevrier's, visits Fellside and falls in love with Lesbia, proposing to her. Lady Maulevrier opposes the marriage and sends Lesbia away for a 'change of air' with the rich and vain Scottish countess Georgina Kirkbank. The two women's journey takes them to Cannes and then to London, where Lesbia becomes the 'beauty of the day' in fashionable Arlington Road. In the meantime the Raja of Bisnagar, Louis Asoph, arrives at Fellside and accuses old Lord Maulevrier of having stolen (with the help of his adulterous mother) the treasure of his dead father forty years before. During a walk to Helvellyn to visit the Red Tarn and Wordsworth's tomb, Hammond proposes to Mary, who agrees to marry him. Mary's meeting with a mysterious old man, who knows many things about the Maulevrier family, causes the stern opposition of Steadman, who advises her not to meet that repulsive man any more and tells her that he is a lunatic relative. Just before the wedding, Hammond confesses to Mary that he is none other than the Earl of Hartfield in disguise, and possessed of a fortune. In the meantime the old and mysterious man who lives near Steadman's garden opens two big trunks of books in front of Mary and Hammond, which contain gold and jewels, offering them as a wedding dowry. In London, Horace Smithson, a came-from-nowhere capitalist famous in the Stock Exchange and capable of making money from practically anything (from gunpowder to slave-trading), proposes to Lesbia, who soon after receives an incredibly high bill for her enormous expenses in luxury goods. Lesbia is thus forced to accept Smithson's second proposal out of economic necessity. Soon after, Lady Lesbia makes the acquaintance of Lord Gomez de Montesma, a rich and romantic Spanish adventurer who was born in Cuba. She immediately falls in love and flirts with this man who is reputed to be a villainous cheat, a bigamist and a slave-trader. During Lesbia and Gomez's trip to France (where they are to be married) on board the *Cayman*, they come across the steam-boat *Persephone* where Hartfield and young Maulevrier, who were chasing them, succeed in convincing Lesbia of Gomez's bad reputation. All of the characters go back to Fellside, where some days afterwards Steadman dies and Lady Maulevrier falls seriously ill. Here the repellent old man discloses his identity as Lord Maulevrier, revealing that the body buried in the Earl's family chapel is Robert Haswell's, a young man from America who died during Lord Maulevrier's stay near Great Langdale on his journey back to Fellside. Lady Maulevrier dies soon after this revelation and everybody agrees to conceal the secret from the world, giving the trunks back to their original owners. The novel closes with Lesbia, now an unmarried and repentant middle-aged lady, teaching young Maulevrier's daughters the pros and cons of London life in high social circles.

Braddon's *Phantom Fortune* is built on a series of chronological, topological, economic and socio-cultural dichotomies: the past (represented by the old aristocracy) is juxtaposed with the present (where social mobility has definitively entered Victorian society and culture), the country estate (which topologically summarises the old values and principles) with metropolitan London (the site of modernity), the late Romantic age (with Wordsworth still alive) with the late Victorian age (where the poet's tomb is only a tourist attraction), the pre-capitalistic accumulation of wealth (represented by Lord Maulevrier as the epitome of the traditional colonial 'usurper')[2] with capitalism (Horace Smithson and Gomez de Montesma). Like many other novels by Braddon, where the categories of right and wrong, moral and immoral, lawful and unlawful can be blurred, all of these stark antitheses will finally be called into question, showing that the material crimes of the past are often projected into the immaterial and 'phantom-like' crimes of the present. As for the novel's characters, Mary embodies traditional familial values associated with nature, juxtaposed with Lesbia as the expression of society[3] and as the exemplary consumer of commodities. Mary and Lesbia are characterised through reference to pictorial images that define their attitudes and their moral status. Like Lady Audley in her notorious portrait (see Chapter 7), the vain Lesbia is also described as a Pre-Raphaelite beauty ('She was to be painted by Millais next year'), while Mary is compared to Joshua Reynolds's comely subjects ('What can any man think except that she is as lovely as the finest of Reynold's [sic] portraits, [. . .] or any example you please to name of womanly loveliness?').[4]

In *Phantom Fortune* Lord Maulevrier is the typical villain whose misdeeds are of a 'colonial' rather than of an 'imperialistic' nature, based on his fraudulent dealings in India. He is accused of having had 'dark transactions' with the native princes probably under pressure from 'a beautiful Ranee, a Creature as fascinating and as unscrupulous as Cleopatra' (p. 9). For this reason he has to answer at the bar of the House of Lords, like Warren Hastings, the first governor-general of India fifty years before, to whom Lord Maulevrier is repeatedly compared.[5] The 'phantom fortune' concealed for forty years in the peaceful retreat of Audley Road (a familiar-sounding name for Braddon readers) is a corrupting moral and economic heredity, which infects the family's life to its roots. Braddon also shows her debt to Wilkie Collins's *The Moonstone* (1868), in which the stolen Indian diamond brings 'a legacy of trouble' to the people who steal it, although she seems to be less ambivalent than Collins on the moral responsibilities of the British rulers. It follows that in *Phantom Fortune* Braddon dramatises a form of 'reverse colonization' (as Stephen Arata defines it) according to which '[in] the marauding, invasive Other, British culture sees its own imperial practice mirrored back in monstrous forms'.[6] This allusion to 'reverse colonization' figures prominently with reference to Gomez de Montesma in the cultural and chronological context of the late eighteen-seventies, where the usurping (colonial) attitudes of the past are replaced by the more hegemonic practices of the (imperial) present, whose economical system is characterised by the 'ghost-like' flow of capital.[7] With his 'olive tint, the eyes of deepest black, the grand form of the head and perfect chiselling of the features' which could belong only 'to the scion of an old Castilian race' (p. 356), Gomez is modelled upon the stereotypical exotic and dangerous alien of imperial (Gothic) fictions and is partially inspired by the Cuban bigamist and villain Captain Manuel in Collins's *Armadale* (1866). In the course of the novel, Gomez denounces the fact that even British capitalists such as Horace Smithson profited from and continue to enjoy the advantages of past colonial crimes, which still condition the economy of late-Victorian England in a more subtle, invisible and 'ghostly' way:

'Everybody in Cuba had a finger in the African trade, before your British philanthropy spoiled it. Mr Smithson made sixty thousand pounds in that line. *It was the foundation of his fortune* [. . .] There are some very black stories in Cuba against poor Smithson. He will never go there again.' (p. 443, my italics)

It is emblematic, therefore, that in order to retrace the criminal acts committed by Gomez de Montesma young Maulevrier does not ask for the help of a traditional detective but of a political economist named Fitzpatrick, who wrote a 'great book upon "Protection *versus* Free trade"' (p. 421). This fact suggests that the new crimes are of an economic rather than of a sexual or familial nature, as was the case with traditional sensation fictions.

Braddon's decision to focus on the late thirties and on the late seventies as the two chronological reference points implies that what happened 'in between' represented a revolutionary change in British society, economy and culture. Indeed, the beginning of the eighteen-forties testified to the rising of the so-called 'middling-classes', together with the increasing fusion of bourgeois landowners with old aristocracy. At the same time the social uprisings and unrest throughout Europe (particularly in France, Germany and Italy) found its most cogent expression in Friedrich Engels's *The Condition of the Working Classes in England* (1845) and in Karl Marx and Friedrich Engels's *The Manifesto of the Communist Party* (1848), whose ideas and rhetoric permeated Victorian England in direct and indirect ways. From a literary point of view, if on the one hand Benjamin Disraeli acknowledged the presence of two socially opposite 'nations' in his *Sybil, or the Two Nations* (1845), on the other Thomas Carlyle denounced (from a conservative point of view) the 'cash nexus' as the prime mover of human relations. In the years that followed, politicians, intellectuals and thinkers gradually came into contact with Marx's reflections on the principles governing capitalistic society summarised in *Capital* (1867). Marx's book was published less than a decade before Queen Victoria was elected Empress of India (1876) through an Act of Parliament, sanctioning the transition from a colonial to an imperial (and capitalistic) economy in Victorian Britain. In a country that hailed the triumph of Samuel Smiles's self-help ideology, promoted an increasing social mobility and was about to become an empire, Marx's thoughts had a slow but steady introduction which reached its peak in 1883 – the year Braddon's novel was serialised – when all of his major publications were (sometimes incompletely) translated. In the words of the theologian and journalist W. Douglas Mackenzie, '[It] is felt by every student and every statesman, even by every one who reads the newspapers, that Socialism is "in the air".'[8] The 'spectre of Communism' Marx evokes at the beginning of the *Manifesto* thus determines the literary and cultural context of Braddon's novel. Consequently, in *Phantom Fortune* Marx's 'phantoms' (the commodities as material objects that tend to become 'mystic' and 'fetishist' entities) haunt the lives of its main dramatis personae in a specular way, from the late-Victorian capitalist who produces commodities (Smithson) to the consumer of luxury goods (Lesbia).

In comparing the past to the present, Braddon's characters both share and challenge the rapidly changing values, the increasing commodification of everyday life and the multiple modalities in which capital is masked, recycled and reduced to an invisible and 'spectral' entity. In a letter Lady Maulevrier writes to Lesbia after the girl's debut at Cannes, and before her success in London, the old lady makes the following remarks:

> '*All things are changed: opinions, manners, creeds, morals even*. Acts that were crimes in my day are now venial errors – opinions that were scandalous are now the mark of "advanced thought". I should be too formal for this easy-going age, should be ridiculed as old-fashioned and narrow minded, should put you to the blush a dozen times a day by my prejudices and opinions.' (p. 169, my italics)

The opinions of Lady Maulevrier as a representative of an old social and economical system paradoxically recall Marx's and Engels's words in *The Manifesto of the Communist Party*:

Constant revolutionizing of production, uninterrupted disturbance of all social conditions, everlasting uncertainty and agitation distinguish the bourgeois epoch from all the earlier ones. All fixed, fast-frozen relations, with their train of ancient and venerable prejudices and opinions, are swept away, all new-formed ones become antiquated before they can ossify. *All that is solid melts into air, all that is holy is profaned, and man is at last combined to face with other senses, his real conditions of life, and his relations with his kind.*[9]

Despite the fact that Braddon's novel does not convey an explicit political message, it is however necessary to try and uncover the 'ideology of form' that determines its themes. According to Fredric Jameson, '[It] is in detecting the traces of that uninterrupted narrative, in restoring to the surface of the text the repressed and buried reality of this fundamental history, that the doctrine of a political unconscious finds its function and its necessity.'[10] In the case of *Phantom Fortune*, the 'socially symbolic theme', embodied by Lesbia's initiation to and relation with the world of London society (and by Mary's renunciation of it), becomes one of the 'forms' behind which the 'ideology' is concealed. As far as characterisation is concerned, Mary has a strict relationship with the natural setting of the Grasmere vale, with its Romantic heritage represented by Wordsworth and, economically speaking, with a rural or at least pre-capitalistic society, where money and tangible goods did not circulate but were simply accumulated from generation to generation. Unlike Mary, Lesbia 'capitalises' herself and 'circulates' in the social 'market', enjoying all of its (expendable) commodities in fashionable late-Victorian London. The antithesis between Mary and Lesbia thus dramatises the ideological, social and economic transition from a naturalistic Romantic culture to a consumerist late-Victorian one, where the principle of credit ruled supreme and whose mode of artistic reproduction mirrored the works of Balzac and Zola.[11]

Lesbia, the consumer of commodities, usually enjoys the company of old Lady Kirkbank, who tries to conceal her age behind a series of 'unnatural' artifices and in a way embodies all the vacuity of London social circles. Here, too, Braddon returns to a pictorial code in order to criticise social conventions, saying that 'if Lady Maulevrier looked like a picture of the Escurial, Lady Kirkbank resembled a caricature in *La Vie Parisienne*'. However, despite Lady Kirkbank's efforts, 'age was made all the more palpable by the artifice which would have disguised it' (p. 113). Like the typical West End shopper, whose condition as *flâneuse* shifted between that of a lady interested in the latest Parisian fashion and a 'streetwalker',[12] Lesbia Haselden epitomises the female consumer of commodities whose life is nothing but a sequence of seemingly

pleasurable events. According to Marx, this relationship between production and consumption takes place because in capitalistically-based
societies '[production] creates the material, as external object, for consumption; consumption creates the need, as internal object, as aim, for
production. Without production no consumption; without consumption, no production'.[13] Always eager to walk aimlessly around London's
fashionable streets and to enter its shops, Lesbia anticipates, among
other things, George Gissing's Nancy Lord in *In The Year of Jubilee*
(1894):

> She flung herself with all her heart and mind into the amusement of the
> moment; she knew neither weariness nor satiety [. . .] And every hour was so
> occupied by pleasure engagements that it was difficult to squeeze in an occa-
> sional morning for shopping – necessary to go to the shops sometimes, or *one
> would not know how many things one really wants* – or for an indispensable
> interview with the dressmaker. Those mornings at the shops were hardly the
> least agreeable of Lesbia's hours. To a girl brought up in one perpetual tête-
> à-tête with green hill-shades and silvery watercolours, the West End shops
> were as gardens of Eden, as Aladdin Caves, as *anything, everything that is
> rapturous and intoxicating.* (p. 231, my italics)[14]

Although magazines such as *The Lady* or *The Queen* suggested how
to dress and where to buy things, many other Victorian periodicals
viewed this interest in independent shopping unfavourably, focusing
on the effects of this practice on middle-class female customers. For
instance, the anonymous writer of an article in *The Graphic* compares
the shoppers' attraction for (and dependence upon) the goods on display
in Whiteley's famous department store to a sexual encounter:

> [What] is the effect? They have not left the halls of temptation; the voice of
> the charmer still rings in their ears [. . .] They return once more to the slaugh-
> ter [. . .] and in the wild and reckless period that follows things are done in
> a financial way which would make the angels weep [. . .] The afternoon's
> excitement has [. . .] all the attraction of a delightful dream, with a slight dash
> of an orgy, leaving a lingering pleasure even over repentance.[15]

Laura's hectic life in London (the love for the latest Parisian fashion,
the flow of people in shops, the ceaseless traffic and a life generally made
more easy and endurable by the advance of technology) reflects that
'experience of modernity' which Marshall Berman describes in the following terms:

> To be modern is to find ourselves in an environment that promises us adven-
> ture, power, joy, growth, transformation of ourselves and the world – and,
> at the same time, that threatens to destroy everything we have, everything we
> know, everything we are [. . .] – to be modern is to be part of a universe in
> which, as Marx said, 'all that is solid melts into air'.[16]

In many of her previous novels, including *Lady Audley's Secret*, Braddon underlined that Victorian women were the principal consumers of commodities, from ordinary products to luxurious ones.[17] Of course, this interest in the possession of material goods was strongly connected to the changing social structure of late-Victorian England, where social status and above all gentility was not related exclusively to a superiority in morality, education and refinement, but to the possibility of purchasing and showing off luxury goods. The perfect wife of early-Victorian England became the perfect lady who was only partially interested in child care and housekeeping; rather, her aim consisted in personal 'ornamentation' as a sign of status enhancement. This reflection applies to those middle-class wives who, through the purchasing of products (from highly-refined dresses to beverages such as hot chocolate and tea) could have the illusion of being 'ladies', as well as to the women from the upper classes who needed to be fashionable and pleasurable to enter aristocratic circles.[18] The proliferation of fashion advertisements in the 1880s and 1890s created a close relationship between the pull to 'beautification' exerted over women, their aspiration to ascend the social ladder and the capillary presence of consumerism.[19] Among the many products targeted at women in department stores and in richly-adorned boutiques, French dresses and luxurious commodities were, along with goods imported from the exploited colonies, the most fashionable and desirable objects for middle- and upper-class female consumers. These goods were complex and articulated signifying systems associated with the potential gentility women like Lesbia (and, before her, Lady Audley) were seeking to attain.

The birth of the figure of the modern consumer pre-supposed the creation of a new system of consumption, whose most emblematic expression in Victorian Britain was the Great Exhibition at Hyde Park held in 1851. By integrating international commercial exchange with spectacle, the Great Exhibition became a paradigmatic model that inspired shoppers and lured consumers. The new glass windows of London shops, whose contents Lesbia enjoys and buys in the fashionable West End, were the most visible signs of this commercial, architectonic and 'libidinal' revolution. Each type and size of product was enclosed and simultaneously put on display in a sort of miniaturised version of the Crystal Palace. This 'spectacularisation' of commodities enhanced the predominance of representation over materiality that allowed (and still allows) capitalistic societies to survive and proliferate: 'Like a modern shopping mall, the Crystal Palace set up an elaborate traffic pattern for channelling people around things.'[20] The 'nation of shopkeepers' Adam Smith alluded to in *The Wealth of Nations* (1776) was slowly turning into Guy Debord's 'Society of Spectacle' and into Jean Baudrillard's consumer society, interested in the acquisition of an object 'without an object', and in the enjoyment of pleasure rather than in the satisfaction of a material need. Lesbia's desires as a consumer ('[It is] necessary to go to the shops sometimes, or one would not know how many things one really wants', p. 231) are not satisfied by a specific commodity but gradually lose their material – in Marx's vocabulary, their 'sensual' – quality, becoming 'phantasmatic' to the point that Lesbia loses control over the real amount of money she is spending. Using a term Braddon will include in the title of her novel, in *Capital* Marx underlines the fact that in capitalistic society material goods acquire a 'phantom-like objectivity', describing commodities as follows:

[An] extremely obvious, trivial thing. But its analysis brings out that it is a very strange thing, abounding in metaphysical subtleties [. . .] So far as it is a use-value, there is nothing mysterious about it [. . .] But as soon as it emerges as a commodity, it changes into a thing which transcends sensuousness.[21]

Commodities are not perceived by consumers (like Lesbia) as mere objects but tend to the status of 'mystical' creations that are 'fetishised'. Borrowing an expression Jacques Derrida uses in *Spectres of Marx* (1993), it is possible to deal with Braddon's 'hauntology' in *Phantom Fortune*, given that this novel seems to be 'talking with the dead' and seems to be evoking those same 'phantoms' of commodities, described as ambiguous fetishist creations, that Marx denounced in *Capital*.[22]

Lesbia's destiny can be read as a parable of the Victorian consumer's fall. An undefended female buyer, she puts herself in the hands of the unscrupulous Jewish dressmaker Madame Seraphine:

Lesbia's first sensation upon having this accomplished person presented to her was one of shrinking and disgust. There was something sinister in the sallow face, the small shrewd eyes, and long hooked nose, the crooked figure, and the claw-shaped hands. (p. 236)[23]

Seraphine convinces Lesbia to buy luxury clothes and accessories on credit, until her final bill amounts to 'twelve hundred and ninety-three pounds seventeen and sixpence' (p. 282) spent in eight weeks. By repeatedly suggesting Lesbia paint her face ('Seraphine ventured to suggest that she would be all the better for a little accentuation of her eyebrows and darkening of her lashes', pp. 236–7), Madame Seraphine anticipates her future prostitution on the London marriage market (prostitutes were in fact usually described as 'the painted women').[24] The connection between marriage, money and Lesbia's sale to Horace Smithson is summarised by Braddon in this brief but meaningful dialogue: '"Will you, Lesbia?,"' [Smithson] repeated earnestly; and she answered softly "Yes." That one brief syllable was more like a sigh than a spoken word, and it seemed to her *as if in the utterance of that syllable the three thousand pounds had been paid*' (p. 300, my italics).

This 'girl of the period' (to use Eliza Lynn Linton's famous phrase) turns into a 'mercenary woman', which was a subject of analysis in the New Woman Fiction of the 1890s by writers such as George Moore and Mona Caird.[25] The final transition of Lesbia from consumer of commodities to consumable product on sale on the Victorian marriage market finds emblematic expression in the image of her photo displayed in London shop windows. Dressed in the latest fashion and ready to be 'put on display' by Smithson on public occasions like another of his prestigious possessions, Lesbia turns into a luxury good:

> Lesbia's Chaumount costume was a success. The women praised it, the men stared and admired. The dark-blue silken jersey, sparkling with closely studded indigo beads, fitted the slim graceful figure as a serpent's scales fit the serpent. The coquettish little blue silk toque, the careless cluster of gold-coloured poppies, against the glossy brown hair [. . .] were all perfect after their fashion; and Mr Smithson felt that the liege lady of his life, the woman he meant to marry nilly willy, would be the belle of the race-course. Everybody in London had heard of Lady Lesbia Haselden. *Her photograph was in all the West-End windows*, was enshrined in the albums of South Kensington and Clapham, Maida Vale and Haverstock Hill. (p. 297, my italics)[26]

Braddon's decision to experiment with new themes and topics is strongly related to her desire to move away from the Lady Audley paradigm and to take inspiration from other literary genres, both national and international, based on detailed characterisation rather than on plot making and melodramatic effects. Her attempt to renew her style was noticed by many contemporary reviewers who, despite the generally negative reception of *Phantom Fortune*, underlined these novelties.[27] As far as Braddon's literary sources are concerned, she owes much to W. M. Thackeray's *Vanity Fair* but, above all, to George Eliot's *Daniel Deronda* (1876), where Gwendolen Harleth was forced to accept Grandcourt's proposal out of economic necessity, becoming a sort of precious jewel owned by her husband. Like Gwendolen, Lesbia reveals her double nature as a consumer of commodities and a consumable luxury on display and sale. Apart from Gwendolen's allusive surname ('Harleth' recalls the word 'harlot'), Eliot and Braddon describe in detail the two women's richly ornamented dresses as seducing signs. Gwendolen and Lesbia are compared to ambiguous, strange, liminal and even dangerous creatures such as snakes ('The dark-blue silken jersey

[. . .] fitted the slim graceful figure as a serpent's scales fit the serpent', p. 297), and Nereids:

> The Nereid in sea-green robes and silver ornaments, with a pale sea-green feather fastened in silver falling backward over her green hat and light-brown hair, was Gwendolen Harleth. She was under the wing or rather soared by the shoulder of the lady who sat by her at the roulette-table.[28]

The influence of *Daniel Deronda* emerges when Lesbia's first real debt to Smithson is occasioned by a game of cards. At the beginning of Eliot's novel Daniel Deronda's first meeting with Gwendolen takes place at a roulette-table, where she receives a letter which reveals her economic ruin. Despite their differences, these two women are consumers of goods who become objects to be consumed, sold on the Victorian marriage market, both executioners and victims of an economic system that is not too different from the one described by Roland Barthes in *The Fashion System*:

> This unavoidable presence of human speech [in advertisements on dress] is clearly not an innocent one. Why does Fashion utter clothing so abundantly? Why does it interpose, between the object and its user, such a luxury of words, such a network of meaning? The reason is, of course, an economic one. *Calculating, industrial society is obliged to form consumers who don't calculate.*[29]

From a formal and narrative point of view, the main sources of inspiration for Braddon's *Phantom Fortune* were French realists such as Émile Zola, for crude naturalism, and Honoré de Balzac, who aimed at portraying (among other things) the moral ambivalence of the rising bourgeois classes. Braddon's rewriting of Flaubert's *Madame Bovary* entitled *The Doctor's Wife* (see Chapter 8) and novels such as *The Golden Calf* (1883), modelled on Zola's *L'Assommoir* (1877), demonstrate the great influence of French novelists upon her. At the time of the composition of *Phantom Fortune*, Braddon was reputed in England to be an expert on French literature, and she was even commissioned to write an article on French novels by the *Fortnightly Review* in 1885 (which remained unpublished because she did not completely share the condemnatory point of view the editor required). As far as *Phantom Fortune* is concerned, Braddon's biographer Robert Lee Wolff finds some similarities with Zola's *La Curée* (1871–2) in the description of Lesbia's fashionable life in London, in the girl's engagement to Smithson and in her elopement with Gomez.[30] Braddon's novel was published only two years after Zola's *Au Bonheur des dames* (*The Ladies' Paradise*, 1881), the eleventh in the Rougon-Macquart cycle, in which Zola focused on Parisian department stores as the new 'commercial cathedrals'. In this novel Zola dealt with the new shopping market, whose clients (and victims) were assertive women of modest origin such as the salesgirl Denise Baudu, whom the owner of the department store tries to seduce:

> The high plate-glass door, facing the Place Gaillon, reached the mezzanine floor and was surrounded by elaborate decorations covered with gilding. Two allegorical figures, two laughing women with bare breasts thrust forward, were unrolling a scroll bearing the inscription: *The Ladies' Paradise* [. . .] With its series of perspectives, with the display on the ground floor and the plate-glass window of the mezzanine floor, behind which could be seen all the intimate life of the various departments, the spectacle seemed to Denise to be endless.[31]

Besides these thematic, rather than technical, similarities *Phantom Fortune* is also inspired by Balzac's peculiar form of realism, which is different from Zola's vivisectionist-like depiction of social life. Indeed, Braddon's novel is suspended between the necessities of the 'novel-with-a-secret' and the urgency to give events an almost symbolic value. For instance, Lesbia's gradual loss of innocence in the London world reminds the reader of Sigismund Smith's fall from artistic grace in *The Doctor's Wife* (1864) and, before him, of Lucien Chardon's slow but inevitable decline in the corrupted Parisian literary scene in Balzac's *Les illusions perdues* (1837–43). Like the reactionary Balzac, Braddon was an open-minded Tory who was capable of portraying and reflecting upon the crisis of traditional social structures in light of the rising social and Socialist turmoil. From a narrative point of view, the close relation-ship between the 'realism' of French novels and of Braddon's *Phantom Fortune* reflects the crisis of the old aristocracy and the consolidation of capitalism, since both elements are mutually dependent. In this sense, money represents a sort of common denominator which is related to what Peter Brooks calls 'the fluidity and vaporousness of things in an economy that can swiftly move from boom to bust and then recycle'.[32]

Horace Smithson is the quintessential came-from-nowhere capitalist who owns a 'phantom fortune' that is as compromising as the one accumulated by Lord Maulevrier. Braddon seems to share Marx's scepticism about the new rising classes, according to which if on the one hand the bourgeois class had the merit of having destroyed the old mediaeval society, on the other the whole existence of the rising middle-class was focused on the acquisition of money:

> The bourgeois, in its reign of barely a hundred years, has created more massive and more colossal power than have all previous generations put together [. . .] The bourgeois has torn apart the many feudal ties that bound men to their 'natural superiors' and left no other bond between man and man than naked interest, than callous cash payment [. . .] The bourgeois has torn

away from the family its sentimental veil and turned the family relation into a pure money relation.[33]

Smithson's behaviour and attitudes are those of the typical late-Victorian capitalist who accumulates material (and political) power with no moral restraints, selling his surplus goods to distant colonies in order to make his capital circulate worldwide. Like many white-collar villains in other Victorian novels,[34] Smithson represents the aspiring bourgeoisie easily entering high-class circles and the London political world, whose crimes – such as slave-trading and dubious economic transactions – are not clearly 'visible'. His capacity to sell his products 'at an almost magical rate' echoes Marx's opinions on the 'magical' and 'mystic' quality of commodities:

> It was in the rise and fall of commodities rather than of stocks and shares that Horace Smithson had made his money. He had exercised occult influences upon the trade of the great city, of the world itself, whereof that city is in a manner the keystone. Iron had risen or fallen at his beck. At the breath of his nostrils cochineal had gone up in the market *at an almost magical rate*, as if the whole civilised world had become suddenly intent upon dyeing its garments red, nay, as if even the naked savages of the Gold Coast and the tribes of Central Africa were bent on staining their dusky skins with the bodies of the female coccus. (p. 241, my italics)

Smithson succeeds in buying Lesbia only because of his riches, sharing (although from a different ideological point of view) Marx's opinion on money as 'the external, universal means and power [. . .] to change representation into reality and reality into mere representation', transforming 'real human and natural faculties into mere abstract representations' as well as 'real imperfections and fancies' into 'real faculties and powers'.[35] The down-to-earth expression of a material possession and an arbitrary sign as well, money was in the Victorian age a referential signifying system which had been gradually losing material form, first with the transition from gold to paper currency (as the example of Lord Maulevrier's fortune demonstrates), and then to capital, as in Smithson's intangible economic transactions. This phenomenon became particularly striking after the introduction of cheques and other modern banking practices, which contributed to enhancing the 'spectral' potentialities of capitals.[36]

The casual incursions of a mysterious and loathsome old man (who is Lord Maulevrier in disguise) suffering from 'fits of madness' – according to a recognisable Lady Audley paradigm – prepare readers for the unveiling of the secret. At the end of *Phantom Fortune* Braddon suggests that the peaceful and isolated Fellside Manor is corrupted at its very core, identified by the concealed wooden cases which contain Indian riches. Like the cursed jewels in Collins's *The Moonstone*, Braddon's cursed riches haunt the places considered by the characters as the safest ones. The building of rooms and walls around the wooden cases coming from India is Lady Maulevrier's unsuccessful attempt to bury the nucleus of past crimes. After the secret is finally revealed, young Maulevrier accuses Lady Maulevrier of having deceived him and of having built the past and present family fortunes upon corrupted and insalubrious foundations:

> 'And so, Lady Maulevrier,' he exclaimed, turning to his grandmother, 'I have borne a title that never belonged to me, and enjoyed the possession of another man's estates all this time, thanks to your pretty little plot. A very respectable position for your grandson to occupy, upon my life!' (p. 461)

Although Smithson's economic rise seems different from Lord Maulevrier's – because it takes place in another chronological, cultural and economic context – Braddon's final message is that the former's 'phantom fortune' is not too dissimilar to the one unlawfully accumulated by Maulevrier during his Madras presidency. Both fortunes are 'ghostlike' and 'spectral'. To quote from Marx again:

> Men make their own history but they do not make it just as they please; they do not make it under circumstances chosen by themselves, but under circumstances directly encountered, given and transmitted from the past. The tradition of all the dead generations weighs like a nightmare on the brain of the living.[37]

Behind Maulevrier's colonial exploitation, Smithson's imperialistic accumulation of capital and Lesbia's corruption, the real mystery of Braddon's novel is represented by Marx's intangible presence, which goes beyond and completes the sensational secret the novel encapsulates. Therefore, in the attempt to escape Lady Audley's narrative ghost, Braddon conjures and evokes Marx's capitalistic spectres.[38] Choosing an oxymoronic title composed of two words graphically different from each other but phonetically associated through alliteration (*Phantom Fortune*), and using a term like 'phantom' (which derives from the Greek verb *phantazo*, meaning 'I show' and 'I appear') Braddon suggests to her readers that the more 'fortunes' seem intangible and 'spectral', the more they are of an ambiguous origin. The fact that *Phantom Fortune* was published in the same year in which Karl Marx died (1883) seems to imply that Braddon followed his spectral steps in a sort of textual séance. Braddon's 'spectral politics' proves in fact that Marx's phantom haunted late-Victorian England in a way that is not too different from the way it still haunts twentieth-first-century readers, intellectuals, citizens and consumers. The more recent 'spectre' of Jacques Derrida admonishes his readers that '[at] a time when a new world disorder is attempting to install its neo-capitalism and neo-liberism, no disavowal has managed to rid itself of Marx's ghosts.'[39]

Braddon's (unexpected) affiliation to Marx is not the ultimate development of a literary production that scanned and scrutinised England in its evolution from a Victorian to a contemporary society. Because of its long chronological setting *Phantom Fortune* can be taken as a model of Braddon's wide and prolific career as an artist writing in a world that was gradually experiencing the end of Victorian expectations and the rise of Postmodern anxieties. Braddon witnessed enormous political, psychological and technological changes, which stimulated her to question her literary and ideological certainties (most importantly the lesson of her master Edward Bulwer Lytton), as well as her successful narrative achievements, most notably *Lady Audley's Secret*. For better or for worse, the novel telling the story of poor Helen Talboys turning into the assertive Lady Audley continues to remain a reference-point for all those readers who want to understand Braddon's problematic and complex relationship with her age, and with ours as well.

Notes

1. See Braddon's negative depiction of the Socialist orator Oliver Greswold in her detective novel *Rough Justice* (see Part II, Chapter 6).
2. Braddon alludes to colonial issues throughout her literary career, from the subtle reference to the well into which George Talboys is thrown in *Lady Audley's Secret* (which is modelled upon the image of the Chawnpore Well of the Indian Mutiny) to *Sons of Fire* (1895), which is partially set in Africa during an expedition that involves its main characters. Africa will indirectly appear also in *Rough Justice*. In one of her last novels, entitled *Dead Love Has Chains* (1907), the seventeen-year-old Irene is sent home from India in disgrace, pregnant and unmarried. Similarly with *Phantom Fortune*, India here represents the site of moral corruption whose main agent is, however, of a British origin.
3. 'The moral implications of the Nature/Society polarity are reflected in the sisters' names: "Mary" is the name of earth and heavenly queens; "Lesbia" the name of an adulterous pagan woman (historically, the unfaithful, aristocrat lover of the Roman poet Catullus' (Marks, 'Seeing into "the Life of Things"', p. 288).
4. Braddon, *Phantom Fortune*, p. 30; p. 51. All quotations will be from this edition. The novel was published in *The Leigh Journal & Times* in twenty-seven weekly parts, from 9 March to 7 September 1883.
5. Warren Hastings, who occupied his position from 1773 to 1784, concluded treaties with various Indian rulers, although in order to wage internal wars

he borrowed (and even extorted) heavily from the Begums of Oudh and the Raja of Benares. For these and other charges he was criticised by philosophers such as Edmund Burke and impeached by Parliament after he had resigned his position. Although his crimes were never totally proved, he was financially and politically ruined (see Kiernan, *The Lords of Human Kind*).

6. Arata, 'The Occidental Tourist', p. 623.
7. '[We] can distinguish between colonization as the take over of territory, appropriation of material resources, exploitation of labour and interference with political and cultural structures of another territory or nation, and imperialism as a global system' (Loomba, *Colonialism/Postcolonialism*, p. 6).
8. Mackenzie, 'The Socialist Agitation', p. 493. For a complete and exhaustive analysis of Mark's presence in Victorian England see Willis, 'The Introduction and Critical Reception of Marxist Thought in Britain'.
9. Marx and Engels, 'The Manifesto of the Communist Party', in *The Marx-Engels Reader*, p. 476, my italics.
10. Jameson, *The Political Unconscious*, p. 20.
11. 'In literary and artistic terms, the shift toward viewing both industry and credit in comparatively positive terms corresponds to the waning of romanticism and the rise of realism [. . .] This evolution corresponded to yet another general shift from the early industrial stress on production to the fin-de-siècle emergence of "consumer society"' (Brantlinger, *Fictions of State*, p. 139). Georg Lukács compared Balzac's treatment of realism (through which he was able to extract the 'inner poetry of life') to Zola's, where '[the] so-called action is only a thread on which the still lives are dispersed in a superficial, ineffective, fortuitous sequence of isolated, static pictures' (*Writer and Critic*, p. 144).
12. 'The West End not only brought the "boulevards of London" by catering to dubious male pleasures. Regent Street shopkeepers actively cultivated a Parisian impression to attract female custom: milliners and dressmakers often adopted French names and stressed the quality and exclusivity of their products by emphasizing their non-British origin' (Walkowitz, 'Going Public', p. 4). In *City of Dreadful Delight*, Walkowitz underlines the association Victorians made between unaccompanied female shoppers and prostitutes, both addressed with the same epithet of 'streetwalkers'.
13. Marx, *Grundrisse*, p. 93. The transition from goods to 'commodities' took place the moment the railway system was introduced, since this technological innovation allowed a more rapid and widespread circulation of objects. On this theme, see also Part I, Chapter 2.
14. Despite her role as independent woman, Nancy Lord in Gissing's *In the Year of Jubilee* is seduced by the image of London celebrating the Victorian Jubilee: 'Nancy forgot her identity, lost sight of herself as an individual. She did not think, and her emotions differed a little from those of any shop-girl let loose. The "culture," to which she laid claim, evanesced in this atmosphere of exhalations. Could she have seen her face, its look of vulgar abandonment would have horrified her' (Gissing, *In the Year of Jubilee*, pp. 61–2).
15. [Anonym.], 'Lunch with the Linedrapers', p. 98. Braddon had already introduced these topics in other texts, most notably in what is recognised

as one of her most important 'novel of manners': *The Lady's Mile* (1866). Published during her so-called 'sensational decade', it anticipates issues that would later reappear in *Phantom Fortune*, such as the image of marriage as an economical bargain (in the case of Florence Crawford and Mr Lobyer), the rise of the figure of the new capitalist (the cotton-trader Mr Lobyer) and the futile existence of many middle- and upper-class women, whose life is compared by Braddon to the 'Lady's Mile' in Hyde Park: 'The lives of the women of the present day are like [the] drive they call the Lady's Mile. They go as far as they can, and then go back again. See how mechanical the horses wheel when they reach the prescribed turning point. If they went any further, I suppose they would be lost in some impenetrable forest depth in Kensington Gardens' (Braddon, *The Lady's Mile*, vol. 1, pp. 17–18).

16. Berman, *All that is Solid Melts into Air*, p. 15.
17. In her essay on the influence of Victorian consumer culture on *Lady Audley's Secret*, Katherine Montwieler asserts that '[the] majority of advertisements were directed toward and depicted women, who were quickly becoming the primary consumers in (and of) English society. The women pictured in Victorian advertisements, rather than being embodiments of evangelical piety, are interested in pleasure, leisure and beautification' ('Marketing Sensation', p. 43). Magazines such as *The Gentlewoman* and *The Queen* included pictures, furniture, books and other cultural objects 'which were paraded before the readers as indicators of taste, culture, and (implicitly) wealth' (Ballaster, Beetham, Frazer and Hebron, *Women's Worlds*, p. 94). See also Baren, *Victorian Shopping*.
18. According to Lori Ann Loeb, '[By] the late nineteenth century, the attainment of the social ideal was determined not only by the cultivation of culturally desirable habits, attitudes, or virtues, but by the acquisition of material things as well' (*Consuming Angels*, p. 10).
19. For Rachel Bowlby, 'there is an obvious connection between the figure of the narcissistic woman and the fact of women as consumers [. . .] The dominant ideology of feminine subjectivity in the late nineteenth century perfectly fitted women to receive the advances of the seductive commodity offering to enhance her womanly attractions' (*Just Looking*, pp. 31–2).
20. Richards, *The Commodity Culture of Victorian England*, pp. 3–4. Judith Flanders argues that '[by] the time of the Great Exhibition it was expected that one's quality of life – one's standard of living – could be judged by the number of possessions one owned, the number of things one consumed. This was an entirely new way of looking at things' (*Consuming Passions*, p. 26). For Erika Diana Rappaport, the enormous department store William Whiteley opened in Bayswater in 1863 was 'a direct descendant of the biggest and most famous mid-Victorian spectacle of all, the Great Exhibition' (*Shopping for Pleasure*, p. 27).
21. Marx, *The Capital*, vol. 1, Penguin edn, p. 164.
22. Derrida suggests that the 'spectres of Marx' were not just those of Communism but also those ghosts that 'inhabited him, the *revenants* with which Marx himself will have been occupied' (*Spectres of Marx*, p. 122).
23. In her physical, moral and even racial attributes as Jewish woman, Seraphine anticipates the characterisation of Lady Adelaide Ducayne in Braddon's vampire story 'Good Lady Ducayne' (1896) (see Part I, Chapter

3). Seraphine is basically 'modelled on the notorious Madame Rachel Leverson, well known to the London *beau monde* and legal authorities for her fashionable but lethal "enamels"' (Marks, 'Seeing into "the Life of Things"', pp. 292–3). Along with selling her beauty products in her New Bond Street shop (which opened in 1863), Madame Rachel was rumoured to practise abortions, and was also a source of inspiration for 'Mother Oldershaw' in Collins's *Armadale*.

24. In her study on the commercial evolution of London's West End and the figure of the new female shopper, Erika Diana Rappaport notes the connection between the customers' gender and Victorian women's habitual buying on credit because of their lack of economic independence (*Shopping for Pleasure*, p. 53).

25. The expression 'girl of the period' was coined by Elisa Linton in her article in *The Saturday Review* published on 14 March 1868. Braddon showed her interest in this topic in the short story 'Milly Darrell' (1871) and in the novels *Taken at the Flood* (1874) and *Dead Man's Shoes* (1876). For Emma Liggins '[discussions] about women's position in the Victorian marriage market straddled both fiction and the periodical press at mid-century, with woman's attractions to mercenary marriages explained either in terms of their frivolity or, more realistically perhaps, in terms of the pressing fear of dependence and poverty' ('Her Mercenary Spirit', p. 76).

26. 'In her search for originality, Lesbia becomes a consumerist artefact in her own right, available to everyone: the kind of democratic classlessness promoted by Wordsworthian spectacle of nature is parodied by the fashionable world, where society photographs replace and replicate the direct, personal experience of nature' (Marks, 'Seeing into "the Life of Things"', p. 295).

27. '[Braddon] has recently devoted much attention to scenery, and has written in a calmer style than that of her earlier manner. In "Phantom Fortune" the old strain comes out again in the midst of a great deal that is of the newest. The very latest and worst development of society in the present day is vigorously presented'([Anonym.], 'Review of *Phantom Fortune*').

28. Eliot, *Daniel Deronda*, Book 1, Chap.1, p. 7.

29. Barthes, *The Fashion System*, p. xi, my italics.

30. Wolff, *Sensational Victorian*, p. 296. For a detailed analysis of the influence of French literature, see Carnell's *The Literary Lives*, pp. 211–21. Carnell's biography includes excerpts from Braddon's unpublished article on French literature entitled 'Émile Zola and the Naturalistic School'.

31. Zola, *The Ladies' Paradise*, p. 4. Zola's 'aseptic' description of Denise – still dressed in black because of her father's recent death – in front of a department store is inspired by his visits to shopping 'institutions' such as the famous Bon Marché, where the writer spent many days in completing his researches for this novel.

32. Brooks, *The Realist Vision*, p. 14. John Vernon considers money as 'one of the most recurring signs of reality in fiction. As a sign of reality, it takes on an ambivalent physical existence. On the one hand, it is an object among other objects and then has a material status [. . .] On the other hand, money is an abstraction, a social power and even (or especially) a sign of the appearances and illusions novelists are fond of stripping from their characters' (*Money and Fiction*, pp. 66–7). Marc Shell says that '[a] piece

of money is almost always a representation, a symbol that claims to stand for something else or to be something else. It is not that paper depicts and represents coins, but that paper, coins, and money, generally, all stand in the place of something else' ('The Issue of Representation', p. 61)

33. Marx and Engels, 'The Manifesto', in *The Marx-Engels Reader*, pp. 473–6.
34. 'Much of Victorian fiction is sustained by the contrast between material wealth and moral worth, and bankers and financiers are more often villainous than virtuous in the pages of novels' (Crosby, 'Financial', p. 235). Mary Poovey writes that '[financial] themes could be easily incorporated into [realist texts] because financial plots lent themselves to this mode of presentation and to the complicated model of causation realism excelled at solving' ('Writing about Finance in Victorian England', p. 33). As far as white-collar crimes are concerned, see Robb, *White-Collar Crime in Modern England*.
35. Marx, 'Economic and Philosophical Manuscripts', in Fromm, *Marx's Concept of Man*, p. 167. Elsewhere, Marx says that '[the] body of money is but a shadow' (*A Contribution to the Critique of Political Economy*, p. 109).
36. It is emblematic that in *The Science of Finance: A Practical Treatise*, Victorian economist R. H. Patterson evoked an imaginary spectator who, after looking at contemporary commercial activities, commented: 'I see no buying and selling [. . .] Where is the money?' (p. 3).
37. Marx, *The Eighteenth of Brumaire of Louis Bonaparte*, in Marx and Engels, *Collected Works*, vol. 11, p. 103.
38. Ann Cvetkovitch suggests reading *Capital* as a sensation novel. The crime that has to be detected is represented in this case by the exploitation of the working classes committed in the factory as the 'hidden abode of production' (*Mixed Feelings*, p. 179).
39. Derrida, *Spectres*, p. 46.

Bibliography

Primary Sources

Andres, Sophia, *The Pre-Raphaelite Art of the Victorian Novel. Narrative Challenges to Visual Gender Boundaries* (Athens: Ohio University Press, 2005).

—, 'Mary Elizabeth Braddon's Ambivalent Pre-Raphaelite Ekphrasis', *Victorian Newsletter*, Fall 2005, www.thefreelibrary.com

[Anonym.], '*Lady Audley's Secret*', *The Times*, 18 November 1862, p. 4.

—, 'Review of *Lady Audley's Secret*', *The Spectator*, 1862, pp. 1196–7.

—, 'Review of *Phantom Fortune*', *Athenaeum*, 29 September 1883, www.sensationpress.com/braddonphantomfortunereviews.htm

—, 'His Darling Sin', *The Spectator*, 4 November 1899, p. 662.

—, 'Miss Braddon at Home', *The Daily Telegraph*, 4 October 1913, p. 19.

Altick, Richard, *Victorian Studies in Scarlet. Murder and Manners in the Age of Victoria* (New York: W. W. Norton and Company, 1970).

—, *Deadly Encounters. Two Victorian Sensations* (Philadelphia: University of Pennsylvania Press, 1986).

Ascari, Maurizio, *A Counter-history of Crime Fiction. Supernatural, Gothic, Sensational* (Basingstoke and New York: Palgrave Macmillan, 2007).

Auerbach, Nina, *Woman and the Demon. The Life of a Victorian Myth* (Cambridge, MA; London: Harvard University Press, 1982).

Austin, Alfred, 'Our Novels: the Sensational School', *Temple Bar*, 29, 1870, pp. 177–94.

Bedell, Jeanne F., 'Amateur and Professional Detectives in the Fiction of Mary Elizabeth Braddon', *Clues: A Journal of Detection*, 4, 1983, pp. 19–34.

Beetham, Margaret, 'Women and the Consumption of Print', in Joanne Shattock (ed.), *Woman and Literature in Britain 1800–1900* (Cambridge: Cambridge University Press, 2000), pp. 55–77.

Braddon, Mary Elizabeth, *Henry Dunbar* (London: Maxwell, 1864).

—, *The Lady's Mile*, 2 vols (Leipzig: Bernhard Tauchnitz, 1866).

—, 'My First Novel: *The Trail of the Serpent*', *The Idler Magazine*, III, February-July 1893, pp. 19–30.

—, *Rough Justice*, 2 vols (Leipzing: Bernhard Tauchnitz, 1898).

—, 'At the Shrine of Jane Eyre', *Pall Mall Magazine*, 37, 1906, pp. 174–6.

—, *Beyond these Voices* (London: Hutchinson, 1910).

—, *Lady Audley's Secret*, ed. David Skilton (Oxford: Oxford University Press, [1862] 1988).

—, *Lady Audley's Secret*, ed. with notes by Jenny Bourne Taylor, with an Introduction by Jenny Bourne Taylor and Russell Crofts (Harmondsworth: Penguin, 1998).

—, *Lady Audley's Secret*, ed. Natalie H. Houston (Peterborough, Ontario: Broadview Press, 2003).

—, *Vixen* (Gloucestershire: Alan Sutton, [1879] 1993).

—, *Eleanor's Victory* (Phoenix Mill: Alan Sutton Publishing, [1863] 1996).

—, *The Doctor's Wife*, ed. with an Introduction and Notes by Lyn Pykett (Oxford and New York: Oxford University Press, [1864] 1998).

—, *Aurora Floyd*, ed. Richard Nemesvari and Lisa Surridge (Peterborough, Ontario: Broadview Press, [1863] 1998).

—, *John Marchmon's Legacy*, ed. with an Introduction and Notes by Toru Sasaki and Norman Page (Oxford: Oxford University Press, [1864] 1999).

—, *His Darling Sin* (Hastings: The Sensation Press, [1899] 2001).

—, *At Chrighton Abbey and Other Horror Stories* (Holicong, PA: Wildside Press, 2002).

—, *The Trail of the Serpent*, ed. Chris Willis, Introduction by Sarah Waters (New York: The Modern Library, [1861] 2003).

—, *Phantom Fortune* (Kessinger Publishing, [1883] 2003).

—, *Thou Art the Man*, ed. with a new Introduction and Notes by Laurence Talairach-Vielmans (Kansas City, MO: Valancourt Books, 2008).

Brantlinger, Patrick, 'What is "Sensational" about the "Sensation Novel"?', *Nineteenth-Century Fiction*, June 1982, pp. 1–28.

Brewer, Pamela Didlake, 'Pre-Raphaelitism in *Lady Audley's Secret*', *Publications of the Arkansas Philological Association*, 19: 1, Spring 1993, pp. 1–10.

Briganti, Chiara, 'Gothic Maidens and Sensation Women: Lady Audley's Journey from the Ruined Mansion to the Madhouse', *Victorian Literature and Culture*, 19, 1991, pp. 189–211.

Carnell, Jennifer, *The Literary Lives of Mary Elizabeth Braddon. A Study of her Life and Work* (Hastings: The Sensation Press, 2000).

Casey, Ellen Miller, '"Other's People Prudery": Mary Elizabeth Braddon', in Don Richard Cox (ed.), *Sexuality and Victorian Literature* (Knoxville: University of Tennessee Press, 1984), pp. 72–82.

Cooke, Simon, 'George du Maurier's Illustrations for M. E. Braddon's Serialization of *Eleanor's Victory* in *Once a Week*', *Victorian Periodicals Review*, 35: 1, Spring 2002, pp. 89–106.

Cropp, Mary Seraly, 'A Detective for Us Ordinary Folk? The Reinscription of the Dupin-esque Detective in Mary Braddon's *Lady Audley's Secret*', *Clues: A Journal of Detection*, 19: 2, Fall-Winter 1998, pp. 87–95.

Cvetkovich, Ann, *Mixed Feelings. Feminism, Mass Culture and Victorian Sensationalism* (New Brunswick, NJ: Rutgers University Press, 1992).

Dingley, Robert, 'Mrs Conyers's Secret: Decoding Sexuality in *Aurora Floyd*', *Victorian Newsletter*, 95, Spring 1999, pp. 16–18.

Donnelly, Brian, 'Sensational Bodies: Lady Audley and the Pre-Raphaelite Portrait', *Victorian Newsletter*, 112, Fall 2007, pp. 69–90.

Fahnestock, Jeanne, 'The Heroine of Irregular Features: Physiognomy and

Conventions of Heroine Description', *Victorian Studies*, 24, Spring 1981, pp. 325–50.

Fantina, Richard and Kimberly Harrison (eds), *Victorian Sensations. Essays on a Scandalous Genre* (Columbus: Ohio State University Press, 2006).

Felber, Lynette, 'The Literary Portrait as Centerfold: Fetishism in Mary Elizabeth Braddon's *Lady Audley's Secret*', *Victorian Literature and Culture*, 35, 2007, pp. 471–88.

Ferguson, Christine, 'Sensational Dependence: Prosthesis and Affect in Dickens and Braddon', *LIT: Literature Interpretation Theory*, 19: 1, January 2008, pp. 1–25.

Fisk, Nicole P., 'Lady Audley as Sacrifice: Curing Female Disadvantage in *Lady Audley's Secret*', *Victorian Newsletter*, 105, Spring 2004, pp. 24–7.

Flint, Kate, *The Woman Reader 1837–1914* (Oxford: Clarendon Press, 1993).

Frye, Lowell T., 'The Ghost Story and the Subjection of Women: the Example of Amelia Edwards, M. E. Braddon and E. Nesbit', *Victorian Institute Journal*, 26, 1998, pp. 167–209.

Garrison, Laurie, 'The Seduction of Seeing in M. E. Braddon's *Eleanor's Victory*: Visual Technology, Sexuality and the Evocative Publishing Context of *Once a Week*', *Victorian Literature and Culture*, 36, 2008, pp. 111–30.

Gilbert, Pamela K., 'Madness and Civilization: Generic Oppositions in Mary Elizabeth Braddon's *Lady Audley's Secret*', *Essays in Literature*, 23: 2, Fall 1996, pp. 218–33.

—, *Disease, Desire and the Body in Victorian Women's Popular Novels* (Cambridge: Cambridge University Press, 1997).

Golden, Catherine J., 'Censoring her Sensationalism. Mary Elizabeth Braddon and *The Doctor's Wife*', in Fantina and Harrison (eds), *Victorian Sensations*, pp. 29–40.

Goodlad, Lauren M. E., '"Go and Marry Your Doctor": Fetishism and "Redundance" at the *Fin de Siècle* and the Vampires of "Good Lady Ducayne"', in Tromp, Gilbert and Haynie (eds), *Beyond Sensation*, pp. 211–34.

Hall, R. Mark, 'A Victorian Sensation Novel in the "Contact Zone": Reading *Lady Audley's Secret* through Imperial Eyes', *Victorian Newsletter*, 98, Fall 2000, pp. 22–6.

Hartman, Mary S., 'Murder for Respectability: the Case of Madeleine Smith', *Victorian Studies*, 16: 4, June 1973, pp. 381–400.

Hatton, Joseph, 'Miss Braddon at Home. A Sketch and an Interview', *London Society*, January 1888, pp. 22–9.

Heilmann, Ann, 'Emma Bovary's Sisters: Infectious Desire and Female Reading Appetites in Mary Braddon and George Moore', *Victorian Review*, 29: 1, 2003, pp. 31–48.

Helfield, Linda, 'Poisonous Plots: Women Sensational Novels and Murderesses of the Victorian Period', *Victorian Review*, 21: 2, Summer 1995, pp. 161–88.

Heywood, Christopher, 'Miss Braddon's *The Doctor's Wife*. An Intermediary between *Madame Bovary* and *The Return of the Native*', *Revue de Littérature Comparée*, 38, 1964, pp. 255–61.

—, 'A Source for *Middlemarch*: Miss Braddon's *The Doctor's Wife* and *Madame Bovary*', *Revue de Littérature Comparée*, 44, 1970, pp. 184–94.

Hopkins, Lisa, *Giants of the Past: Popular Fictions and the Idea of Evolution* (Lewisburg, PA: Bucknell University Press, 2004).

Howard, Greg, 'Masculinity and Economics in *Lady Audley's Secret*', *Victorian Institute Journal*, 27, 1999, pp. 33–53.

Hughes, Winifred, *The Maniac in the Cellar. Sensation Novels of the 1860s* (Princeton, NJ: Princeton University Press, 1980).

—, 'The Sensation Novel', in Patrick Brantlinger and William B. Thesing (eds), *A Companion to the Victorian Novel* (Oxford: Blackwell, 2002), pp. 260–78.

Huskey, Melynda, 'No Name: Embodying the Sensation Heroine', *Victorian Newsletter*, 8, 1992, pp. 5–13.

James, Henry, 'Miss Braddon', *The Nation*, 9 November 1865, pp. 593–4.

Johnson, Heidi H., 'Electra-fying the Female Sleuth: Detecting the Father in *Eleanor's Victory* and *Thou Art the Man*', in Tromp, Gilbert and Haynie (eds), *Beyond Sensation*, pp. 255–75.

Jones, Anna Maria, *Problem Novels: Victorian Fiction Theorizes the Sensational Self* (Columbus: Ohio State University Press, 2007).

Jones, Susan, '"Stepping out of the Narrow Frame": Conrad's Suspence and the Novel of Sensation', *Review of English Studies: A Quarterly Journal of English Literature and the English Language*, 49, August 1998, pp. 306–21.

Kaplan, Joel H., 'Exuming Lady Audley: Period Melodrama for the 1990s', in James Redmond (ed.), *Melodrama* (Cambridge: Cambridge University Press, 1992), pp. 143–60.

Kolentsis, Alysia, 'Home Invasions: Masculinity and Domestic Power in the Supernatural Fiction of Elizabeth Gaskell, Mary Elizabeth Braddon and Rhoda Broughton', in Sladja Blazan (ed.), *Ghosts, Stories, Histories: Ghost Stories and Alternative Histories* (Newcastle Upon Tyne: Cambridge Scholars, 2007), pp. 60–80.

Kucich, John, *The Power of Lies. Transgression in Victorian Fiction* (Ithaca, NY; London: Cornell University Press, 1994).

Langland, Elizabeth, 'Enclosure Acts: Framing Women's Bodies in Braddon's *Lady Audley's Secret*', in Tromp, Gilbert and Haynie (eds), *Beyond Sensation*, pp. 3–16.

Liggins, Emma, 'Her Mercenary Spirit: Women, Money and Marriage in Mary Elizabeth Braddon's 1870s Fiction', *Women's Writing*, 11: 1, 2004, pp. 73–87.

Lindemann, Ruth Burridge, 'Dramatic Disappearances: Mary Elizabeth Braddon and the Staging of Theatrical Character', *Victorian Literature and Culture*, 25: 2, 1997, pp. 279–91.

Loesberg, Jonathan, 'The Ideology of Narrative Form in Sensation Fiction', *Representations*, 13, Winter 1986, pp. 115–38.

Lynch, Eve, 'Spectral Politics: the Victorian Ghost Story and the Domestic Servant', in Nicola Bown, Carolyn Burdett and Pamela Thurschwell (eds), Foreword by Gillian Beer, Afterword by Steve Connor, *The Victorian Supernatural* (Cambridge: Cambridge University Press, 2004), pp. 67–86.

Mangham, Andrew, '"Murdered at the Breast": Maternal Violence and the Self-Made Man in Popular Victorian Culture', *Critical Survey*, 16: 1, 2004, pp. 20–34.

—, *Violent Women and Sensation Fiction. Crime, Medicine and Victorian Popular Culture* (Basingstoke: Palgrave Macmillan, 2007).

—, 'Life after Death: Apoplexy, Medical Ethics and the Female Undead', *Women's Writing*, 15, 3, December 2008, pp. 282–99.

Mansel, Henry Longueville, 'Sensation Novels', *Quarterly Review*, 113, April 1863, pp. 481–514.

Marks, Patricia, '"The Boy on the Wooden Horse": Robert Audley and the Failure of Reason', *Clues: A Journal of Detection*, 15: 2, Fall-Winter 1994, pp. 1–14.

—, 'Seeing into "The Life of Things"': Nature and Commodification in *Phantom Fortune*', *Studies in the Novel*, 33: 3, Fall 2001, pp. 285–305.

Mattacks, Kate, 'After Lady Audley: M. E. Braddon, the Actress, and the Act of Writing in *Hostages to Fortune*', in Emma Liggins and Daniel Duffy (eds), *Feminist Readings of Victorian Popular Texts: Divergent Femininities* (Aldershot: Ashgate, 2001), pp. 69–88.

Matus, Jill M., 'Disclosure as "Cover-up": The Discourse of Madness in *Lady Audley's Secret*', *University of Toronto Quarterly*, 62: 3, Spring 1993, pp. 334–56.

—, *Unstable Bodies. Victorian Representations of Sexuality and Maternity* (Manchester: Manchester University Press, 1995).

Maunder, Andrew, *Varieties of Women's Sensation Fiction, 1855–1890: Volume 1. Sensationalism and the Sensation Debate* (London: Pickering and Chatto, 2004).

Miller, D. A., *The Novel and the Police* (Berkeley; Los Angeles; London: University of California Press, 1988).

Mitchell, Sally, 'Sentiment and Suffering: Women's Recreational Readings in the 1860s', *Victorian Studies*, 21, 1977, pp. 29–45.

Montwieler, Katherine, 'Marketing Sensation: *Lady Audley's Secret* and Consumer Culture', in Tromp, Gilbert and Haynie (eds), *Beyond Sensation*, pp. 43–62.

Morris, Virginia B., *Double Yeopardy: Women who Kill in Victorian Fiction* (Kentucky: The University Press of Kentucky, 1990).

Nemesvari, Richard, 'Robert Audley's Secret: Male Homosocial Desire in *Lady Audley's Secret*', *Studies in the Novel*, 27: 4, Winter 1995, pp. 515–28.

—, '"Judged by a Purely Literary Standard". Sensation Fiction, Horizons of Expectation and Generic Construction of Victorian Realism', in Fantina and Harrison (eds), *Victorian Sensations*, pp. 15–28.

Odden, Karen M., '"Reading Cooly" in *John Marchmont's Legacy*: Reconsidering M. E. Braddon's Legacy', *Studies in the Novel*, 27: 1, Spring 2004, pp. 21–40.

Ofek, Galia, 'Sensational Hair. Gender, Genre, and Fetishism in the Sensational Decade', in Fantina and Harrison (eds), *Victorian Sensations*, pp. 102–14.

Oliphant, Margaret, 'Sensation Novels', *Blackwood's Edinburgh Magazine*, 91, May 1862, pp. 564–80.

—, 'Our Female Sensational Novelists', *Christian Remembrancer*, 46, 1863, pp. 209–236.

—, 'Novels', *Blackwood's Edinburgh Magazine*, 102, September 1867, pp. 257–80.

Onslow, Barbara, 'Sensationalising Science: Braddon's Marketing of Science in *Belgravia*', *Victorian Periodicals Review*, 35: 2, Summer 2002, pp. 160–77.

Pallo, Vicki A., 'From Do-Nothing to Detective: the Transformation of Robert

Audley in *Lady Audley's Secret*', *Journal of Popular Culture*, 39: 3, June 2006, pp. 466–78.

Petch, Simon, 'Robert Audley's Profession', *Studies in the Novel*, 33: 1, Spring 2000, pp. 1–13.

Pykett, Lyn, *The 'Improper' Feminine. The Women's Sensation Novel and the New Woman Writing* (London and New York: Routledge, 1992).

—, 'Sensation and the Fantastic in the Victorian Novel', in Deirdre David (ed.), *The Cambridge Companion to the Victorian Novel* (Cambridge: Cambridge University Press, 2001), pp. 192–211.

Radford, Andrew, *Victorian Sensation Fiction. A Reader's Guide to Essential Criticism* (Basingstoke: Palgrave Macmillan, 2009).

Rae, Frances W., 'Sensation Novelists: Miss Braddon', *North British Review*, 43, September 1865, pp. 180–204.

Rance, Nicholas, *Wilkie Collins and Other Sensation Novelists. Walking the Moral Hospital* (London and Basingstoke: Macmillan, 1991).

Robinson, Solveig, 'Editing *Belgravia*: M. E. Braddon's Defense of "Light Literature"', *Victorian Periodicals Review*, 28, 1995, pp. 108–22.

Schipper, Jan Davis, *Becoming Frauds. Unconventional Heroines in Mary Elizabeth Braddon's Sensation Fiction* (San Jose; New York; Lincoln; Shanghai: Writers Club Press, 2002).

Schroeder, Natalie and Ronald A. Schroeder, *From Sensation to Society: Representations of Marriage in the Fiction of Mary Elizabeth Braddon, 1862–1866* (Newark: University of Delaware Press, 2006).

Sears, Albert C., 'Mary Elizabeth Braddon and the "Combination Novel". The Subversion of Sensational Expectation in *Vixen*', in Fantina and Harrison (eds), *Victorian Sensations*, pp. 41–52.

Showalter, Elaine, *A Literature of Their Own. From Charlotte Brontë to Doris Lessing* (London: Virago, 1978).

—, *The Female Malady. Women, Madness and English Culture 1830–1980* (London: Virago, 1985).

Sparks, Tabitha, 'Fiction Becomes Her: Representations of Female Character in Mary Braddon's *The Doctor's Wife*', in Tromp, Gilbert and Haynie (eds), *Beyond Sensation*, pp. 187–210.

Swenson, Kristine, 'The Menopausal Vampire: Arabella Kenealy and the Boundaries of True Womanhood', *Women's Writing*, 10:, 1, 2003, pp. 27–46.

Taylor, Jenny Bourne, *In The Secret Theatre of Home: Wilkie Collins, Sensation Narrative and Nineteenth-Century Psychology* (London and New York: Routledge, 1988).

Terry, R. C., *Victorian Popular Fiction, 1860–80* (London: Macmillan, 1983).

Tilley, Elizabeth, 'Gender and Role-playing in *Lady Audley's Secret*', in Valeria Tinkler-Villani and Peter Davidson, with Jane Stevenson (eds), *Exhibited by Candlelight. Sources and Developments in the Gothic Tradition* (Amsterdam and Atlanta, GA: Rodopi, 1995), pp. 197–204.

Trodd, Anthea, *Domestic Crime in the Victorian Novel* (London: Macmillan, 1989).

Tromp, Marlene, Pamela K. Gilbert and Aeron Haynie (eds), *Beyond Sensation. Mary Elizabeth Braddon in Context* (Albany: State University of New York Press, 2000).

Tromp, Marlene, *The Private Rod. Marital Violence, Sensation and the Law in Victorian Britain* (Charlottesville and London: University of Virginia Press, 2000).

Wagner, Tamara S., '"Magnetic Clues to the Past": Reinvestigating the Victorians' Regency Period in *Eleanor's Victory*', *Clues. A Journal of Detection*, 'Theme Issue: Victorian Detective Fiction, Part 1', 25: 1, Fall 2006, pp. 81–95.

Willis, Chris, 'Braddon and Burne-Jones. The Original of Lady Audley's Portrait?', www.chriswillis.freeserve.co.uk/sidonia.htm

Wolff, Robert Lee, '"Devoted Disciple": the Letters of Mary Elizabeth Braddon to Sir Edward Bulwer-Lytton, 1862–1873', *Harvard Library Bulletin*, 22, 1974, pp. 5–35; pp. 129–61.

—, *Sensational Victorian. The Life & Fiction of Mary Elizabeth Braddon* (New York and London: Garland Publishing, 1979).

Wynne, Debrah, *The Sensation Novel and the Victorian Family Magazine* (London: Palgrave Macmillan, 2001).

Secondary Sources

A. A., *The Christian Observer*, XIV, 1815, p. 512.

Altick, Richard, *The English Common Reader. A Social History of the Mass Reading Public, 1800–1900* (Chicago and London: University of Chicago Press, 1957).

[Anonym.], 'Lunch with the Linedrapers', *The Graphic*, 3 August 1872, p. 98.

Arata, Stephen D., 'The Occidental Tourist: *Dracula* and the Anxiety of Reverse Colonization', *Victorian Studies*, 33, 1990, pp. 621–45.

Armstrong, Nancy, *Desire and Domestic Fiction: a Political History of the Novel* (New York and Oxford: Oxford University Press, 1987).

—, *Fiction in the Age of Photography* (Cambridge, MA; London: Harvard University Press, [1999] 2002).

Ascari, Maurizio, *La leggibilità del male: genealogia del romanzo poliziesco e del romanzo anarchico* (Bologna: Patron Editore, 1998).

Auerbach, Nina, *Our Vampires, Ourselves* (Chicago: University of Chicago Press, 1995).

Austen, Jane, *Pride and Prejudice*, ed. Mary Lascelles, new Introduction by Peter Conrad (London: Everyman's Library, [1813] 1978).

—, *Northanger Abbey, Lady Susan, The Watsons, and Sanditon*, ed. with Notes by John Davie and an Introduction by Terry Castle (Oxford and New York: Oxford University Press, [1798–1803] 1990).

Avery, Simon, '"Some Strange and Spectral Dream": the Brontës' Manipulation of the Gothic Mode', *Brontë Society Transactions*, 23: 2, 1998, pp. 120–35.

Bailin, Miriam, *The Sickroom in Victorian Fiction: the Art of Being Ill* (Cambridge: Cambridge University Press, 1994).

Bakhtin, Mikhail M., *The Dialogic Imagination. Four Essays*, ed. Michael Holquist, transl. Caryl Emerson and Michael Holquist (Austin: University of Texas Press, [1981] 1996).

Ballaster, Ros, Margaret Beetham, Elizabeth Frazer and Sandra Hebron,

Women's Worlds: Ideology, Femininity and the Women's Magazine (Hong Kong: Macmillan Education Ltd, 1991).

Baren, Maurice, *Victorian Shopping* (London: Michael O' Mara Books Ltd, 1998).

Barreca, Regina (ed.), *Sex and Death in Victorian Literature* (Bloomington and Indianapolis: Indiana University Press, 1990).

Barringer, Tim, *Pre-Raphaelites: Reading the Image* (London: The Everyman Art Library, 1998).

Barthes, Roland, 'The Photographic Message', in *Image, Music, Text*, transl. Stephen Heath (New York: Noonday Press, 1977), pp. 15–31.

—, *The Fashion System*, transl. Matthew Ward and Richard Howard (New York: Hill and Wang, 1983).

—, 'The Reality Effect', in Tzvetan Todorov (ed.), *French Literary Theory Today*, transl. R. Carter (New York: Cambridge University Press, 1982), pp. 11–17.

Bartram, Michael, *The Pre-Raphaelite Camera: Aspects of Victorian Photography* (Boston: Little Brown, 1985).

Bauman, H.-Dirksen L., 'Towards a Poetics of Vision, Space and the Body. Sign Language and Literary Theory', in Lennard J. Davis (ed.), *The Disability Studies Reader*, 2nd edn (London and New York: Routledge, 2006), pp. 355–66.

Beebe, Thomas O., *The Ideology of Genre. A Comparative Study in Generic Instability* (University Park: Pennsylvania State University Press, 1994).

Beer, Gillian, *Darwin's Plots: Evolutionary Narrative in Darwin, George Eliot and Nineteenth-Century Fiction* (London: Routledge and Kegan Paul, 1983).

Bell, Alexander Graham, *Memoir upon the Formation of a Deaf Variety of the Human Race* (Washington, DC: Alexander Graham Bell Association for the Deaf, [1883] 1884).

Bell, Charles, *The Anatomy and Physiology of Expression as Connected with the Fine Arts* (London: George Hill and Sons, 1844).

Benjamin, Walter, *Charles Baudelaire: a Lyric Poet in the Era of High Capitalism*, transl. Harry Zohn (London: Verso, 1983).

Berman, Marshall, *All that is Solid Melts into Air: the Experience of Modernity* (New York: Simon and Shuster, 1982).

Biberman, Matthew, *Masculinity, Anti-Semitism and Early Modern English Literature. From the Satanic to the Effeminate Jew* (Aldershot: Ashgate, 2005).

Blaker, C. P., *Eugenics: Galton and After* (Cambridge, MA; London: Harvard University Press, 1952).

Bloom, Harold, *The Anxiety of Influence. A Theory of Poetry*, 2nd edn (Oxford and New York: Oxford University Press, [1973] 1997).

Botting, Fred, *Gothic* (London and New York: Routledge, 1996).

Bowlby, Rachel, *Just Looking: Consumer Culture in Dreiser, Gissing and Zola* (New York: Methuen, 1985).

Brantlinger, Patrick, *Rule of Darkness: British Literature and Imperialism, 1830–1914* (Ithaca, NY; London: Cornell University Press, 1988).

—, *Fictions of State: Culture and Credit in Britain, 1694–1994* (Ithaca, NY; London: Cornell University Press, 1996).

—, *The Reading Lesson. The Threat of Mass Literacy in Nineteenth-Century*

British Fiction (Bloomington and Indianapolis: Indiana University Press, 1998).

Briggs, Asa, *Victorian Things* (Chicago: University of Chicago Press, 1989).

Brontë, Charlotte, *Villette* (Ware: Wordsworth, [1853] 1993).

Brooks, Peter, *Reading for the Plot. Design and Intention in Narrative* (Cambridge, MA; London: Harvard University Press, 1992).

—, *Body Work. Objects of Desire in Modern Narrative* (Cambridge, MA; London: Harvard University Press, 1993).

—, *The Melodramatic Imagination. Balzac, Henry James, and the Mode of Excess* (New Haven, CT; London: Yale University Press, [1976] 1995).

—, *The Realist Vision* (New Haven, CT; London: Yale University Press, 2005).

Brown, Andrew, 'Bulwer's Reputation', in Christensen (ed.), *The Subverting Vision of Edward Bulwer Lytton*, pp. 29–37.

Bulwer Lytton, Edward, *Paul Clifford* (Boston, MA: Adamant Media Corporation, [1830] 2001).

Bulwer Lytton, Rosina, *A School for Husbands: or Molière's Life and Times*, 3 vols (London: Skeet, 1852).

—, *A Blighted Life: A True Story*, with a new Introduction by Marie Mulvey Roberts (Bristol: Thoemmes, 1997 [1880]).

Burt, Richard and John Michael Archer (eds), *Enclosure Acts: Sexuality, Property and Culture in Early Modern England* (Ithaca, NY; London: Cornell University Press, 1994).

Byerly, Alison, *Realism, Representation and the Arts in Nineteenth-Century Literature* (Cambridge: Cambridge University Press, 1998).

Calanchi, Alessandra, *Quattro studi in rosso. I confini del privato maschile nella narrativa vittoriana* (Cesena: Il Ponte Vecchio, 1997).

Carter, Ian, *Railways and Culture in Britain. The Epitome of Modernity* (Manchester: Manchester University Press, 2001).

Chambers, Robert, *Vestiges of the Natural History of Creation*, 6th edn (London: John Churchill, [1844] 1847).

—, *Vestiges of the Natural History of Creation and Other Evolutionary Writings*, ed. James A. Secord (Chicago, IL: University of Chicago Press, 1994).

Chase, Karen and Michael Levenson, *The Spectacle of Intimacy: a Public Life for the Victorian Family* (Princeton, NJ: Princeton University Press, 2000).

Christ, Carol T. and John O. Jordan (eds), *Victorian Literature and the Victorian Visual Imagination* (Berkeley; Los Angeles; London: University of California Press, 1995).

Christensen, Allan Conrad (ed.), *The Subverting Vision of Edward Bulwer Lytton. Bicentenary Reflections* (Newark: University of Delaware Press, 2004).

Christie, Agatha, 'Greenshaw's Folly', in *Double Sin and Other Stories* (New York: Berkley Books, [1961] 1984), pp. 119–50.

Cobbold, Lord, 'Rosina Bulwer Lytton: Irish Beauty, Satirist, Tormented Victorian Wife, 1802–1882', in Christensen (ed.), *The Subverting Vision of Edward Bulwer Lytton*, pp. 147–58.

Collins, Wilkie, *The Woman in White* (Harmondsworth: Penguin, 1994).

—, *No Name*, ed. with an Introduction and Notes by Mark Ford (Harmondsworth: Penguin, [1862] 1994).

—, *The Moonstone*, ed. with an Introduction and Notes by John Sutherland (Oxford and New York: Oxford University Press, [1868] 1999).

—, *Armadale*, ed. Catherine Peters (Oxford and New York: Oxford University Press, [1866] 1999).

Costantini, Mariaconcetta, *Venturing into Unknown Waters: Wilkie Collins and the Challenges of Modernity* (Pescara: Tracce, 2008).

Craig, Patricia and Mary Cadogan, *The Lady Investigates: Women Detectives and Spies in Fiction* (Oxford and New York: Oxford University Press, 1986).

Crary, Jonathan, *Techniques of the Observer. On Vision and Modernity in the Nineteenth Century* (Cambridge, MA; London: MIT Press, 1992).

Crosby, Christina, 'Financial', in Tucker (ed.), *A Companion to Victorian Literature and Culture*, pp. 225–43.

Daly, Nicholas, 'Blood on the Tracks: Sensational Drama, the Railway, and the Dark Face of Modernity', *Victorian Studies*, 42:, 1, Autumn 1998–9, pp. 47–76.

Darwin, Charles, *The Descent of Man, and Selection in Relation to Sex*, 2 vols (London: John Murray, 1871).

—, *Correspondence of Charles Darwin*, ed. F. Burkhardt and S. Smith, 3 vols (Cambridge and New York: Cambridge University Press, 1988).

—, *Charles Darwin's Letters: a Selection*, ed. Frederick Burkhard (Cambridge and New York: Cambridge University Press, 1996).

—, *The Origin of Species*, ed. Gillian Beer (Oxford and New York: Oxford University Press, [1859] 1996).

—, *On the Origin of Species by Means of Natural Selection*, ed. Joseph Carroll (Peterborough, Ontario: Broadview Press, 2003).

Davenport-Hines, Richard, *Gothic. Four Hundred Years of Excess, Horror, Evil and Ruin* (New York: North Point Press, 1998).

Davie, Neil, *Tracing the Criminal: the Rise of Scientific Criminology in Britain* (Oxford: Bardwell Press, 2006).

Davis, Lennard J., *Enforcing Normalcy: Disability, Deafness and the Body* (London: Verso, 1995).

Davison, Carol Margaret, *Anti-Semitism and British Gothic Literature* (Basingstoke: Palgrave Macmillan, 2004).

Deane, Bradley, *Making of the Victorian Novelist: Anxieties of Authorship in the Mass Market* (London and New York: Routledge, 2003).

Delany, Paul, *Literature, Money and the Market: from Trollope to Amis* (Basingstoke: Palgrave Macmillan, 2002).

Derrida, Jacques, *Of Grammatology*, transl. Gayatri Chakravorty Spivak (Baltimore and London: The Johns Hopkins University Press, [1967] 1976).

—, 'The Law of Genre', transl. Avital Ronell, *Glyph*, 7, 1980, pp. 202–32.

—, *Spectres of Marx. The State of Debt, the Work of Mourning and the New International*, transl. Peggy Kamuf (New York and London: Routledge, [1993] 1994).

Devey, Louisa, *Life of Rosina, Lady Lytton: A Vindication* (London: Sonnenschein, 1887).

Dickens, Charles, *Bleak House*, ed. Stephen Gill (Oxford and New York: Oxford University Press, [1854] 1998).

—, *Dombey and Son*, ed. with an Introduction and Notes by Andrew Sanders (Harmondsworth: Penguin, [1848] 2002).

—, *Our Mutual Friend*, ed. Michael Cotsell (Oxford and New York: Oxford University Press, [1864] 1989).

Dickerson, Vanessa, *Victorian Ghosts in the Noontide: Women Writers and the Supernatural* (Columbia: University of Missouri Press, 1996).

Dolin, Tim, *Mistress of the House. Women of Property in the Victorian Novel* (Aldershot: Ashgate, 1997).

Doyle, Sir Arthur Conan, *The Adventures of Sherlock Holmes*, ed. Julian Wolfreys (Ware: Wordsworth Classics, 1992).

—, *The Hound of the Baskervilles, with 'The Adventure of the Speckled Band'*, ed. Francis O'Gorman (Peterborough, Ontario: Broadview Press, [1901] 2006).

Eco, Umberto and Thomas A. Sebeok (eds), *The Sign of Three. Dupin, Holmes, Peirce* (Bloomington and Indianapolis: Indiana University Press, 1983).

Eliot, George, 'Silly Novels by Lady Novelists', *Westminster Review*, 86, 1856, pp. 442–61.

—, *The George Eliot Letters*, ed. Gordon S. Haight (New Haven and London: Yale University Press, 1954).

—, *George Eliot, A Writer's Notebook, 1854–1879, and Uncollected Writings*, ed. Joseph Wiesenfarth (Charlottesville: University Press of Virginia, 1981).

—, *Adam Bede*, ed. Stephen Gill (Harmondsworth: Penguin, [1859] 1985).

—, *The Mill on the Floss* (Harmondsworth: Penguin, [1860] 1994).

—, *Daniel Deronda* (Ware: Wordsworth Classics, [1876] 1996).

Ellis, Havelock, *The Criminal* (Montclair, NJ: Patterson Smith, [1890] 1975).

Ellis, Kate Ferguson, *The Contested Castle: Gothic Novels and the Subversion of Domestic Ideology* (Urbana: University of Illinois Press, 1989).

Ellmann, Richard, *Oscar Wilde* (Harmondsworth: Penguin, 1987).

Engels, Friedrich, *The Condition of the Working Class in England*, transl. W. O. Henderson and W. H. Chaloner (Stanford, CA: Stanford University Press, 1958).

Ermarth, Elizabeth Deeds, *Realism and Consensus in the English Novel: Time, Space and Narrative* (Edinburgh: Edinburgh University Press, 1998).

Felman, Shoshana, 'Women and Madness: the Critical Fallacy', *Diacritics*, 5: 4, Winter 1975, pp. 2–10.

Flanders, Judith, *Consuming Passions. Leisure and Pleasure in Victorian Britain* (London: Harper Press, 2006).

Flint, Kate, *The Victorians and the Visual Imagination* (Cambridge: Cambridge University Press, 2000).

—, 'Disability and Difference', in Bourne Taylor (ed.), *The Cambridge Companion to Wilkie Collins*, pp. 153–67.

Flow, John, *Genre* (London and New York: Routledge, 2006).

Forster, John, *The Life of Charles Dickens*, 2 vols (London: J. M. Dent and Sons, [1876] 1966).

Foucault, Michel, *Histoire de la folie à l'age classique* (Paris: Gallimard, 1972).

—, *La volonté de savoir* (Paris: Gallimard, 1976); English edn, *The History of Sexuality, Vol. 1: An Introduction*, transl. Robert Hurley (New York: Random House, 1978).

—, *Language, Counter-Memory, Practice: Selected Essays and Interviews*, ed. Donald Bouchard (Oxford: Blackwell, 1977).

—, 'About the Concept of the "Dangerous Individual" in Nineteenth-century

Legal Psychiatry', transl. Alain Baudot and Jane Couchman, *International Journal of Law and Psychiatry*, 1, 1978, pp. 1–18.

—, *The Birth of the Clinic. An Archeology of Medical Perception*, transl. A. M. Sheridan (London and New York: Routledge, [1963] 1989).

—, *Discipline and Punish. The Birth of the Prison*, transl. by Alan Sheridan (New York and London: Vintage, [1975] 1995).

Fowler, Alastair, *Kinds of Literature. An Introduction to the Theory of Genres and Modes* (Oxford: Clarendon Press, 1982).

Fowler, D. P., 'Narrate and Describe: the Problem of Ekphrasis', *The Journal of Roman Studies*, 81, 1991, pp. 25–35.

Frank, Lawrence, 'Reading the Gravel Page: Lyell, Darwin, and Conan Doyle', *Nineteenth-Century Literature*, 44, December 1989, pp. 364–87.

—, 'The Hound of the Baskervilles, the Man on the Tor, and the Metaphor for the Mind', *Nineteenth-Century Literarature*, 54: 3, December 1999, pp. 336–72.

—, *Victorian Detective Fiction and the Nature of Evidence: the Scientific Investigations of Poe, Dickens and Doyle* (London and New York: Palgrave Macmillan, 2003).

Frazer, George Henry, 'The Condition of Authors in England, Germany and France', *The Frazer's Magazine*, 35, 1847, pp. 285–95.

Freeman, Michael, *Railways and the Victorian Imagination* (New Haven and London: Yale University Press, 1994).

Freud, Sigmund, *The Standard Edition of the Complete Works of Sigmund Freud*, ed. James Strachey (London: Hogarth Press, 1955).

Fromm, Eric, *Marx's Concept of Man* (New York: Frederic Ungar, 1968).

Furst, Lilian R., *All is True. The Claims and Strategies of Realist Fiction* (Durham, NC: Duke University Press, 1995).

Gallagher, Catherine, *The Body Economic: Life, Death and Sensation in Political Economy and the Victorian Novel* (Princeton, NJ: Princeton University Press, 2005).

Gallagher, Catherine and Stephen Greenblatt, *Practicing New Historicism* (Chicago: University of Chicago Press, 2000).

Galton, Francis, *Inquiries into Human Faculty and its Development* (London: J. M. Dent, 1883).

Gaskell, Elizabeth, *Wives and Daughters*, ed. Angus Easson (Oxford and New York: Oxford University Press, [1864–6] 1991).

Gelder, Ken, *Reading the Vampire* (London and New York: Routledge, 1994).

Genette, Gérard, *Narrative Discourse: an Essay in Method* (Ithaca, NY; London: Cornell University Press, [1972] 1980).

—, *Palimpsestes. La littérature au second degrée* (Paris: Éditions du Seuil, 1982).

—, *Seuils* (Paris: Éditions du Seuil, 1987).

—, *Paratexts: Thresholds of Interpretation*, transl. Jane E. Lewin (Cambridge: Cambridge University Press, [1987] 1997).

Gilman, Sander L. (ed.), *The Face of Madness: Hugh W. Diamond and the Origin of Psychiatric Photography* (New York: Brunnel-Mazel, 1976).

Gilman, Sander L., *The Jew's Body* (London and New York: Routledge, 1991).

Gissing, George, *In the Jear of Jubilee* (New York: Dover, [1894] 1985).

Greenblatt, Stephen, 'Psychoanalysis and Reinassance Culture', in Patricia

Parker and David Quints (eds), *Literary Theory/Renaissance Texts* (Baltimore and London: The Johns Hopkins University Press, 1986), pp. 210–24.

Green-Lewis, Jennifer, *Framing the Victorians. Photography and the Culture of Realism* (Ithaca, NY; London: Cornell University Press, 1996).

Greimas, Algirdas Julien, *Du Sens* (Paris: Seuils, 1970).

Gribble, Jennifer, *The Lady of Shalott in the Victorian Novel* (London and Basingstoke: Macmillan, 1983).

Harrington, Ralph, 'The Railway Accident: Trains, Trauma and Technological Crisis in Nineteenth-Century Britain', www.york.ac.uk/inst/irs/irshome/papers/rlyacc.htm

Harrowitz, Nancy, 'The Body of the Detective Model: Charles S. Peirce and Edgar Allan Poe', in Eco and Sebeok (eds), *The Sign of Three*, pp. 179–97.

Hartley, Lucy, *Physiognomy and the Meaning of Expression in Nineteenth-Century Culture* (Cambridge: Cambridge University Press, 2001).

Heffernan, James A. W., *Museum of Words. The Poetics of Ekphrasis from Homer to Ashbery* (Chicago: University of Chicago Press, 1993).

Heilmann, Ann and Valerie Sanders, 'The Rebel, the Lady and the "anti": Femininity, Anti-feminism, and the Victorian Woman Writer', *Women's Studies International Forum*, 29, 2006, pp. 289–300.

Heller, Tamar, *Dead Secrets. Wilkie Collins and the Female Gothic* (New Haven, CT; London: Yale University Press, 1992).

Hobbes, Thomas, *Leviathan*, ed. C. B. Macpherson (Harmondsworth: Penguin, [1651] 1968).

Hollingworth, Keith, *The Newgate Novel* (Detroit, MI: Wayne State University Press, 1963).

Howells, Coral Ann, *Love, Mystery and Misery. Feeling in Gothic Fiction* (London: The Athlone Press, 1978).

Hughes, Kathryn, *The Victorian Governess* (London and New York: Hambledon, 1993).

Hurley, Kelly, *The Gothic Body. Sexuality, Materialism and Degeneration at the Fin de Siècle* (Cambridge: Cambridge University Press, 1996).

Irons, Glenwood (ed.), *Feminism in Women's Detective Fiction* (Toronto: University of Toronto Press, 1995).

Jackson, Arlene, 'Photography as Style and Metaphor in the Art of Thomas Hardy', in Norman Page (ed.), *Thomas Hardy Annual 2* (London: Macmillan, 1984), pp. 91–109.

Jackson, Rosemary, *Fantasy: The Literature of Subversion* (London: Methuen, 1981).

Jameson, Frederic, *The Political Unconscious. Narrative as a Socially Symbolic Act* (London: Methuen, 1981).

Jann, Rosemary, 'Darwin and the Anthropologists: Sexual Selection and its Discontents', *Victorian Studies*, 37: 1, Autumn 1993, pp. 287–306.

Jordanova, Ludmilla, *Sexual Visions. Images of Gender and Science in Medicine between the Eighteenth and the Twentieth Centuries* (New York; London; Toronto; Sydney; Tokyo: Harvester Wheatsheaf, 1989).

Kauvar, Elaine, 'Jane Austen and *The Female Quixote*', *Studies in the Novel*, 2, Spring 1970, pp. 211–20.

Kavles, Daniel J., *In the Name of Eugenics: Genetics and the Use of Human Heredity* (New York: Alfred A. Knopf, 1985).

Kayman, Martin A., *From Bow Street to Baker Street: Mystery, Detection and Narrative* (New York: St Martin's Press, 1992).

Kearns, Katherine, *Nineteenth-century Literary Realism: Through the Looking Glass* (Cambridge: Cambridge University Press, 1996).

Kenealey, Arabella, 'A Beautiful Vampire', *The Ludgate Magazine*, 3 (1896), pp. 35–46.

Kiernan, V. G., *The Lords of Human Kind: Black Men, Yellow Men, and White Men in the Age of Empire* (New York: Columbia University Press, [1969] 1986).

Kilgour, Maggie, *The Rise of the Gothic Novel* (London and New York: Routledge, 1995).

Klein, Kathleen Gregory, *The Woman Detective: Gender and Genre* (Urbana: University of Illinois Press, 1988).

Knight, Stephen, *Form and Ideology in Crime Fiction* (London: Macmillan, 1980).

Kristeva, Julia, *Powers of Horror: an Essay on Abjection*, transl. L. Roudiez (New York: Columbia University Press, [1980] 1982).

Lacan, Jacques, 'Le séminaire sur *La Lettre volée*', in *Écrits* (Paris: Seuils, 1966), pp. 11–61.

Larson, Magali Sarfatti, *The Rise of Professionalism: a Sociological Analysis* (Berkeley: University of California Press, 1977).

Lavater, Johann Kaspar, *Essays on Physiognomy: for the Promotion of the Knowledge and the Love of Mankind*, transl. and ed. Thomas Holcroft, 3 vols (London: G. and G. Robinson, 1789–93).

Le Fanu, Sheridan J., *Carmilla*, in Robert Tracy (ed.), *In A Glass Darkly* (Oxford and New York: Oxford University Press, [1872] 1999).

Lennox, Charlotte, *The Female Quixote* (Oxford and New York: Oxford University Press, [1752] 1991).

Levine, George, *The Realistic Imagination: English Fiction from Frankenstein to Lady Chatterly* (Chicago: University of Chicago Press, 1981).

—, 'Dickens and Darwin, Science, and Narrative Form', *Texas Studies in Literature and Language*, 28: 1, Spring 1986, pp. 250–80.

—, *Darwin Among the Novelists: Patterns of Science in Victorian Fiction* (Chicago: University of Chicago Press, 1988).

—, *Darwin Loves You. Natural Selection and the Re-Enchantment of the World* (Princeton, NJ; Oxford: Princeton University Press, 2006).

Lewes, George Henry, 'Realism in Art: Recent German Fiction', *Westminster Review*, 70, 1858, pp. 488–518.

Lewis, Matthew G., *The Monk*, ed. Howard Anderson (Oxford and New York: Oxford University Press, [1796] 1973).

Lodge, David, 'Thomas Hardy and Cinematographic Form', *Novel*, 7, Spring 1974, pp. 246–54.

Loeb, Lori Ann, *Consuming Angels: Advertising and Victorian Women* (Oxford and New York: Oxford University Press, 1994).

Loomba, Ania, *Colonialism/Postcolonialism* (London and New York: Routledge, 1998).

Lukàcs, Georg, *Studies in European Realism*, transl. Edith Bone (London: Hillway, 1950).

—, *Writer and Critic*, ed. and transl. Arthur K. Dahn (London: Merlin Press, 1970).

Lyell, Charles, *Principles of Geology*, ed. James A. Secord (Harmondsworth: Penguin, [1831–3] 1997).

Mackenzie, W. Douglas, 'The Socialist Agitation', *Westminster Review*, May 1890, pp. 492–5.

Mandel, Ernest, *Delightful Murder: a Social History of the Crime Story* (London: Pluto, 1984).

Mantell, Gideon Algernon, *The Wonders of Geology; or, A Familiar Exposition of Geological Phenomena; Being the Substance of a Course of Lectures Delivered at Brighton*, 2 vols (London: Relfe and Fletcher, 1839).

Marroni, Francesco, *Miti e mondi vittoriani. La cultura inglese dell'Ottocento* (Rome: Carocci, 2004).

Marx, Karl, *A Contribution to the Critique of Political Economy* (New York: International Publishers, 1970).

—, *Grundrisse: Foundations of the Critique of Political Economy* (New York: Vintage, [1858] 1973).

—, *Capital*, vol. 1 (Harmondsworth: Penguin, [1867] 1976).

—, *Capital*, vol. 1, transl. from the 3rd German edition by Samuel Moore and Edward Aveling (New York: International Publishers, 1987).

Marx, Karl and Friedrich Engels, *The Marx-Engels Reader*, ed. Robert C. Tucker (New York: Norton, 1978).

—, *Collected Works*, 11 vols (New York: International Publishers, 1979).

Massé, Michelle A., *In the Name of Love: Women, Masochism and the Gothic* (Ithaca, NY; London: Cornell University Press, 1992).

Matus, Jill L., 'Trauma, Memory and Railway Disaster: the Dickensian Connection', *Victorian Studies*, 43: 3, Spring 2001, pp. 413–36.

Maudsley, Henry, *The Physiology and Pathology of Mind* (London: Macmillan, 1867).

—, 'Galstonian Lecture II: on the Relations between Body and Mind', *The Lancet*, 30 April 1870, pp. 609–12.

Mavor, Carol, *Pleasures Taken: Performances of Sexuality and Loss in Victorian Photography* (Durham, NC: Duke University Press, 1995).

McGowan, John P., *Representation and Revelation: Victorian Realism from Carlyle to Yeats* (Columbia: University of Missouri Press, 1986).

Messac, Régis, *Le 'Detective Novel' et l'influence de la pensée scientifique* (Paris: Champion, 1929).

Mighall, Robert, *A Geography of Victorian Gothic Fiction. Mapping History's Nightmares* (Oxford and New York: Oxford University Press, 1999).

Milbank, Alison, 'The Victorian Gothic in the English Novels and Stories, 1830–1880', in Jerrold E. Hogle (ed.), *The Cambridge Companion to Gothic Fiction* (Cambridge: Cambridge University Press, 2002), pp. 145–66.

Miller, Andrew H., *Novels behind Glass: Commodity Culture and Victorian Narrative* (Cambridge: Cambridge University Press, 1995).

Mitchell, Leslie, *Bulwer Lytton: the Rise and Fall of a Victorian Man of Letters* (London and New York: Hambledon, 2003).

Moers, Ellen, *Literary Women. The Great Writers* (Garden City, NY: Doubleday, 1976).

Moretti, Franco, *Signs Taken for Wonders: Essays in the Sociology of Literary Form* (London: Verso, 1988).

Morson, Gary Saul and Caryl Emerson, *Mikhail Bakhtin. Creation of a Prosaics* (Stanford, CA: Stanford University Press, 1990).

Oppenheim, Jane, *The Other World: Spiritualism and Psychical Research in England 1850–1914* (Cambridge: Cambridge University Press, 1985).

—, *'Shattered Nerves': Doctors, Patients and Depression in Victorian England* (Oxford: Oxford University Press, 1990).

Otis, Laura (ed.), *Literature and Science in the Nineteenth Century. An Anthology* (Oxford and New York: Oxford University Press, 2002).

Ousby, Jan, *Bloodhounds of Heaven. The Detective in English Fiction from Godwin to Doyle* (Cambridge, MA; London: Harvard University Press, 1976).

Page, Norman (ed.), *Wilkie Collins. The Critical Heritage* (Boston and London: Routledge, 1974).

Patterson, R. H., *The Science of Finance: A Practical Treatise* (Edinburgh: William Blackwell, 1868).

Pick, Daniel, *Faces of Degeneration: A European Disorder, c. 1848–c. 1918* (Cambridge: Cambridge University Press, [1989] 1996).

Pollock, Giselda, 'Woman as Sign in Pre-Raphaelite Literature. The Representation of Elizabeth Siddall', written in collaboration with Deborah Cherry, in Giselda Pollock, *Vision and Difference. Feminism, Femininity and the Histories of Art*, with a new Introduction by the Author (London and New York: Routledge, [1988] 2003), pp. 128–62.

Pontrandolfo, Luisa, *Railway mania. Gioie e paure 'ferroviarie' nella letteratura inglese dell'Ottocento* (Bari: Graphis, 2001).

Poovey, Mary, '"Scenes of Indelicate Character": the Medical "Treatment" of Victorian Women', *Representations*, 14, Spring 1986, pp. 137–68.

—, *Uneven Developments. The Ideological Work of Gender in Mid-Victorian England* (London: Virago, 1998).

—, 'Writing about Finance in Victorian England: Disclosure and Secrecy in the Culture of Investment', *Victorian Studies. Special Issue: 'Victorian Investments'*, 45: 1, Autumn 2002, pp. 17–42.

Porter, Dennis, *The Pursuit of Crime: Art and Ideology in Detective Fiction* (New Haven, CT; London: Yale University Press, 1991).

Pullan, Matilda, *Maternal Counsels to a Daughter* (London: Darton, 1855).

Pykett, Lyn, *Wilkie Collins. Authors in Context* (Oxford and New York: Oxford University Press, 2005).

Priestman, Martin, *Crime Fiction from Poe to the Present* (Plymouth: Northcote House, 1998).

—, *Detective Fiction and Literature: the Figure on the Carpet* (London: Macmillan, 1990).

— (ed.), *The Cambridge Companion to Crime Fiction* (Cambridge: Cambridge University Press, 2003).

Rappaport, Erika Diana, *Shopping for Pleasure: Women in the Making of London's West End* (Princeton, NJ: Princeton University Press, 2000).

Rayner, B. F., *The Dumb Man of Manchester. A Melodrama in Two Acts* (London: Thomas Hailes Lacy, [1837] 1838).

Reddy, Maureen T., *Sisters in Crime. Feminism and the Crime Novel* (New York: Continuum, 1988).

Redmond, James, *Melodrama* (Cambridge: Cambridge University Press, 1992).

Reitz, Caroline, *Detecting the Nation. Fictions of Detection and the Imperial Venture* (Athens: Ohio University Press, 2004).

Reynolds, Joshua, *The Literary Works of Sir Joshua Reynolds*, 2 vols (London: Bohn, 1852).

Richards, Thomas, *The Commodity Culture of Victorian England. Advertising and Spectacle, 1851–1914* (Stanford, CA: Stanford University Press, 1990).

Ridding, Lady Laura, 'What Should Women Read?', *Women at Home*, 37, 1896, pp. 932–4.

Riffaterre, Michel, *The Semiotics of Poetry* (Bloomington: Indiana University Press, 1978).

—, *Fictional Truth* (Baltimore and London: The Johns Hopkins University Press, 1990).

Robb, George, *White-Collar Crime in Modern England: Financial Fraud and Business Morality 1845–1929* (Cambridge: Cambridge University Press, 1992).

Rose, M. A., *Parody/Metafiction* (London: Croom Helm, 1979).

Rosenman, Ellen Bayuk, '"Mimic Sorrows": Masochism and the Gendering of Pain in Victorian Melodrama', *Studies in the Novel*, 35:, 1, Spring 2003, pp. 22–43.

Rousset, Jean, *Forme et Signification. Essais sur les structures littéraires de Corneille à Claudel* (Paris: Librairie José Corti, 1962).

Ruskin, John, *The Complete Works of John Ruskin*, ed. E. T. Cook and Alexander Weddenburn, 39 vols (London: George Allen, 1903–7).

—, *Selected Writings*, ed. Dinah Birch (Oxford and New York: Oxford University Press, 2004).

Said, Edward, *Orientalism. Western Conceptions of the Orient* (Harmondsworth: Penguin, [1978] 1995).

Sanders, Andrew, *Charles Dickens. Authors in Context* (Oxford and New York: Oxford University Press, 2003).

Schmitt, Cannon, *Alien Nation: Nineteenth-Century Gothic Fictions and the English Nationality* (Philadelphia: University of Pennsylvania Press, 1997).

Schmitt, Cannon, Nancy Henny and Arondekar Anjali (eds), *Victorian Studies*. 'Special Issue: Victorian Investments', 45: 1, Autumn 2002.

Schor, Naomi, *Reading in Detail. Aesthetics and the Feminine*, Foreword by Ellen Rooney (London and New York: Routledge, [1987] 2007).

Sebeok, Thomas A. and Jean Umiker-Sebeok, '"You Know My Method": a Juxtaposition of Charles S. Peirce and Sherlock Holmes', in Eco and Sebeok (eds), *The Sign of Three*, pp. 11–54.

Secord, James A., *Victorian Sensation. The Extraordinary Publication, Reception and Secret Authorship of 'Vestiges of the Natural History of Creation'* (Chicago, IL: University of Chicago Press, 2000).

Sedgwick, Eve Kosofsky, *Between Men: English Literature and Male Homosocial Desire* (New York: Columbia University Press, 1985).

—, *The Coherence of Gothic Conventions* (New York and London: Methuen, [1976] 1986).

Sekula, Allan, 'The Body and the Archive', *October*, 39, 1987, pp. 3–64.

Shell, Marc, *The Economy of Literature* (Baltimore and London: The Johns Hopkins University Press, 1993).

—, 'The Issue of Representation', in Martha Woodmansee and Mark Osteen (eds), *The New Economic Criticism: Studies at the Intersection of Literature and Economics* (London and New York: Routledge, 1999), pp. 44–64.

Schivelbusch, Wolfgang, *The Railway Journey. The Industrialization of Time and Space in the 19th Century* (Berkeley and Los Angeles: University of California Press, [1977] 1986).

Showalter, Elaine, *Sexual Anarchy: Gender and Culture at the Fin de Siècle* (New York: Viking, 1990).

Shuttleworth, Sally, 'Female Circulation: Medical Discourse and Popular Advertising in the Mid-Victorian Era', in Mary Jacobus, Evelyn Fox Keller and Sally Shuttleworth (eds), *Body/Politics. Women and the Discourses of Science* (New York and London: Routledge, 1990), pp. 47–68.

—, 'Preaching to the Nerves: Psychological Disorder in Sensation Fiction', in Martha Benjamin (ed.), *A Question of Identity: Women, Science, Literature* (New Brunswick: Rutgers University Press, 1993), pp. 192–244.

Small, Helen, *Love's Madness. Medicine, the Novel and Female Insanity 1800–1865* (Oxford: Clarendon Press, 1996).

Smith, Andrew, *Victorian Demons. Medicine, Masculinity and the Gothic at the 'Fin-de-siècle'* (Manchester: Manchester University Press, 2004).

Smith, Lindsay, *Victorian Photography, Painting and Poetry. The Enigma of Visibility in Ruskin, Morris and the Pre-Raphaelites* (Cambridge: Cambridge University Press, 1995).

Spencer, Herbert, 'The Social Organism', in *Essays: Scientific, Political, and Speculative*, 3 vols (London: Williams and Norgate, 1891).

Spencer, Kathleen L., 'Purity and Danger: *Dracula*, the Urban Gothic and the Late Victorian Degeneracy Crisis', *ELH*, 59: 1, Spring 1992, pp. 197–225.

Spiegel, Alan, *Fiction and the Camera Eye: Visual Consciousness in Film and Modern Novel* (Charlottesville: University Press of Virginia, 1976).

Stang, Richard, *The Theory of the Novel in England: 1850–1870* (London: Routledge and Kegan Paul, 1961).

Stevenson, Robert Louis, *R. L. Stevenson on Fiction. An Anthology of Literary and Critical Essays*, ed. Glenda Norquay (Edinburgh: Edinburgh University Press, 1999).

Stewart, R. F., *. . . And Always a Detective: Chapters on the History of Detective Fiction* (Newton Abbot: David and Charles, 1980).

Stoddard Holmes, Martha, *Fictions of Affliction. Physical Disability in Victorian Culture* (Ann Arbor: The University of Michigan Press, 2004).

Stoker, Bram, *Dracula*, ed. Glennis Byron (Peterborough, Ontario: Broadview Press, [1897] 2000).

Stone, Lawrence, *The Family, Sex and Marriage in England 1500–1800* (Harmondsworth: Penguin, 1990).

Stott, Rebecca, 'Darwin's Barnacles: Mid-century Victorian Natural History and the Marine Grotesque', in Roger Luckhurst and Josephine McDonagh (eds), *Transactions and Encounters. Science and Culture in the Nineteenth Century* (Manchester: Manchester University Press, 2002), pp. 151–81.

—, *Darwin and the Barnacle. The Story of One Tiny Creature and History's Most Spectacular Scientific Breakthrough* (London: Faber and Faber, 2003).

Stratmann, Linda, *Chloroform: the Quest for Oblivion* (London: Alan Sutton, 2003).

Surrige, Lisa, *Bleak Houses: Marital Violence in Victorian Fiction* (Athens: Ohio University Press, 2005).

Symons, Julian, *Bloody Murder: from the Detective Story to the Crime Novel* (Harmondsworth: Penguin, 1974).

Tagg, John, 'Power and Photography, Part I: A Means of Surveillance: the Photograph as Evidence in Law', *Screen Education*, 36, 1980, pp. 17–56.

Taylor, Jenny Bourne (ed.), *The Cambridge Companion to Wilkie Collins* (Cambridge: Cambridge University Press, 2006).

Tennyson, Alfred, *The Poems of Tennyson*, ed. Christopher Ricks (London: Longmans, Green and Co., 1969).

—, *Complete Poems and Plays*, ed. T. Herbert Warren, revised and enlarged by Frederick Page (Oxford and New York: Oxford University Press, 1971).

Thackeray, William Makepeace, *Vanity Fair* (Boston: Houghton, [1847–8] 1963).

Thomas, R. Ronald, 'Minding the Body Politic: the Romance of Science and the Revision of History in Victorian Detective Fiction', *Victorian Literature and Culture*, 19, 1991, pp. 233–54.

—, 'The Fingerprint of the Foreigner: Colonizing the Criminal Body in 1890s' Detective Fiction and Criminal Anthropology', *ELH*, 61: 3, Autumn 1994, pp. 653–81.

—, 'Victorian Detective Fiction and Legitimate Literature: Recent Directions in the Criticism', *Victorian Literature and Culture*, 24, 1996, pp. 366–79.

—, *Detective Fiction and the Rise of Forensic Science* (Cambridge: Cambridge University Press, 1999).

—, 'The Moonstone, Detective Fiction and Forensic Science', in Bourne Taylor (ed.), *The Cambridge Companion to Wilkie Collins*, pp. 65–78.

Thoms, Peter, *Detection and its Designs: Narrative and Power in Nineteenth-century Detective Fiction* (Athens: Ohio University Press, 1998).

Tillotson, Kathleen, 'The Lighter Reading of the Eighteen-Sixties', in Wilkie Collins, *The Woman in White* (Boston: Houghton, 1969), pp. ix–xxvi.

Todorov, Tzvetan, *The Fantastic: a Structural Approach to a Literary Genre* (Ithaca, NY; London: Cornell University Press, 1973).

—, 'The Typology of the Detective Fiction', in *The Poetics of Prose*, transl. Richard Howard (Oxford: Blackwell, [1971] 1977), pp. 42–52.

— (ed.), *French Literary Theory Today*, transl. R. Carter (Cambridge: Cambridge University Press, 1982).

—, *Genres in Discourse*, transl. Catherine Porter (Cambridge: Cambridge University Press, 1990).

Trollope, Anthony, *An Autobiography*, ed. Michael Sadleir and Frederick Page, Introduction and Notes by P. D. Edwards (Oxford and New York: Oxford University Press, [1883] 1999).

Tucker, Herbert F. (ed.), *A Companion to Victorian Literature and Culture* (Oxford: Blackwell, 2005).

Vernon, John, *Money and Fiction: Literary Realism in the Nineteenth and Early Twentieth Centuries* (Ithaca, NY; London: Cornell University Press, 1984).

Walkowitz, Judith R., *City of Dreadful Delight: Narratives of Sexual Danger in Late-Victorian London* (Chicago: University of Chicago Press, 1992).

—, 'Going Public: Shopping, Street Harassment and Streetwalking in Late Victorian London', *Representations*, 62, Spring 1998, pp. 1–30.

Weeks, Jeffrey, *Sexuality and its Discontents: Meanings, Myths and Modern Sexualities* (London: Routledge and Kegan Paul, 1985).

Welsh, Alexander, *George Eliot and Blackmail* (Cambridge, MA; London: Harvard University Press, 1985).

—, *Strong Representations: Narrative and Circumstantial Evidence in England* (Baltimore and London: The Johns Hopkins University Press, 1992).

Welsh, Susan, 'Bodies of Capital: *Great Expectations* and the Climacteric Economy', *Victorian Studies*, 37, 1993, pp. 73–97.

Wicke, Jennifer, *Advertising Fictions: Literature, Advertisement and Social Reading* (New York: Columbia University Press, 1988).

Wiesenthal, Chris, *Figuring Madness in Nineteenth-century Fiction* (London and New York: Macmillan, 1997).

Williams, Anne, *Art of Darkness. A Poetics of Gothic* (Chicago: University of Chicago Press, 1995).

Willingham-McLain, Gary, 'Darwin's "Eye of Reason": Natural Selection and the Mathematical Sublime', *Victorian Literature and Culture*, 25: 1, 1997, pp. 67–85.

Willis, Kirk, 'The Introduction and Critical Reception of Marxist Thought in Britain 1850–1900', *The Historical Journal*, 20: 2, June 1977, pp. 417–59.

Wilson, Elizabeth, *Through the Looking Glass: a History of Dress from 1860 to the Present Day* (New York: Parkwest; London: BBC Books, 1991).

Wilton, Andrew, *The Life and Works of J. H. W. Turner* (London: Academy Editions, 1979).

Wolfreys, Julian, 'Preface: "I Could a Tale Unfold", or The Promise of Gothic', in Ruth Robbins and Julian Wolfreys (eds), *Victorian Gothic. Literary and Cultural Manifestations in the Nineteenth Century* (Basingstoke: Palgrave Macmillan, 2000), pp. xi–xx.

Wollstonecraft, Mary, *Maria, or the Wrongs of Women*, ed. Gary Kelly (Oxford and New York: Oxford University Press, [1788–98] 1976).

Wood, Mrs Henry (Ellen), *East Lynne*, ed. Norman Page and Kamal Al-Solaylee (London: Everyman, [1862] 1994).

Zaczek, Barbara Maria, *Censored Sentiments. Letters and Censorship in Epistolary Novels and Conduct Materials* (Newark: University of Delaware Press, 1997).

Zola, Émile, *The Ladies' Paradise*, transl. with an Introduction and Notes by Brian Nelson (Oxford and New York: Oxford University Press, [1881] 1998).

Index